# WITH OR WITHOUT GOD

# GRETTA VOSPER

# WITH or WITHOUT GOD

## WHY THE WAY WE LIVE IS MORE
## IMPORTANT THAN WHAT WE BELIEVE

HARPER PERENNIAL

*With or Without God*
Copyright © 2008 by Gretta Vosper.
Foreword © 2008 by John Shelby Spong.
All rights reserved.

Published by Harper Perennial, an imprint of HarperCollins Publishers Ltd

Originally published in Canada in hardcover by HarperCollins Publishers Ltd: 2008
This Harper Perennial trade paperback edition: 2009

HARPER ● PERENNIAL® is a registered trademark of HarperCollins Publishers.

Grateful acknowledgement is made to the following for permission to reprint previously
published material:

Houghton Mifflin Harcourt Publishing Company. Excerpt from *The God Delusion*
by Richard Dawkins. © 2006 by Richard Dawkins. Reprinted by permission of
Houghton Mifflin Harcourt Publishing Company. All rights reserved.
House of Anansi Press Inc. Excerpt from *A Short History of Progress* by Ronald Wright,
© 2004 by Ronald Wright. Reprinted by permission of House of Anansi and the author.
Oxford University Press, Inc. Excerpt from *Lost Christianities* by Bart D. Ehrman,
© 2003 by Bart D. Ehrman. Reprinted by permission of Oxford University Press, Inc.
Perseus Books Group. Excerpt from *Birth of a Worldview* by Robert Doran,
© 1995 by Robert Doran. Reprinted by permission of Perseus Books Group.
SCM Press. Excerpt from *Honest to God* by John A.T. Robinson,
© 1963 by John A.T. Robinson. Reprinted by permission of SCM Press.
West Hill United Church. "As I Live" by Scott Kearns and Gretta Vosper,
©2005. Reprinted by permission of West Hill United Church and the authors.

Every reasonable effort has been made to establish, locate, and obtain
permission from the copyright owners of works cited in this book.
The publisher welcomes information relating to any copyright owner
who may have been omitted or incorrectly acknowledged.

HarperCollins books may be purchased for educational, business,
or sales promotional use through our Special Markets Department.

HarperCollins Publishers Ltd
2 Bloor Street East, 20th Floor
Toronto, Ontario, Canada
M4W 1A8

*www.harpercollins.ca*

ISBN 978-1-55468-400-7

Library and Archives Canada Cataloguing in Publication is available.

Printed and bound in the United States
RRD 9 8 7 6 5 4 3 2 1

Text design by Sharon Kish

# CONTENTS

To John Shelby Spong,
who deserves all the credit
and none of the blame.

And to all those
born into light
yet ever seeking it.

# WITH OR
# WITHOUT
# GOD

# FOREWORD

I first heard Gretta Vosper speak when the Canadian Centre for Progressive Christianity was publicly launched in the facilities of a United Church congregation in Mississauga, Ontario. She was chosen for this task and introduced by James R. Adams, a retired Episcopal priest and founder of America's Center for Progressive Christianity.

Gretta rose to speak. After five minutes, I knew that I was watching a star being born to a national audience, indeed to an international audience. Gretta's gifted and well-read mind synthesized the issues that differentiate modern people from traditional religious forms. She quoted notable figures from my own Christian formation, individuals such as Dietrich Bonhoeffer, Paul Tillich, John A.T. Robinson, and Friedrich Schleiermacher. I soon discovered, however, that she was determined to push the insights drawn from these giants into dimensions of truth and experience beyond anything I had yet embraced. She made me realize just how much real work still needed to be done to bring about a reformation in Christianity that would ensure its vibrancy well into the twenty-first century. I was absolutely stunned by her brilliance and by the comprehensiveness of her far-reaching intellect.

In the years since that day in 2004, I have observed the development of this gifted woman. Unlike so many theologians who speak and write only for members of the academia, Gretta serves a living congregation. I have watched her call this community of faith into her vision, challenging and enabling it to move with her into a new place. She has done this with rare sensitivity and great courage. The members of her congregation know her, love her, and trust her. They have indicated not just a willingness to walk with her, but great joy in doing so.

As she progressed with her work, her ideas began to disperse and to be noticed in the body politic of her United Church of Canada. Suddenly, traditionalists actually listened to what she was saying, and their small theological worlds began to shake. They struck back, in the time-honoured way of frightened people: those who cannot deal with the message always attack the messenger.

The *Observer*, the national magazine of The United Church of Canada, was filled with evangelical and fundamentalist attacks on Gretta Vosper. The bad news was that, for the most part, none of her critics appeared to understand what she was saying; they knew only that they were against it. The good news was that the *Observer* escaped its formerly routine and boring content and became exciting to read, filled as it was with the vitality and life of a genuine debate.

Most people do not understand the truth that organized religion will die of boredom long before it dies of controversy. Gretta's critics, like all people who feel threatened, called for the removal of what threatened them, proposing that Gretta resign or, if she would not, that she be ousted from their church for heresy. To their abundant credit, her church's leaders were not the slightest bit interested in Gretta's removal. Instead, they recognized in her a new voice that had the capacity to help them move toward a new future.

Now, Gretta has put her ideas into this book in a systematic way, filled it with scholarly insight and fascinating prose. Through the process of writing it, she has issued a very public challenge to which her church now has a chance to respond. Not coincidentally, she has also placed her life and her career squarely on the line. Her church has a choice to make. It can either follow Gretta's lead and venture into unknown waters or it can begin the process of marginalizing her. What remains certain is that, with the publication of this book, nothing will ever be the same, not for Gretta, nor for The United Church of Canada, perhaps not even for Christianity.

This is a powerful book, a provocative book, a book that needs to be read and debated. Gretta Vosper writes to make the God she worships clear. This God does not look like the God of traditional Christianity. Some will think this is the book's fatal flaw. I could not disagree more with that assessment. The traditional understanding of God has changed many times in the past, even in the Bible. The God who sent plagues of horror on the Egyptians and who stopped the sun in the sky to allow the slaughter of the Ammonites at the time of Joshua, quite frankly, does not look like the God of Jesus who enjoined us to love our enemies. The experience of God is surely eternal, but the form in which this God-experience is understood in any age is always bound and warped by time. Gretta calls for her readers and for the Christian Church to be open to the eternal God-experience that has been translated in radically different ways during our walk through history. Our future as Christians depends in large measure on how we respond to new insights.

As I near the end of my public career, nothing thrills me more than to see people such as Gretta Vosper, who is younger even than my youngest daughter, driving the consciousness of the Christian West to places it has never gone before. I enormously admire this rising voice of new Christian possibilities, and I commend her for her penetrating insights into this new generation of spiritually aware and spiritually open people. For some, this will not be an easy book to read, but it is a book that will resonate with many as it calls our generation to a new religious authenticity.

—John Shelby Spong
Morris Plains, New Jersey, 2008

# IT'S TIME
## THE FREEDOM AND RESPONSIBILITY
## TO RECONSTRUCT CHURCH

In moments of utter chaos, great things *can* happen. The dissolution of order allows for new patterns to emerge, new relationships to form. Stereotypes and expectations slip beyond our reach and disappear into cocoons of "what might be." Former structures crumble and give way, and in the remaining mixture of dust and sweat, things that once seemed outrageously improbable suddenly emerge as the next best, in fact, the *only*, thing you could possibly expect.

None of us are very comfortable in the midst of chaos. We prefer knowing what's going to happen next. We like to think we can trust our responses in any given situation, and often we can. We know how we'll react to certain kinds of events, or to hearing particular bits and pieces of news. Someone's daughter is moving to Africa; someone else's dad has gone into long-term care; the house down the street sold for a phenomenal sum. Few of us, though, are ever able to prepare for the really big "come what mays" and we don't want them. The desire to wake up to a wildly different world than the one we fell asleep in is very likely limited to the discontented and the recently arrested. For the most part, we like things to stay the same on a day-to-day basis.

Our hesitation about chaos is exactly because great things *can* happen. There is no such thing as great things *will* happen. It's not a given. Dreadful things happen, too, and, from the last scan of my field of reference, with more frighteningly disproportionate regularity. "Can" is never prescribed. "Can" only means there are lots of possibilities, only a few of which might end up being something exquisitely beautiful and deeply worthy of the disturbing sensations with which chaos takes its hold. "Can" means we have choices. We do.

Chaos has erupted in the mainline church. Things may still look pretty much the same—the slowly receding congregations, the reverential whispers, the soft light filtered through stained-glass saints—but beneath the veneer of our obligatory "Good morning"s ferments a newly mixed potion for which the church has not prepared itself. Critical thought has seeped in, mingled with centuries-old formulae for "what we believe," and begun a reaction the likes of which any explosives chemist would be proud.

The Christian Church, as we have built it and known it, has outlived its viability. Less and less vulnerable to religion's absolute and supernatural claims, people are no longer content with its ethereal promises. Evangelical, liberal, and sacramental expressions of Christianity scrabble for relevance in a world that they are, for the most part, ill suited to address. And yet, it is precisely because of the challenges present in today's world that we most need the strength church might be able to offer should it survive the mess in which it currently finds itself.

## AN INVITATION TO CHANGE

Can the church slough off the encrustations of two millennia of ecclesial doctrine and theology in order to address the world's most urgent needs? Can it let itself dissolve into the pool of ideals, passion, and hope-filled primordial elements out of which it once grew and find in a new mix, in new combinations of those elements, something of value to offer the world? Can we who work in it, worship in it, watch it, and critique it open ourselves to what might emerge from that chaotic pool? And should we find whatever it is that emerges worthy, can we, regardless of our ideologies, shelter it and support it until its own strength can match the needs to which it must respond? This is an enormous challenge. This is almost too many "cans" for us ever to dream the likelihood of a positive outcome. The effort even seems ridiculous when so many argue change is unnecessary. But I am convinced that we must try and that we must try now.

As we consider the possibilities inherent in this new entity that may emerge from the chaos, there are many characteristics we will hope to find, things that, should we see evidence of them coalescing, we already know we must encourage, feed, help grow. Many of them have been part of our spiritual journeys, our reflective lives already: tools for creating and strengthening community; opportunities to gather for ethical exploration and challenge; time set aside for corporate and personal spiritual nurture and comfort; voices united in advocacy for justice; and compassionate efforts to heal and help others near and far. Perhaps as these things develop they will unfold in kaleidoscopic patterns and styles, offering myriad ways to explore, engage, and embrace. To be effective, for this new thing to do the work it needs to do, its many offerings will have to be supportive of humanitarian values and be inclusive of people of all faiths, philosophies, or worldviews who seek to live by those values.

There will be, however, other things that, should they begin to appear, we will have to diligently oppose. This will be difficult, for many of these will be things we will recognize, things we know and are comfortable with—the language, the rituals, the beliefs we have travelled with these many years. For millennia, these things have divided, excluded, disillusioned, and hurt many, even as they attempted, and succeeded, in including and comforting some. If we are to alter our self-destructive course, we must learn the lessons of our past and live by what we learn. Religious declarations and promises based entirely on speculation or individual experience or that claim a supernatural authority must be identified for what they are; we must refuse to grant them an authority they do not deserve. We have the right and the responsibility to draw the necessary line.

What the world needs in order to survive and thrive is the radical simplicity that lies at the core of Christianity and so many other faiths and systems of thought—an abiding trust in the way of love as expressed in just and compassionate living. Out of the multitude of understandings of religion, spirituality, and faith; out of the varying views of the origins, nature, and purpose of life; out of the countless individual experiences of what might be called divine; out of it all may be distilled a core that, very simply put, is love. This core message carries its own authority. It needs no doctrine to validate it, no external expert or supernatural authority to tell us it is right. Love is quite demanding enough as a foundation, sufficiently complex and challenging without the requirement of additional beliefs, unbelievable to many. The *church* the future needs is one of people gathering to share and recommit themselves to loving relationships with themselves, their families, the wider community, and the planet.

Such a church need not fear the discoveries of science, history, archaeology, psychology, or literature; it will only be enhanced by such discoveries. Such a church need not avoid the implications of critical thinking for its message; it will only become more effective. Such a church need not cling to and justify a particular source for its authority; it will draw on the wisdom of the ages and challenge divisive and destructive barriers. Such a church, grown out of values that transcend personal security, self-interest, and well-being, could play a role in the future that is not only viable but radically transformative and desperately needed.

In order for this sort of church to arise out of the chaos we are experiencing, the foundation of the church will have to shift from where it has been to someplace quite different, though perhaps even more deeply rooted in our human story. It must shift from its time-bound biblical and doctrinal base to a broader base of timeless, life-enhancing values—a base that would include all peoples of the world who embrace humanitarian and ecologically sound ideals, which, although differently interpreted and applied, are commonly held. It's a broad vision, but a beautiful one.

## Change Is Needed

Broad-vision change is not "new curtains" window-dressing change but real, deep down, "this is going to hurt" change. It can be liberating and refreshing, but it comes with costs. Without it, there is not only no future for the mainline church, there is also no need for one.

For the many still working hard to keep the church alive, imagining no need for the church is simply outrageous. For those who have long since written off the church as archaic and self-absorbed, it is a no-brainer. Between these two disparate reactions lies the possibility of the kind of church about which I speak and, too, the courage to bring it about. It will require asserting our *right* to assess the church's claims and our *responsibility* to do so. Prepared for this new role, we will be able to look at what the church professes to believe, what it says, what it represents, and test those things for relevance, veracity, and value. What is irrelevant, refutable, or simply wrong we have to consign to the historical record. Those things that are worthy of being carried into the future will become the core of the church's teachings and strength. It is a distillation process that must be employed over and again as new awareness, new knowledge, and new challenges become known. Much will be lost, now and in the future, but it will have been sacrificed for our own good and for the good of the planet that sustains us and all the life we know.

Since humanity is a decidedly self-centred life form, the sacrifice of what is no longer able to sustain or comfort us would seem to be a reasonable trade-off. At issue, however, is more than just our own personal comfort—it's our sense of security. We don't toy lightly with our lives. In healthy, supportive environments, children at a very early age learn that life is precious, but shortly after that, they also learn how unpredictable it can be. We find we are never completely secure in this life. Indeed, we aren't going to make it out alive.

We have contrived, however, beyond the bounds of natural biology, a supernatural realm in which we believe our ultimate safety *can* be secured regardless of what happens to us or those we love throughout the course of our natural lives. We have called it "heaven," and those who feel certain of achieving it may be less likely to lament the loss of a sustainable planet or the struggles of humanity. Intentionally dulling ourselves to the instinctual awareness of our dependency upon one another and the earth, we have shifted our need for security to what comes after this life as we know it and have found there what the church calls our "certain hope."

Self-preservation is always capable, if not needful, of violence. The natural world is one great canvas of violent beginnings and endings through which life extends itself. Extrapolated into the afterlife, beyond the need for earthly things, self-preservation acquires an urgency capable of greater and greater violence. The church, and, in a broader sense, religion, has made its living nurturing that urgency. Finding in our most primal, universal need for security an unchanging rock upon which to build itself, the church has become both the proprietor and the agent of that otherworldly security. The billions who profess belief in a supernatural being are not comforted solely by this-worldly security.

They will work, argue, fight, and die for a security for which there is no proof other than what they have been taught by the church or one of the other multitude of religions that barter the wares of the afterlife. For this reason, the idea of change in the church's message will be anathema to many, for it will require a dismantling of that promised otherworldly safety and a willingness to risk living in whatever fragile, evasive security we can manage on this compromised planet we share.

Perhaps a greater challenge than the one being issued to the church is the one being issued to those who have left the church, those who have determined there is no God they can believe in, only a scientifically evolving world and the complexities of the life forms that exist upon it. Their explorations into and beyond the issues of faith are worthy and have helped prod the church to much self-discovery. But it is time for all of us to stop pointing fingers and guffawing. It is time for humanists and atheists, skeptics and agnostics to see they *share a common future* with the many who are still comforted by their religious beliefs. In the face of that future, harmony, not acrimony, understanding, not mockery, will make our coexistence so much more than merely palatable. We all have much to offer one another: not supernatural beings to whom we can offload our problems, but spiritual tools and practices that can help us know and honour our shared and richly human experiences of life.

## Talking Change

When church-change gurus get together, they often talk about paradigm changes—the tectonic-sized shifts in perspective that unsettle the way we understand things. The term *paradigm* is used in the sense popularized by Thomas Kuhn in the late 1960s and refers to the particular concepts that are held within a discipline during a certain period of time. Kuhn was talking about scientific paradigms, charting and identifying the changes that happened within the scientific body of knowledge as new discoveries were made. He noted that scientific knowledge, rather than building progressively upon itself, stepped from paradigm to paradigm, each new set of concepts complete in and of itself and *replacing*, not simply adding to, previous knowledge, if that "knowledge" was now outdated.

In *The Future of the Christian Tradition*, Richard Holloway, retired Bishop of Edinburgh and Primus of the Scottish Episcopal Church, notes that paradigm shifts do not happen within religious, cultural, and social settings in the same clear-cut way they happen in science. The former don't come out quite as clean as the latter. In fact, they don't come out clean at all. There's stuff left hanging about—bits and pieces of detritus that don't get properly cleared away—things we no longer actually believe but have not officially so declared.

When a scientific paradigm's day is done, it dies. If you are being educated as a scientist today, as Holloway explains, you don't start with Aristotle's paradigm and work up to the scientific approach that prevails today; you start in with the current paradigm. Unlike scientific paradigms, social, religious, and cultural paradigms seem to hang around forever. Though they may have only a shadowy existence, they never really die, are never really abandoned when a new paradigm appears. Rather, they get stacked up like trays in a self-service cafeteria.[1]

Each of the major Christian paradigms that has existed throughout the history of Christianity continues to be found in one form or another within contemporary expressions of the faith. Not one of them has been entirely replaced. Dogma from each lingers, stalking any effort to bring new understandings, new ideas, and new beliefs to what continues to be referred to as a single monolithic faith—Christianity. Endeavouring to preserve our spiritual values, we hold on to the religious dogma with which they have long been fused.

Holloway seeks to explain why it is that we can't let go of

what has gone before; why it is that we get stuck with all these paradigms, one atop the other, each proposing real but differing understandings of Christianity; why it is that the gospel story of the early church hasn't long since been bypassed in favour of an empirically sound one. He sums it up: humans don't like change.

Drawing from Marx and Nietzsche, Holloway points out that not only do we dislike change itself, but the *way* change happens reinforces our distaste for it. Marx, whom he calls the "last and greatest of the Hebrew prophets," taught us that change comes from the victims of the ruling power system.[2] Those victims challenge the power structure that has oppressed them, eventually overturning it. Such change is an affront to what has gone before and calls it aberrant or wrong. For most scientists, even those who initially resist new understandings, the replicable evidence of the new paradigm eventually convinces them of its validity. It becomes, then, a whole new world, a fascinating opportunity for further discovery. For the theologian, whose trade is debatable ideas, the new paradigm remains an unprovable accusation. It challenges and exposes chauvinistic thinking; it labels the old as an insult to those it sought to oppress. Up until now, the only way to answer that accusation and preserve self-respect has been to deny it, hold on to what has been, and attempt to use new words to explain and justify it; and so the paradigms stack up.

Progressive paradigms have matured the Christian faith over the centuries, but that work is constantly held hostage by those paradigms we have been hesitant, if not loath, to release. Emerging Christian movements, popularized by the disparate writings of evangelicals, such as Leonard Sweet, and mainline scholars, such as Marcus Borg, are the latest attempts to create a seemingly new church that can still coexist with all the previous incarnations that have gone before. Sweet holds on to the evangelical gospel message of exclusive salvation while co-opting contemporary post-modern language to communicate relevancy; Borg holds on to the archaic worship forms and language while re-explaining and retrofitting the gospel message with a view to pluralist sensitivities. (Borg's and Sweet's efforts are explored in more detail in Chapters Three and Seven.) Sweet's refusal to grapple with the anthropological genesis of God and Borg's enchantment with the ecclesial encrustations the church has endured keep the church tied to aspects of the past that we can and must move beyond. Sweet, Borg, and others might work hard to dress the church up for the future, but I believe the future requires much more. Their attempts suggest that the church is willing and able to change itself from within, but they are desperate last efforts to hang on to old paradigms the world has moved far beyond. The critically observant remarks of Sam Harris, author of *The End of Faith*, ring balefully true:

> We have to be honest about why [religions] are evolving. The door leading out of religious literalism doesn't open from the inside. These religions have been moderated because of the pressure of modernity. It's secular politics and a conception of human rights and our growing scientific understanding of the universe.... This [evolution] is not to be credited to faith. This is the legacy of faith continually losing the argument to science, and secular politics, and common sense.[3]

Faced with the challenges brought to us from the outside, we'll change as much as we feel we have to; but like Scarlett O'Hara in *Gone with the Wind*, we are only too happy to put off until tomorrow the creative, at-the-roots change that is ours to bring about. We lament that so many in the larger world are not interested in our message and are unwilling to join our worldview. Yet the minor accommodations we are willing to make leave the trays stacked up and the old paradigms in place, as we attempt relevance in a world laden with twenty-first-century–sized maladies.

## Change Is Possible

There is a growing threat inside the church, however, that might now turn into an opportunity. Nietzsche noted that the victims of power structures often align themselves with others within the system who are willing to be unfaithful to it, either through moral weakness or because they are "intellectually restless" and eager to break rank with the increasing stupidity that is characteristic of strong but homogenous systems.[4] Those on the inside of the church who have seriously challenged the system have always had to be cautious, keenly aware of the colleagues and mentors whom they love and who might be unsettled, or even harmed, by any sort of assault on the underlying assumptions, the foundations of the Christian fort. They have often stopped, necessarily, just shy of aligning themselves with those who have been victimized by the church—Aboriginal populations, women, non-Christians, gays, lesbians, bisexuals, and transgenders (GLBT)—sparing the institution their deepest accusations and most critical exposés. But the vital critique they have offered has cranked open the windows, stopped a few doors just short of latching, and let in fresh air. Along with that fresh air came women.

Once ordained,* women gained access to a power structure they had recognized from the outside as displaying many of the features of archaic institutions; they saw where it was hierarchical, self-preserving, bigoted, chauvinist, and dulled by successive gen-erations of leaders whose circumcised intellect prevented them from exploring beyond their own reiterated dogma and canoni-cal laws. Their loyalties to the power structure are weak. They are not viscerally committed to preserving it. They, who were

---

*Women were first ordained by The United Church of Canada in 1936, the Anglican Church of Canada in 1975, and the Evangelical Lutheran Church in Canada in 1976. The Church of England ordained its first woman in 1994 amid enormous protest. Many Christian denominations and institutions continue to deny access to ordained leadership to women, including the Roman Catholic Church, Eastern Orthodoxy, the Church of Jesus Christ of Latter-Day Saints, and the Southern Baptist Convention.

so recently outside it themselves, can still hear the voices of the victims who look for someone inside the fort to help them bring down its oppressive power structures.

And that is likely why it's a woman writing this book. We women who are intellectually restless, who, historically, may be morally more susceptible to what we find to be true than to privilege and power, are now on the inside. We're ready to cooperate with the victims, align ourselves with those who are eager for change, and destabilize the archaic power structure that Christianity has been. Not only for the victims who have been and are, but for the world that is to come.

As any "good woman" well trained in a powerful patriarchal system will do, I head straight for the dirty, piled-up trays in Holloway's cafeteria. It's time to address them, to deal with the paradigmatic leftovers and wipe the counters clean. Leftovers lying around are only an invitation to vermin—the big, fat, licking-their-lips ones and the teeny-tiny microbial ones. Women know how that works. It's not just about keeping the scavenging rodents out on the porch. It's also about saving ourselves from our own self-consuming bacteria. Without a clean sweep, without ridding ourselves of previous unhelpful paradigms and forcing ourselves into the most current understanding of faith, we're going to be eaten.

That's what this book is about—living in the current paradigm, being progressive enough to let go of the beliefs and traditions to which we've had to tip our hats and curtsy in the past but which can no longer prevail in our contemporary world. It is about finding a way to be a church that knows its past but respects the present enough to leave the past where it belongs and not use it as the litmus test for any new idea we might want to propose. The future of any discipline does not survive wrapped in the trappings of the past; it can come about only when the carapace is cracked and something new, related to but distinct from what went before, is freed and allowed to thrive. And so the church, freed from its absolute and supernatural claims with which it has obligated its members, would be able to deliver a clear message of justice and compassion and play a dynamic role in the mending and re-creation of a sustainable social world and a planet with which we might live in right relationship. The church must learn to lead in the areas of ethics, relationships, meaning, and values that are solidly rooted in our own best thinking and not contrived to align with whatever biblical verses can be construed to support them. The church could help us set the ideals by which we wish to live and then challenge us to do so. This would be honourable work and worthy of our energy, allegiance, and support.

Those of us who speak out against change are often confronted by the arguments stating that, if we wish to remain Christian, we will have to respect our traditions. Those who bring these chal-lenges are often comfortable with the way the cafeteria looks. They do not see the dangers inherent in the piles of leftover paradigms congesting the countertops and making it difficult to move. They have found their security in the established power structure and are more comfortable staying with what they know than tampering with it, even though they may see hints of how ineffective it is in the outside world. They feel the whole fabric will be destroyed by change, for they believe that the doctrine, the dogma, is foundational.

When confronted by such a critique, our instincts are to be polite, to accede to those who challenge us, to commit to find ways to honour and stay connected to what went before. But when we think about it, are such challenges valid? Do we have to respect all of our traditional beliefs, many of which are problem-atic, and some of which are heinous and lie in the shadows of the most horrific periods in human history? Are we really nourished only by our past—the idea of slavery, an ethic of self-revulsion, the subjugation of women, incest, and misogyny? Have we not been confronted and nurtured in each of those areas by what came to us from *outside* the church rather than from within it, those changes in our beliefs made necessary, as Sam Harris says, because of science, or politics, or common sense? It's time to stop deferring to those who wish to salvage the church by preserving its every paradigm.

I write as a woman who represents a generation of female presence in the church and is intent on finding the inside knob on Harris's door to change—a knob that will open the church fully to the twenty-first century and forever more allow it to move forward on its own impetus, rather than as the result of outside influences. I write, too, as a woman who is a practitioner in the church, who works with real people in a real congregation in a real, mainline denomination. I am not an academic; indeed, I believe the work of challenging the church cannot be done by those who write within the confines of institutions of higher learning. There, writing becomes part of the preservation of what is being challenged—language seems to become increasingly elitist and inaccessible to those who are crying out for change but who can make neither heads nor tails of the academic papers and tomes that argue whether it should or should not happen. These pages are for those who want to stay in the church but desire deeply that their church have an immediate integrity, not a questionable comfort with its words and rituals that they can achieve only after weeks of reading and translating or listening to privately shared intimations from pastoral staff. As well, these pages are for those who in the past needed the church to be there for them but, upon finding the church was mostly there for itself, have left. And these pages are for those who may never have felt any need for church but find it an interesting anomaly in contemporary society and who might, upon reading this book, see some benefit in church if it were able to address some of society's most pressing issues with a relevant, comprehensible message of justice and compassion. These are not academic pages. They are meant for ordinary people who care about themselves, one another, and the planet and who might see the church as part of that process of care. They are an invitation to what might be.

I write as a minister who has moved from the centre of liberal Christian thought to the bleeding edge of Christianity, struck by the complacency with which I had accepted the liberal framework and shamed by it as well. I write as a woman who is providing leadership in the progressive movement, a movement that pulls us away from the comfortable into the scary but satisfying and exciting world of what we now know and that I expect (and hope) will also one day progress. I write as a woman who has challenged and been challenged by individuals and a community of faith willing to struggle with difficult questions and assert equally difficult answers. I write as a pastor who celebrates with those for whom life is a journey of discovery and delight. I write as that same pastor who also ministers to those for whom life is gut-wrenchingly difficult, those who lose much but who recognize—with love, and support, and encouragement—that the only hope worth holding on to is the hope we have in our own hands and who then, sometimes in the midst of their deepest losses, find the courage to commit to living that hope into being in the world. And I write as a woman who, as a mother, cannot push the difficult things into tomorrow. Like Scarlett O'Hara, who in her final scene opts for a new coping strategy, I, too, can now see that tomorrow may very well *not* offer the church, or even the world, another day. Today is the day in which we must think and see and address our situation. Tomorrow, my children, all our children, may suffer for want of the action that might have been taken today. I cannot risk that. I will not risk that. This book is a testament to that belief.

## Basic Assumptions

My basic assumptions, as I head into this work, can and will be disputed by those who hold different theological and philosophical perspectives. There would be no need for a great many books if we all saw the world in exactly the same way. It is my hope that by setting out the basic context from which my thoughts arose, it might allow you to more easily find some commonality with my subsequent arguments.

I believe all human beings have what I call a spiritual dimension to their lives. Within that dimension we know and celebrate relationships, explore meaning, develop our value systems, and experience love. That spiritual dimension is not some sacred, special place inside us that pulls us apart from the world, though. Too much that is labelled spirituality tends to split us into two natures—an earthly, cravings-based one and a spiritual, dispassionate one. The spiritual "realm" of which I speak is no less connected to who I am than is my emotional or psychological dimension. It is integral to my structure, my experience of life.

This spiritual dimension causes us to explore what is utterly beyond description; we try to pin it down with words such as *spirit*, the *Ground of all Being*, *Ultimate Concern*, the *Divine*, and *God*. The question of whether or not those ideas or names point to actual entities, either outside or within us, is beyond the scope of this book. The peace and passion that alternately soothe and animate me may be described as gifts or challenges from a being or force remote from myself, but they are complex responses to my awareness of my inner needs and those of the community, whose needs transcend my own. Is that the working of the Spirit? Of spirit? I feel it takes place within my spirit, but whether it comes from somewhere else, I cannot say. I just don't know. And although I seek to know what can be known, I am content not to know what I cannot.

Further, and perhaps more controversially, I know no proof

of God beyond personal experience, and I cannot acknowledge that proof as substantial. Personal experience is the most often claimed reason for belief in God, Allah, Krishna, or Raven, but it is also the most often claimed reason for the lack of belief in those same deities—something those who claim their experience is proof of God's existence regularly fail to acknowledge. I prefer to acknowledge my ignorance in regard to matters of which I can have no reproducible evidence. Even when experiments produce results, I am wary of attributing cause or meaning to it. I know there exists a world beyond me—the "other"—but whether that other includes another kind of being, I simply don't know. These matters have been debated for millennia, with conclusions posited along a continuum. How some people sense a true "presence," how others sense other dimensions, how some have a clear sense of connection, how others hold to exemplary values in spite of the cost—these experiences I cannot explain and do not presume to rate them as more or less spiritual. What I need to understand is how I may continue to develop myself spiritually, open myself to learning, and stay committed to living with integrity.

Admitting unorthodox views ushers in a barrage of labels from many directions. "Oh, then, you're an atheist." "Or an agnostic." "A non-Christian." "A heretic." "A New Ager." "A Unitarian." "A progressive." Labels are, by their nature, exclusive. We listen to someone's "beliefs" and slot them under a label, seeking to accept or reject them (either is a possible reaction toward the labels above). Some readers may dismiss my thoughts because the label they will readily attribute to me is one they already object to having a place in the Christian Church. Others may apply a label, but it will be a positive one to them; they'll be happy to include those under that label. Still others, if they can suspend a possible negative reaction to the label hanging above them about to descend and capture them, may find that they are there, to their surprise, in full view right beside me. The church has in its knowledge banks the information to validate these views, and thereby these people. Its role as spiritual leader is diminishing as a result of its inability to share the truth it knows instead of the "Truth" it pretends to know. Harsh? So has been the affect on many who fail to "believe" the Truth presented by the church but who passionately seek truth for living. This truth must be explored within the church, spoken in the church, and celebrated in the church. The church needs to be the place where this happens.

I am not, in any way, attempting to wrest from anyone his or her sense of a relationship with God or Jesus. If that sense moves people to live lives of justice and compassion, I heartily celebrate it. They live with God and honour life through their belief. My intention is, rather, to provide a model for a way of life, a way of faith, a way of gathering together for those who either do not believe in the supernatural elements of religion or do believe but do not feel we can make absolute, universal claims about it; for those who cannot accept church doctrines but who deeply and passionately believe in the goodness and rightness of love; for those who have to ignore, reword, or quietly object to much of what is said in a typical liberal church service, and long to listen, learn, sing, pray, and speak in terms that make sense in the pew, the home, the workplace, and in the quest for a more humane world; for those who see religion as a way of living oriented to ultimate life-enhancing values or for those who live this way but don't like the word *religion;* for those who have no need of "God"—it is for these people I write.

## Change Is Challenging

You have before you a confrontation. I hope it challenges you. I hope it disturbs you. I hope it changes something in you and gives you the permission to let go of some of the things you've long doubted but always thought you were supposed to hang on to. I hope it leads you to stand in church as who you are, knowing what you know, and demand that it hear *you* and see *you*, that it help you when you need to be helped, inspire you when you need to be inspired, challenge you when you need to be challenged, and hold you when you need to be held. I hope that when the things I say hurt or make you angry they also challenge you to find out why it is you are responding that way and how you can turn that pain or anger into a productive way of moving toward a better future. I hope this confrontation helps you articulate the things you never had words for and gives you the strength to say them over and over again. And when you do, when you talk about these things with others, especially those in the church, and you are put down or challenged or told you aren't a Christian any more, as you will be, remember the words from a song that has become inspirational for me. They are from the Dixie Chicks' wonderfully strident response to being blacklisted by the American radio industry for a remark deemed to be unpatriotic. Their song is called "Not Ready to Make Nice."[5] Think about it. "Making nice" suggests keeping quiet about something extremely important solely to please those who wish to or have the influence to keep that important something quiet. Sometimes making nice just isn't the right thing, the good thing, the necessary thing to do. Sometimes being difficult is the only way forward. I know this book is difficult. I know it will cost much to those of you who are active in the church. But I hope you agree that the price is not too high if, in exchange for your losses, you are impassioned by these pages to help build a church that is ready to inspire the world of tomorrow with beauty, justice, integrity, and a constant yearning after truth.

## OVER TIME

It has taken millennia to arrive where we are. The concepts that frame our religious understandings have evolved as slowly as our technological capacity to control our world—up until the last century, that is. What we have come to understand outside our beliefs has had an enormous effect on them without seeming to have had any effect on them at all. It is a paradox the church can no longer live with and remain whole.

## God, Over Time

Long ago, when we were afraid and unsure, we came to know God. We came to understand the world as having been created by God, ourselves as God's most precious creations, and the rest of the world a gift to us from that God. When we were beset by troubles and conflict, it was God we heard urging us to have faith. When we triumphed, it was to God we made our thanksgiving. God became such a big part of our world that, for as long as we can remember, it has been bigger than anything else we could imagine. We like it like that. It makes us feel safe.

But God isn't as big as it* was before. Though we are still often afraid and unsure, this smaller version isn't nearly as comforting as its bigger predecessor. Over the past several centuries, the concept of God has been whittled down by questions we have not been able to settle. Those questions touch such subjects as human suffering and the presence of evil in the world, God's apparent absence from our lives, God's ongoing silence, and the apparent goodness of many who do not believe in the "crucial" aspects of God's message and who refuse God's protection. The ages during which God sheltered us from life's cruel twists and turns have passed and we find we must move on, many of us without its warm

---

*Gender-inclusive language has long challenged us to think about what pronoun we should use for *God*. When I use the term *God*, I will almost always be referring to a *concept* of God. Concepts are not gender-specific, so, discomfiting as it may be, I use the pronoun *it* for God. On occasion, you'll see me use *he*, but please recognize that when I do, it is to deliberately place you in the context in which the ideas I explore were created. When I got to the point of using *god* with no capitalization, you will know there are no remaining traces of deity left in it at all.

embrace. Indeed, to be true, that warm embrace has never proven to be the shelter we once believed it to be—not in our ancient past, not in the savagery of the Dark Ages, not in the increasingly complex and expanding world of the modern era, not in the frightening realities of today's world.

The anxiety of living without a big God to protect us has become overwhelming. Bishop John Shelby Spong, in his book *A New Christianity for a New World*, names this anxiety as the source of many of our self-destructive habits—addictions to caffeine, alcohol, tobacco, drugs—and the rise of clinical depression in our society.[6] We need to find something that will help us address and resolve the urgent issues facing society and our world. For those whose absolute, unquestioned trust in that big God remains, no work need be done, except the many necessary explanations for why things often work out so very badly. But there are many who need something instead of that God, instead of that being who has proven unable or unwilling to rescue us not only from life's challenges (disease, illness, senility, family problems, failed dreams) but, ultimately, from ourselves.

It may seem an impossible task, but we're lucky. The fact that our *primitive* minds were able to grasp a being that ensured our psychological survival into the twenty-first century bodes well for the important work our contemporary minds are now called to do. Add that neural capacity to the fact that many have already been thinking about just such a thing, and our work should be, well, not easy, but much clearer than it has been in the past.

When God was still big within the Christian world, it was the church—not any single church, but the worldwide Christian Church—that became its agent. The church created a vast and intricate system of belief to streamline the understanding of our relationship with God and its influence on our lives. That system is crumbling. Schisms have fragmented it; intellectuals have left it; apologists, those whose role is to make its beliefs appear reasonable, are the only ones who seem able to still flourish within it. Coming under scrutiny from many different directions, the church's insistence on ignoring or stifling challenges to its self-granted authority may, ironically, be what has fatally weakened it. Even when criticism has come from within the institution itself, sources it might have trusted, its responses have proven too habitual to change; the challenges and those who made them were rejected. The lumbering giant now threatens its own existence. In reiterating its same claims, its same arguments, its same effect and beliefs, it has failed to grow into the present age. God, writ large, has been lost; god, writ small, may yet disappear.

## Voices Over Time

Today, the church faces an incredibly long list of challenges. Actually, for many, many years, decades, even centuries, the church's claims have been challenged. Within the institution, however, these challenges have often been stifled behind the church's massive doors and whispered among the theological elite but kept far from the ears of the laity, many of whose own doubts and concerns might have been illuminated by what they were not told. The voices raising these challenges now are full and rich. As they call the church to account, they echo loudly in its often empty sanctuaries.

Some of these voices urge the church toward a critique of its main source of revelation and inspiration—the Bible—and are raised by those who have examined scripture for years and found that its origins, together with the contradictions and repetitions within it, explain it as the construction of human, not divine, hands. The church is also being called to account by others who have noted that the defence of a document's truth cannot be found exclusively within itself and demand that the church acknowledge its circuitous reasoning. It is called to account by those who have sifted through the sands of the Middle East, eager to find some kind of proof for the burden of both testaments, and who found, once those sands have filtered through their fingers, few grains of fact remaining. Those whose questions about the nature of reality the church either could not answer or answered in ways that held no meaning for them—they, too, ask for an accounting. As do those who have found too many of the Bible's moral messages, in the light of the call to love one's neighbour, not merely irrelevant but actually life denying. The call comes from those who were excommunicated from the established church for thinking outside the church's interpretation of faith, for daring to confront, to argue, to think critically, and to act bravely. It comes from those who, outside of the church's version of Christian legitimacy, have still lived the values of love and justice, compassion and forgiveness. Time and time again, the church has been called to meet these challenges. Yet even when the call has been heard, the church has too often shied away.

In the preface to his iconoclastic book published in 1963, *Honest to God*, John A.T. Robinson, the then Bishop of Woolwich in South London, wrote these words:

> I suspect that we stand on the brink of a period in which it is going
> to become increasingly difficult to know what the true defence
> of Christian truth requires. There are always those . . . who see
> the best, and indeed the only, defence of doctrine to lie in the
> firm reiteration, in fresh and intelligent contemporary language,
> of "the faith once delivered to the saints." And the Church has not
> lacked in recent years theologians and apologists who have given
> themselves to this task. Their work has been rewarded by a hungry
> following, and there will always be need of more of them.
>
> At the same time, I believe we are being called, over the years
> ahead, to far more than a restating of traditional orthodoxy in
> modern terms. Indeed, if our defence of the Faith is limited to this,
> we shall find in all likelihood that we have lost out to all but a tiny

religious remnant. A much more radical recasting, I would judge, is demanded, in the process of which the most fundamental categories of our theology—of God, of the supernatural, and of religion itself—must go into the melting. Indeed, though we shall not of course be able to do it, I can at least understand what those mean who urge that we should do well to give up using the word "God" for a generation, so impregnated has it become with a way of thinking we may have to discard it if the Gospel is to signify anything.[7]

Robinson's words were brilliant splashes of hope against a bleak and sterile ecclesial backdrop for the many who wished to see his challenge accepted by the church. He was vilified by others for his vision and his challenge to organized Christianity. Yet he ended the preface of his groundbreaking book with these prescient words: "The one thing of which I am fairly sure is that, in retrospect, [my words] will be seen to have erred in not being nearly radical enough."[8]

I hope the voices raised have proved him right. There have been more than forty years of scholarship and argument heard since Robinson wrote, yet we are still inclined to shrink from his vision. We must not. We must look at it directly and rise to his challenge, recasting our understanding of Christianity, examining the structures that have supported it, clearing away those things that would keep us from seeing it clearly; for it is time to step more boldly into the realities of this world as we experience them, to open ourselves to an honest critique of our Christian heritage, and to expose ourselves to the light of new understandings that so many have placed before us. It's time.

When we have constructed dogma—demanded something be considered absolute and universal—out of personal experiences of God or the spiritual realm and created rituals with which to relate to it, we have called it "religion." There are, of course, many definitions of religion, some of which differ substantially.

Some definitions require belief in the supernatural; others only in a set of ultimate values that orient one's life. By any definition though, religion seems to be mandated by our peculiar human need to make sense of our world. We have constructed our institutions and traditions according to our beliefs as we understood them. But we have held to those institutions and traditions until they no longer make any sense for most of us, until we no longer recognize them as meaningful. The church has often refused to see this irrelevancy, refused to bend, change, or accommodate; it requires that one generation's idea of the appropriate approach to its particular concept of the divine must hold for the next generation, arguing the original was based on a sanctioned authority that still holds. Yet just as every other field of knowledge has changed as we have learned, our faith communities have not only the freedom but the supremely important responsibility to work at our message and our expression of it—to align and realign it with the best available knowledge and the highest, healthiest vision we can develop of the sacredness of life, the sacredness of community.

For generations, working within the confines of traditional Christianity as lay leaders or ordered ministry personnel has meant operating in a language of faith that grew out of a beautifully rich belief system—a religion known and celebrated through millennia. The exquisite nature of this language—be it music, prayer, imagery, ritual, or art, with the assurance of comfort and security woven deep into its folds—has strengthened a vast host of believers. For them, it has become very powerful. There exists, however, another vast host of people who have searched for meaning in the midst of a chaotic world and struggled but failed to embrace the things Christian authorities call "truth"; for them, healing and a truth they can embrace may yet be distant. The view of history held by the church, the language that was intended to bring stability, beauty, and understanding, has served only as a strong and inviolable barrier to Christianity and its communities of faith. They have been labelled unsaved, unenlightened, un-Christian. Even though we on the inside may have derived a certain amount of security and comfort in glossing over discrepancies, it is no longer helpful or healthful for us to stick with the familiar statements of faith and to try to explain these peculiar words and requirements to newcomers. If we are to be an influence for good, for comfort, for strength, for growth, we must use the language of those who come to us, not require that they come to understand ours.

## Timely Changes

By changing the language, I do not mean merely renaming the sanctuary "the Celebration Room" or the narthex "the lobby." We have lost too many years worrying about such things, important though they are.* I am also not simply referring to gender-inclusive language; that should now be a given. We need to release words, statements, and concepts that reiterate dogma we no longer (and maybe never did) truly believe ourselves. I'm calling for a conscientious clearing of the house of faith, a sweeping away of language that suggests salvation from hell in return for a belief in the sacrifice of Jesus for our sins. I'm talking about being willing to give up the public singing of hymns—no matter how dear to our hearts—that reiterate that bargain and celebrate Christianity's march across the globe, triumphantly bringing its patronizing "light of the world" to all the nations. I'm urging us to stop referring to God, casually or reverently, as someone who sends or doesn't send favourable weather; grants or does not grant

---

*Many congregations, in attempts to be more "accessible" to the general public, have stopped using archaic language to describe the various parts of the church building and the worship space inside it, formerly called the nave. The lobby was known as the narthex; the area at the front, the chancel. Various other terms, such as the lychgate, have gone out of common use. The move to replace those terms with more colloquial language is very important if we are to be at all welcoming to those who don't normally attend.

our prayers; saves or does not save a loved one from harm, for reasons "only God knows" but that we most certainly will not understand yet must accept as evidence of God's wisdom, power, and love. And I'm suggesting that we boldly, comfortably, and confidently write our own sacred wisdom *again*, this time gleaning from scripture all that is life-enhancing—*but none that is not*— discovering new and not so new spiritual expressions that come to us from other traditions and ideologies and stretching ourselves to seek new sources of inspiration. We can do this. We should do this. We must do this.

We need to be ruthlessly honest, to state who we are, what we believe or don't, and what we don't yet understand. We need to work together to discover new ways to find meaning in the world, new strength to engage its too inhumane systems, and new joy in the experience we call life. We have much on which to build. We hold deeply sacred beliefs about the value of life and the value of community. We hold deeply sacred beliefs about our responsibility for one another. None of these will be left behind.

The church will never change without a rethinking and re-equipping of congregational leaders. We need to offer them new tools for use in study, worship, and community leadership. Worship leaders will need to be brave enough to let go of their traditional liturgy, even traditional liturgy restated in postmodern language, and reach within themselves to the core of their being from which can well up incredibly rich and fresh language, imagery, poetry, music. It will not be easy—many of us have become numb to some of our own creative instincts—but it is essential. I hope beyond that place of numbness to find a place of wonder and beauty.

There are so many moments, points in our lives, where we plunge into a spiritual realm, moments that pull us to consider meanings deeper than those readily apparent and that challenge us to question purpose. We are inspired by these moments to stretch past the boundaries of our own egos and see ourselves as part of a vast and intricately interwoven whole. They place before us the simple truth that we are responsible not only for ourselves but for our brothers and sisters and the earth. Interconnection has a way of coming back on us, calling us to a never-ending cycle of introspection and conviction, forcing us to see and name our complicity in relationship.

We seek out these moments, intentionally create them when we can, and use them to gain strength, to evaluate our lives, to refocus on what we want to place at the centre of our lives, to recognize and give thanks for those who have touched us and brought clarity or peace to our souls, to reconnect with what or who is precious to us—to name it sacred, holy. Birth, coming of age, declarations of love and commitment, the changes inherent in the passing of years, the end of life as we know it—all these things we need to hallow, to hold dear and ensure they are not squandered in a world with other interests. We need to find new ways to honour life and its many quests, to dignify our common search and celebrate life's holy moments.

To do that re-thinking and re-tooling, to create those new forms of celebration, to honour life's holy moments in some significant way, we will need communities of faith that speak a language that is open to intellectual exploration, spiritual quest, and whatever experiences of the divine are brought to them. Those communities will need resources to encourage critical thinking and gather people together to engage in conversation about the big things, issues that matter—values, meaning, relationships—the things we call "of the spirit."

We are not forced to deal with those big issues if our created belief system designates a divine being as the origin of all blessing and curse in our universe. With such a being in place, we can passively turn to it with either thanksgiving or lament, depending on what the day has unfolded for us. Following any natural disaster, newspapers are filled with stories and pictures of people thanking God for their survival. The feeling is natural, but the attribution is highly problematic. It is as though they are utterly oblivious to the loss or death of their neighbours, of children and the elderly—who have succumbed to conditions they'd previously seen only on TV. We must listen to the words we so commonly use and hear within them the silent implication that if God chose to save us from the flood, God must have also chosen not to save the person who drowned next door. Our Christian belief system reinforces that we, if believers, are privileged, that God is on our side, that we are saved because God loves us better than whoever that other poor wretch may have been. We explain the tragedy of death by assuring ourselves that God, in love, took the deceased home to heaven. It is crucial that we peel away the interventionist deity concept from our belief systems and face reality. *We* are the origin of blessing and curse in our world, not some otherworldly deity—not in Christianity, not in Judaism, not in Hinduism, not in Islam, not anywhere.

Some might look at hurricanes and landslides and want to add nature as co-creator of blessing and curse, too; however, despite the fact that lately we've been found to be terribly responsible for what nature has been handing us,[9] I would argue that what nature doles out is neither blessing nor curse—it just is. How we deal with it, how we respond to it, how we pull ourselves and others out of it—either working together to survive or using each other to reap personal benefit, either welcoming others into our hearts or behaving bitterly toward them—that is where blessing and curse originate, not in global weather patterns and tectonic shifts.

Can someone's concept of a guiding, loving God be a source of help to them in difficult situations? Absolutely. Does everyone experience help in this way? Of course not. Should the church declare and guarantee not only that an omnipotent, omniscient

God will help everyone in this same way (when clearly it does not) but that everyone *should* seek guidance from it? Absolutely not. Could the church help us figure out how to choose to be a blessing instead of a curse? How to open ourselves to another's plight instead of retreating into a guarded self-protection? How to open our hands instead of closing them *whether or not we believe in God?* I certainly hope so. If not, we might be sunk.

Articulating a new vision is tricky. As soon as we think we've figured it out, another problem peeks around the doorway. Our message will be less distinct than an approved systematic theology or creed. It will vary from place to place, from voice to voice. We see things and experience things differently from one another. How to spell that all out in a cohesive way is one of our bigger challenges.

## Time to Focus on the Core

But there is another tricky challenge involved. The Christian Church, and almost every other faith tradition, too, has argued since time began that it held the absolute and only truth, the keys to the kingdom. We would be able to access that truth, that kingdom, if we believed the right message about salvation and participated in rituals, sacraments, services, and duties that were ascribed to us by the Church to ensure our sins were forgiven and our souls properly prepared for a blissful eternity enfolded in God's arms. It was an absolute message. There was no other way. The truth was known and we had to follow it.

Is it any wonder so many have run, screaming in protest, to the relativist's perspective? Relativism teaches that there are no absolute truths, that there are as many experiences of something as there are people experiencing it. That being the case, we can't really say anything definitive about anything, name any creed as absolute, or judge any behaviour as inherently bad or good. In relativism, we can find truth in so many different places, almost all of them, nowadays, outside the church. We see truth in the faith traditions to which others hold, in the mystic traditions, and eastern philosophies. We find it in economic principles and our lover's eyes. We nurture it in our gardens and weep when we hear its chords stretched from the strings of a cello. Truth, whatever each of us means by that, is available to us everywhere, and one cannot be the judge of what another finds to be the central core of the truth he or she follows. We simply cannot fully see the world from another's perspective.

So we have created what we refer to as a politically correct world in which we attempt to honour what it is that others follow as their route to spiritual growth and happiness. Put in such simple terms, of course we would agree that each person should be allowed the space, tools, and opportunity to find their own spiritual path and follow it. It is a liberal's dream.

But, faced with the possibilities of living in such a relativist world, we have reason to be scared. If we embed in our societies the individual's right to pursue any spiritual path, we must be prepared for whatever direction that path takes, and I'm not sure we are ready for that. Upholding freedom of choice alone, we'd have to embrace suicide-bombing, wife-burning, ritualized sex, and self-mutilation. We must be ready for polygamy, the carrying of concealed weapons, the denial (or acceptance) of same-sex marriage, the shrouding of women, and the inhumane treatment of animals. The list could go on and on. Some choices you may agree with; others you would outright reject. But we would have to grant safe passage to a whole host of behaviours, prejudices, and rituals that would be considered consistent with whatever an individual believed to be an integral part of his or her spiritual path.

Of the panoply of values available to us, *none* actually carry inherent authority. We give a value its authority over us, by choosing it as good and right. Nothing is inherently good (not even chocolate). Nothing is inherently bad (not even chocolate). Yet, there are values I believe we must *choose* and on to which we must fervently hold. I propose that these values could be the foundation for the future assessment of our beliefs and practices, affirming those things that ennoble the human spirit and sifting out those things that diminish it.

Of course, to choose a value such as love and say it is absolute for us immediately conjures the questions "What is love?", "For whom?", "When and where?" To say "life-enhancing values" immediately raises voices that will call out, "*Whose* life?" The discussion of how values are to be applied cannot ever be final, for we are on an evolutionary trail and forget that at our peril. But the discussion is vital, for we are always choosing, every day, both in the small details and in the big decisions.

In a workshop on critical thinking offered at a conference hosted by the Canadian Centre for Progressive Christianity, a group of clergy and laypeople were asked to compile a list, using non-religious language, of what they considered to be of utmost importance in life, what they would not want to risk losing, what they hoped their great-great-grandchildren would still be living by. The list is by no means exhaustive, but as I read it again, I am deeply aware that, should we lose even one of these things, the world would be a very different place: hope, peace, joy, innocence, delight, forgiveness, caring, love, respect, wisdom, honour, creativity, tranquility, beauty, imagination, humour, awe, truth, purity, justice, courage, fun, compassion, challenge, knowledge, daring, artistry, wonder, strength, and trustworthiness.

Not one of these values could be called dogma, doctrine, or a theological term. All are common not only to most religions but also to all who embrace humanitarian ideals. When we look closely, we see that while a belief in a supernatural deity would not diminish the list, neither is such a belief necessary in order to embrace any or all of them. Some people may call them religious words, some spiritual, others human. They are, I believe, simply words that unite rather than divide.

A church that promotes the way of life portrayed in values such as those above rather than approved doctrines, holy books, or teachers is what the future desperately needs. The church can get there. It's time. It must be time.

## Church Past and Present

Memory connects many to a time when the church was a vibrant and wonderful place. Gracious, spire-topped buildings were filled with hundreds, if not thousands, of parishioners; a preacher that could stir one's heart as it has never since been stirred; and organ music that transported the whole congregation straight to heaven, once a week beginning at eleven o'clock Sunday morning. People actually came to church on Sunday mornings, afternoons, evenings, and often, because everything revolved around this awe-inspiring edifice, days and evenings during the week. It was an amazing place.

You went to church because everyone went to church. To avoid it brought untold dangers upon your head—business decline, refused birthday party invitations, harassment by the local clergy. And those were just the social risks. The possibility of eternal damnation weighed in rather heavily as well. The risk was just too great for many; so buildings swelled beyond capacity, generous donations helped build extensions, and all was well.

That memory, which makes many a long-time churchgoer smile wistfully, isn't all that "once upon a time" ago. In fact, in terms of the length and breadth of church history, it is from a very recent time and a very specific geographical area—North America in the 1950s and 1960s. There, in two countries founded on secular values,* the church's influence deepened and spread as, following the Second World War, the population bulged, and the strength of the nuclear family became tied to its scrubbed-clean understanding of religion.

And scrubbed-clean it was. Gone were any traces of the brutal ages of the faith. Families worshipped together in the soft light of stained-glass windows oblivious to the history that had left deep and permanent stains upon the flesh-and-blood saints whose glass counterparts now blindly stared down on them: the power-mongering that accompanied the creation of the official "scriptures," the heinous ecclesial activities of the Dark Ages, the witch trials, the Inquisition, the brutal child-rearing practices, the missionary zeal that annihilated whole cultures, the deep anti-Semitism that culminated in blind-eyes turned toward Nazi Germany just a few short years before. No traces of these things remained in the churches of the 1950s and 1960s—nothing but a gracious God who loved us and that beautiful, oh so beautiful, music.

I was sitting, back then, in a United Church of Canada congregation in a massive limestone building—one of three that stood within six blocks of one another. Ours had a tall, silver-grey spire gleaming against the blue sky. The children, robed in crisp white gowns still emanating the starched scent of their mothers' hot irons, sang from the balcony, where many had to sit because the pews below were groaning with the weight of hundreds of people. The organist, like his predecessor, was world renowned; the

---

*The Christian right in America is fond of challenging the U.S. government to return to the Christian principles upon which it was founded. Those who wrote the Constitution, however, insisted that the document include religious freedoms, as several were Deists and Unitarians. Controversy continues to foment around Article XI of the American Treaty with Tripoli, written in 1796 under the presidency of George Washington, himself misrepresented by an early biographer as a devout Christian. That article, in its efforts to assure religious freedom to Tripoli's Muslims, stated clearly that the United States "is not in any sense founded on the Christian Religion." Rob Boston, "Joel Barlow and the Treaty with Tripoli: A Tangled Tale of Pirates, a Poet and the True Meaning of the First Amendment," *Church & State*, June 1997.

preacher, a most literate man, soothed the polished wood of the exquisite pulpit with his hands as he delivered his painstakingly crafted oration each week. Stillness stole into each heart there, and we were awed by the majesty of the Sunday morning experience. In church school, I was among the first students who studied under the New Curriculum, a Sunday school program that drew intense criticism from evangelical Christians, particularly the Baptist Church, with whom the United Church had previously co-operated on educational materials. (That relationship was eventually severed as a result of the publication.) To the dismay of conservative leaders and denominations within the country, much of what had been identified early in the century as fundamental to Protestant belief * had been expunged from the New Curriculum. [10] Liberal Christianity was turning away from the heavily doctrinal books of the New Testament, such as John's Gospel and the Epistles, and grounding its theology in the stories of the life and acts of Jesus as found in the synoptic Gospels.[11] The curriculum acknowledged the findings of contemporary scholarship, a reality completely unacceptable to more conservative denominations.

So I learned many stories from the Bible but wasn't forced to memorize its books. I learned to see Jesus as a wise and loving man who did his best for everyone, but I was left without that soul-galvanizing belief that he had died for my sins. I integrated his teachings about justice and compassion, but not the ones about everlasting punishment. The Jesus I was introduced to was so kind that, on a blistering cold day, out on the rink my mother had poured in our backyard, under the shadow of that awesome spire, he took time out from his otherworldly duties to teach me to skate. Being a first-century Middle Easterner, his knowledge

---

*The five fundamentals are the acceptance of (1) the Bible as inerrant; (2) the virgin birth and the divinity of Jesus; (3) the doctrine of substitutionary atonement through God's grace and human faith; (4) the bodily resurrection of Jesus; and (5) the veracity of the miracles (for some, it is Jesus' pre-millennial second coming).

of skating was limited, of course, and I never did get very good at it, but his heart was such that he would be there for me when I needed him, and I knew it.

## SECLUDED STUDY

So it didn't seem too strange later on when I learned that while I had been ingesting a Sunday school version of what some might call "Christianity lite," theologians of the 1950s and 1960s were poring over and pouring out material that questioned the "truth" asserted in the Bible, the foundation upon which all that beauty and well-being rested. Quietly, within the dimly lit corridors of theological colleges, seminaries, and universities, far away from any instruments of detection, scholars, professors, and students had begun earnestly listening to voices that had been urging alternative perspectives for centuries. They started discussing such ideas as the human construction of the Bible, the historical person who might have been Jesus, the context of Israel in which the authors of the scriptures had written, and the prejudices those early authors brought with them. All of these discussions, for all the years before and every year since, follow the ebb and flow of reason in the church, welling up and dying off as the questions that prompt them, the threats inherent in them, and the courage of those who address them fluctuate.

But the fact that scholarly exploration was happening did seem strange to many. That 1950s and 1960s scrubbed-clean version of Christianity has been handed down through another generation since my childhood, and most of those to whom it has been handed have not been inclined to seek out anything more than what has landed in their lap. Indeed, for many, it was an unwelcome inheritance, and they quickly dispensed of it. A theological education is not the norm for the North American, so the understanding that the typical liberal Christian has of their faith has come to them from their congregational leaders, a recollection of church they have received from a parent or grandparent (actual attendance at church has fallen to the point that many people no longer have a first-hand experience of its teaching),[12] or the media's presentation of it. The average North American has not followed the conversations that have taken place within academia; many do not know that most contemporary scholarship has undermined the classic claims of Christianity and they do not care. For them, the Bible is the Word of God. God is God when they need him and pretty much not an issue when they don't. And Jesus is a nice guy who would like us to be good. It's as simple as that.[13] (A recent *Newsweek* poll found that 79 per cent of Americans believe the details of Jesus' life, including his virgin birth, as they are found in the Bible.)[14]

For the Christian with evangelical roots, the uprising of liberal biblical scholarship that took place in the 1950s and 1960s was perceived to threaten humanity's very relationship with God and needed to be utterly denied. Evangelicals believe that we simply cannot question the Bible, which they understand to contain the exclusive keys to a personal relationship with the Creator and, for those who believe, the subsequent salvation that awaits beyond the struggles of this mortal existence. The scrubbed-clean North American version of Christianity handed down through the evangelical tradition again ignores much of Christianity's dark past. While continuing to claim the inerrancy of the Bible, a book riddled with gory descriptions of the vengeful acts of a jealous God, evangelicals are able to overlook its horrors by reading everything through the lens of the loving sacrifice of the Jesus found in the New Testament. Rather than focusing on the stories about his life and teaching and the consequent need to perform "good works" on their way to heaven as liberals were wont to do, evangelicals internalized the theology of John and Paul and argued that since no one's good works are good enough, they can't get you into heaven; God offers the gift of salvation, and belief in that promise is itself its assurance. It is only if one *believes* Jesus graciously took his or her own personal sins upon him that forgiveness is possible and the assurance of an eternal relationship with the Father in heaven is granted. Jesus became the ultimate mediator of sacrificial love, the extreme gift of a God who calls us to him, lovingly and devotedly. His presence is palpable, and his guidance an absolute in an otherwise threatening and evil-soaked world.

For many Christians with roots in more sacramental traditions, such as the Roman Catholic Church, the Orthodox churches, and some Protestant denominations, even the thought of looking at the Bible to study it would have seemed somewhat strange. Within those traditions, persons who are ordained have been understood to be the authority on the scriptures. Typical laypeople, while they would undoubtedly have a Bible in their homes and perhaps regularly read from it, would not normally have undertaken to discover what its words meant for themselves personally, let alone what the words meant for the authors originally. All that worrisome work could be left to church officials, who would tell the laypeople what they needed to know. The essential teaching of the sacramental church is that, through the temporal and spatial mystery of the Eucharist, one's sins are atoned for by being added to those Jesus willingly took upon himself at the Crucifixion.[15] Since the Eucharist is made available from each denomination as often as it is deemed necessary for salvation, there is little else with which one needs to be concerned.[16] The rise of liberal biblical scholarship in the 1950s and 1960s wasn't even a blip on the screen for those who gathered weekly for the distribution of the Eucharist.

## Into the Open

But it was only a matter of time before someone opened the sluice gates and the scholarship spilled out into the light of day. And that's exactly what John A.T. Robinson did in the 1960s when he called for "[a] much more radical recasting [of the faith] . . . in the process of which the most fundamental categories of our theology—of God, of the supernatural, and of religion itself—must go into the melting."[17] Rapidly claimed by thirsty clerics everywhere, *Honest to God* presented Robinson's very real questions about the doctrines of the church. He showed how, over the course of its history, the church had made subtle shifts in what it understood the Bible to be saying, and he queried the incongruous demand that the Bible be recognized as the authoritative Word of God.

Robinson's book was a much needed first step, but, like so many first steps, it was followed by a thud. The book received censure from church authorities, some of whom, although they stated that they agreed with Robinson's perspective, aimed their attacks at the lack of clarity they found within his syntax. Even the academic C. S. Lewis dismissed the import of the conversation Robinson sought to stimulate. Using the royal "we," he projected his own highly educated understanding of God upon all unsuspecting "Christian laymen." "We have long abandoned belief in a God who sits on a throne in a localized heaven," he said. "[Robinson's] view of Jesus . . . seems wholly orthodox." Lewis's dismissal of Robinson's insights is reflected in the continued arrogance of the ecclesial elite.[18] The controversy wound down slowly, and, although *Honest to God* continues to be a source of inspiration to many, it was unable to significantly alter the publicly stated beliefs of the ecclesia.

Within theological colleges, seminaries, and training centres, however, progressive voices persisted. In each of the four major areas of study—theology, the Bible, church history, and practical ministry—scholars and practitioners continued to add to the corpus of progressive scholarship that had already seriously undermined many of the assumptions of Christianity. But almost no one outside of church theological circles knew anything about it.

Contemporaneous German theologians Paul Tillich, Rudolf Bultmann, Dietrich Bonhoeffer, and Karl Barth all struggled in the early mid-century with the challenges of reconciling twentieth-century worldviews and the rise and realities of Fascism with a first-century biblical witness. Barth severed the cord that had previously tethered theological suppositions to the inerrancy of the Bible, arguing, despite his belief that God used the Bible to make his revelations to humanity, that if it was a human construction, as he believed it was, it could never take the true place of divine revelation. While Tillich attempted to recast the main theological precepts of Christianity in more accessible terms in order to help the laity understand and thereby accept the Christian faith, Bultmann worked to take the incredulity out of the Bible's stories by identifying them as myths. Tillich's name for the deity, "Ground of All Being," was the first broadly accepted, non-theistic image of God and continues to be widely used today.[19] Bonhoeffer, hanged just before the end of the Second World War for his participation in plots to kill Adolf Hitler, tried to inspire his own church in its ongoing struggle with the Nazi state and articulated the tension between cheap and costly grace. All four of these theologians began writing before Robinson—Tillich was one of his influences—but their work remained central to the training of mainline congregational leaders in the last half of the century.

Other theologians brought different perspectives to the universities. The provocative Roman Catholic Hans Kung stretched his church's patience by reiterating the call for reformation that came out of the Second Ecumenical Council of the Vatican in 1965. He addressed an ecclesia that too soon began to focus its energy on trying to pretend the council hadn't happened. In the 1980s, another Roman Catholic theologian, Matthew Fox, countered the church's doctrine of original sin with his book *Original Blessing*. In 1988, he was silenced for one year following the publication of *The Coming of the Cosmic Christ*. The Roman Catholic

Congregation for the Doctrine of the Faith (formerly the Office of the Holy Inquisition), under the leadership of Josef Ratzinger, then cardinal but now known as Pope Benedict XVI, had been investigating Fox for some time prior to his first publication and eventually expelled him from the Domincan Order. (The Vatican had been murdering, excommunicating, and silencing its detractors for centuries.[20] In the twentieth century, they ceased the first order of action, as far as we know, but they continue to silence theologians who do not conform to papal authority. Most recently, theologian Jon Sobrino has been disciplined, though not yet silenced, for his work in the field of liberation theology.)[21]

In the area of biblical studies, scholars such as Rolf Rendtorff, a student of Old Testament scholar Gerhard von Rad, disturbed the almost universally held (in the liberal church at least) Documentary Hypothesis in which the Old Testament is argued to be the work of at least four distinct authors. One of the gifts his work has given the religious community was his doggedly determined effort to scrape the Christian perspective from the Hebrew scriptures. Literary theorist Northrop Frye, an ordained minister of The United Church of Canada, added a twist to the study of scripture by introducing cross-disciplinary studies, examining the Bible for themes previously confined to the study of literature. His work has validated the examination of scripture as story and continues to strongly affect how it is addressed within congregations.

By the 1980s, biblical criticism was finally getting the full brunt of feminist critique, introduced to the church a couple of decades before by theologian Mary Daly. Roman Catholic scholar Elizabeth Schüssler Fiorenza sternly marched her colleagues back to the Bible and demanded that they read it again, this time from a woman's perspective. Rosemary Radford Ruether exposed the sexism prevalent in church language and introduced the concept of Womenchurch, a theology incarnate in today's Womenpriest movement. As the stirrings of feminist theology rumbled through the church, however, womanist theologians started similar rumblings within the feminist movement itself, as black women called attention to feminist theology's lack of attentiveness to the experiences of women of colour.[22]

Church historians, the majority of whom had previously used history to bolster doctrinal and ecclesial beliefs, broke free from their apologetic role and began to study the early days of the church without projecting their own twentieth-century questions and perspectives onto it.[23] This more objective eye exposed the great interweaving of political, economic, and theological interests in the development of the church through the ages. By the 1960s, most mainline scholars recognized this complexity, and students in seminaries had their elementary picture of a heaven-sent church replaced with something that, although never able to be perfect, more accurately reflected its all-too-human origins.

In 1986, Robert Funk founded the Westar Institute and its Jesus Seminar as an advocate for religious literacy. It hoped to open wide the doors of academia so the public could access the scholarly quest for the historical Jesus, trying to discover who the man who is said to have started all this really was and what he might have really intended to do.

Since that time, theology, church history, and critical study of the Bible written for the public has exploded. Ecospirituality theologians Thomas Berry and Brian Swimme have pointed out the beauty and intricacies of the universe. In their work, they have shown that life is more than merely a debased and transitory journey toward everlasting pleasures or tortures, and they have helped us to see all of creation, our human bodies included, as a thing of wonder and beauty. Carter Heyward, feminist, activist, and theologian, writes about the realities of oppression and names our visceral reaction to the lurch it causes in our stomachs: God. Richard Holloway, former Bishop of Edinburgh, let people know that biblical scholars believe that human thinking influenced not only our own understanding of God but that of the original authors of scripture. In 2002, Andrew Furlong, a priest in Ireland, came before an ancient tradition in the form of a heresy trial for making this same call to us. His resignation, an act of personal preservation from a frightened and reactionary church, was publicized in his book *Tried for Heresy*. Don Cupitt, founder of the Sea of Faith, an international organization formed to explore and promote religion as a human construction, and Lloyd Geering, a New Zealand theologian, author, and contributor to the Sea of Faith movement, push the envelope even further, asking the questions that those who wish to remain comfortably in the pews are loath to ask: what does the church look like beyond Christianity, and, more radically yet, what does Christianity look like beyond God? Perhaps the most outspoken and widely read of those who seek to make contemporary Christian scholarship accessible to the public is retired Bishop of the Episcopal Diocese of Newark John Shelby Spong. In the face of massively difficult ecclesial and social issues presented to the church, this first recipient of the Westar Institute's John A. T. Robinson Award for unrelenting honesty in both spoken and written word continues to pour out his life energy in a provocative call to the church from within the church. His encyclopedic knowledge of the Bible and his commitment to hauling Christianity out of the first century and into the twenty-first have made him one of Christianity's most maligned authors.

## Accessible but Not

So it was that scholarship, both within academia and beyond it, that was at odds with the doctrinal positions of every single Christian denomination active in the world was being read. While there had been a lag time of several decades, by the late 1980s, those with theological training and those without it *could be*, in terms of access to resources, on equal footing.

Could be. Access always introduces the concept of "could be." Some will access the resources, some will not. The books were out there; there was no doubt about that. Anyone who took a pensive stroll through the corridors of their favourite bookstore or library would have come across at least one or two. And those training for leadership within the church were certainly aware of them, too. Indeed, for some in the more liberal colleges and training centres, progressive perspectives were on the required reading list.[24] But for the massive majority of churchgoing Christians, even the massive majority of liberal churchgoing Christians, access wasn't the issue. When you don't know something exists, your chances of intentionally accessing it are nil. And accidentally taking the wrong book out of the library changes very few lives. One cannot rely on serendipity to get crucial knowledge out to the populace.

Now, it is possible that, next to electronic and print media, there may be no better, more organized, regularly attended place than the church from which large amounts of information can be transmitted reliably to adults. Every Sunday morning, millions gather in buildings around the world to participate in church services, of which a portion of each is almost always oratorical. That period of oratory, the sermon, provides church leaders with weekly opportunities to address their congregants. So, it would seem that, since information about biblical scholarship, church history, and theology is most pertinent in that setting, the church would be the very best place from which such information could be released.

Alas, it was not to be. As Jack Good notes in *The Dishonest Church*, "A silent pact often exists between pastor and congregation, a pact in which certain difficult issues are to be left unmentioned."[25] Those issues span everything from the origins of scripture to the nature of God. As long as the laity don't have to think about it, pastors don't have to talk about it. As long as pastors don't talk about it, the laity don't think about it. A tidy, mutually beneficial agreement. In almost every church, what the preacher says is entirely up to her or him, as long as it is consistent with the teachings of their denomination and it isn't going to incite the congregation to riot. Most preachers find themselves constrained by the first obligation; and most of those who do not, by the second. What they say, too often, is entirely in keeping with Good's "silent pact."

Liberal mainline denominations have been seriously wounded by their refusal to state what they actually believe. We have all watched the gaping wound in the right grow as those who want the "truth" laid out for them more clearly have left for more conservative denominations and community churches happy to give it to them. But the wound in the left has gone unnoticed and has hemorrhaged into nothingness as spiritual quests have become personal pursuits unconnected with church for those who could no longer abide the church's theological dithering. As society has become more secular and less focused on religion and religious values, it has become more acceptable, if not preferable, to claim no religious affiliation at all than to identify oneself as a Christian. In 2001, the category "Jedi" was added to the list of religions in the U.K. after 390,000 Brits identified themselves as Jedi Knights in the national census. British officials were quick to note that the inclusion of the category in census reporting did not denote official religious status.[26] It is likely, however, that very few, if any, of those who identified themselves as Jedi Knights on the census form would actually do the same on admittance forms at a local emergency room, particularly if the hospital had a psychiatric ward. In other words, they don't really think they are Jedi Knights; they were merely enjoying the hoax. Their interest in religion is slight.

The memories of church attendance in the 1950s and 1960s stand in stark contrast to the fifty or sixty people or even the few hundred sprinkled across mainline sanctuaries built to echo the sounds of many more voices raised in praise. On their own, the costs of maintaining the pipe organs designed and handcrafted to accompany those voices have choked many a congregation. Fuel bills and rising personnel costs, failing roofs and crumbling mortar all challenge congregations' futures. Those of us who remain, afraid we won't make it, acquire a survivor mentality. We look around for the perpetrators of our demise so we can finally cast the blame, fix the problem, and turn things around. We distribute that blame regularly at board meetings and council meetings, gatherings of the elders and the deacons, in parking lot discussions, and from behind a wagging finger in the doorway of the pastor's office. And we give it, essentially, to anyone we can, anyone we think might have taken the sheen off what we remember church to have been: those who have stopped choosing the old hymns; who have introduced inclusive language; who put their kids in sports teams that practise Sunday mornings; who don't wear ecclesial garb; who won't help out in the Sunday school; who are gay or lesbian and have forced their way into the pews and pulpits of the nation; who sing secular music in the sanctuary; who try to be multicultural; who aren't multicultural enough; who play pianos, guitars, keyboards, and drum kits in the church; who come from other countries and just don't want to learn about Jesus; who run around in the basement and don't clean up after themselves; who clap during the service; who won't come because there's no parking; who voted for Sunday shopping; who don't give enough money; who bring their kids into the service and then just keep whispering "Shhhh!"; who won't sing; who won't make crafts for the bazaar; who let the neighbourhood kids use the building; who don't want to hear about social justice; who only have a social justice axe to grind; and . . . you get the picture. Too often we set our sights based on what has been and not what might be.

It is that vision I am arguing for—what the church might be, not what it was, as precious as that has been to many. To lose that vision would be to lose whatever the church might bring to the future, and I believe that can be much. To find that future will require that the church let go of much of the past and, like each and every one of us does each and every morning, wake up to the realities this day brings and try to steer them toward a just and fruitful tomorrow. It is the best we can do.

## THE "OFFENCE" OF PROGRESSIVE CHRISTIANITY

As a young girl, I was the recipient of my mother's lessons on etiquette and appropriate social behaviour. I learned that, especially around older people, it was more respectful to walk than to run, to talk softly than to shout; that expecting less than I hoped for in any situation meant that whatever I was given I would receive with an appropriate show of appreciation; and that sharing was a good thing, particularly if it was with a whining brother or sister. I learned how to interact politely with my parents' acquaintances, relatives, and even people I did not like. I learned that if I was lost and needed someone to help me find my way home, it was better to ask a girl than a boy. I learned that it wasn't always a good thing to read road signs out loud, especially if the writing was done with spray paint. There were many diverse lessons, and I absorbed them as well as any young girl can do.

Sharing a birthday with my grandmother offered me an annual opportunity to hone my tea and cookie serving skills. I quickly learned that when transporting a cup filled with tea from my mother's silver service to an aged and elegant guest, one should look not at the teacup but toward the person, thereby reducing the amount of tea sloshed into the saucer. I gained an enormous sense of accomplishment from these lessons.

## A Mother's Lessons

But my mother had far more lessons to offer her children than proper social skills. Indeed, some of her characteristic behaviours are now so natural to my own behaviour, I would not be the least surprised to discover they were passed on genetically rather than learned at the hem of her skirts.

Looking back upon the awe-inspiring congregational experience that I grew up with—rich music; challenging, erudite preaching; a nurturing, loving environment—it is easy to believe that church was perfect and clean and pure. But over the years, I came to be aware of times when things weren't all that blissful. I can remember my mother, not all that infrequently, being irritated, even angry, about things that happened there. We children waltzed back and forth across the street to the church in a bit of a happy fog as far as church politics went, completely unaware that such a thing controlled and manipulated many congregations. But my mother was often caught in its web, fastened by the sticky pull of many difficult issues, caught by a clear vision of what church should be.

Similarly, she became embroiled in the many challenges she encountered as a teaching master at our local community college, where she taught and mentored those who would be caring for my generation's children in daycares and nursery schools. These challenges weren't brought to her by her students. They came from a myopic institutional administration, fellow teachers, and ineffectual leaders. In both places, and I am sure many others, my mother's perspective on what things should be like, on what they could be, and how they might get there, was irrepressible. There was no possible way for her to stifle what she felt needed to be said.

## The Elephant

You will likely have heard of the elephant in the middle of the room—so big there is hardly room for anyone else to be in the space or move around it comfortably—yet no one will admit to seeing it. Families, congregations, institutions, and workplaces all have difficult issues no one wants to address. And while my mother, like all of us, has elephants with which she has negotiated a comfortable coexistence, at the church and at her workplace, elephants, for her, were intolerable.

Often the results were humiliating for her children, particularly when we were teens and young adults. Mother would rise at a meeting, take a deep breath and a longer pause, tilt her head to one side, and start describing that day's particular beast as she saw it—size, colour, age, caretakers. Her descriptions were so complete that no one could argue the elephant didn't exist. Exposed, it stood in the middle of the room, waiting to be coaxed away and leave the space clear for whatever right relationship my mother believed was achievable.

The problem was no one *would* admit they actually saw the elephant—not in the meeting. Afterwards, while washing coffee cups or stacking chairs, individuals would creep up to her, thank her for her courageous words, and slip away, unidentified in the congregational minutes. Frustrated and often in tears, my mother would bear the ache of a dissonant church experience as she longed for spiritual integrity and struggled with congregational evasion.

When all is said and done, I might look back and wish that my mother had passed on to me her silver tea service rather than her penchant for saying what needs to be said. But truth be told, there is a lot more need for that irrepressible honesty these days than there is for silver tea services.

## Ecclesial Mammoths

Some of the elephants that I am least tolerant of are in the church. They loom large at many congregational, denominational, and ecumenical gatherings. Grown and usually well-educated men and women work their way around these elephants with skilled

ease. There are few who are not graced with some skill at nego-
tiating space in the narrow margins left by the wrinkled, ecclesial
mammoths.

Early on in my student days, I employed my negotiation skills
with a certain aplomb. In a seeming paradox, I used the skill I had
learned from my mother to avoid having to deal with elephants
I didn't want to address. Effortlessly pointing to one or another
of the smaller elephants, much to the discomfort of my fellow
students and then colleagues, I colluded with them in ignoring
the herd of bigger elephants that I did not have the fortitude to
confront. I was able to satisfy my own penchant for hard truths
and avoid having to wrestle with them all at the same time. It was
the best of both worlds.

The issue about which I was the most articulate (and annoying)
was *de rigueur* for enlightened women at the time of my theological training—gender-inclusive language. Aware of the pervasive exclusivity of the language of scripture and academia, and
the male-centric metaphors used by most of my professors, I was
drawn over and again into my mother's infamous role. Once, in
a worship class, a fellow student inquired after the correct pro-
nunciation of the word *Amen*. Before I could put a sock in it, I
quipped that it depended upon whether one was female or male,
suggesting that feminists may like to start using "Ah-women" for
a refreshing change. So pervasive was exclusive language and so
predictable my protest to it that I was soon dismissed as a single-
issue nitpicker.

On other matters more closely related to the essence of
Christianity, I said nothing. The camaraderie of silence works its
charm meticulously in the hallowed halls of both the academy
and the ecclesia. Affirmations of faith, both spoken and unspoken,
draw students, professors, and clergy into complicit alliances, co-
conspirators who cannot acknowledge the existence of even, or
especially, the largest of the elephants.

## Two Analogies: The Code and the Post

Two analogies will help to identify this issue. The first lies enfolded in discussions about Dan Brown's blockbuster hit *The Da Vinci Code*. Many streams of Christianity have denounced *The Da Vinci Code* because it suggests that some of the significant ideas about Jesus may not be true. Much of the intrigue in the novel is introduced through an interpretation of the painting *The Last Supper* by Leonardo da Vinci. My guess is that those churches most concerned with the book and the movie are threatened by the thought that their adherents might be lured into believing something other than what the church tells them. But the results of misbelieving are not as drastic as what the church makes them out to be, because, essentially, the ideas Dan Brown put in his novel can be considered to be made up.

Follow me here. In an effort to dismiss the implications Dan Brown alludes to in *The Da Vinci Code*, it has been pointed out that even if what the novel says is true and da Vinci *did* put a coded message into his painting, it is absolutely possible that da Vinci made it up. We are talking fiction after all. In fact, even if Brown and da Vinci both believed what the code suggests was true, it would not necessarily mean that it was true. Therefore, one can dismiss whatever faith-shattering errors are presented by the book and movie because they are—in light of what is believed to be the truth of the Gospels, in the reasoning of the church, and according to the characteristics of the medium in which they are found—fiction, that is, made up.

The interesting thing about this logic is the strength of its braking system. Those who use it are generally unable or unwilling to extrapolate their reasoning beyond Brown's novel, so they slam on the brakes and stop at the end of the previous paragraph. But watch this: using their logic we could argue that just because the apostles wrote the Gospels the way they did doesn't mean they didn't make them up. And even if the authors believed what they wrote, it doesn't mean it is true. Someone else might have made it all up before then. After all, they certainly had ample time between the death of Jesus and whenever it all finally got written down.[27]

It doesn't take long for us to realize that everything upon which we have based our Christian worldview can be examined in this manner. Having done so, one has to decide whether or not one wishes to believe the worldview that the church presents, and it may be that he or she does. What we can no longer do, however, is present that worldview as fact, especially when the questions of logical reasoning are applied. Belief? Go ahead and enjoy it as such if you like, but do not present it as absolute truth and require that anyone (much less everyone) believe it, too.

The other analogy is a post in the middle of a field. The post represents the fundamentals of Christianity. Around the post are those who adhere to the faith. Some are holding on to it. Some are close, but not touching. Some are at quite a distance, and some can barely see the post at all. But all of them use it as a frame of reference for their lives.

This analogy was offered by a colleague at a denominational event to suggest that, despite the great distance between me and the post, I still belonged. Its telling was a gesture of kindness. But I am uncomfortable with it, for it assumes the post *will* never and *should* never be moved, much less *re*moved. Its permanence is assumed, validating its orthodoxy and ignoring the reality that it was humans who drove it into the ground in the first place. And it leaves us vulnerable to those who would quickly draw a line at some arbitrary circumference, thereby determining who "really" belongs and who doesn't.

Other posts represent the worldviews for other faith systems or ideologies. The people closest to the post are the ones who believe in the most things nailed to the post—the fundamentals (and, yes, there are many arguments about what actually belongs on the post and what doesn't).

Those who raise liberal voices within Christianity call for the inclusion of all, even those who are at great distances from the post. It is time, however, to move beyond the liberal argument and call for the post's complete removal, for it should no longer serve as the point of reference. To understand why, we must examine what the post presents as our Christian worldview. What is inscribed upon it that we are using to orient our lives?

Well, the first order of belief is that God created the universe and everything in it. The second is that the Bible is TAWOGFAT (the authoritative word of God for all time).[28] The third is that we, as we are, are unworthy of God's love. The fourth is that Jesus is the one and only Son of God come to Earth to live and die for us. The fifth is that we can be forgiven our sinful natures by believing Jesus offered himself as a sacrifice for our sins. And on and on. Over the centuries, many things have been nailed to the post and used to establish the orthodox Christian world-view. But those who have even a rudimentary understanding of astronomy, science, history, anthropology, archaeology, or any number of disciplines, who have read the Bible and examined it with the help of critical contemporary scholars, and who have applied critical thinking to the basic tenets of Christianity will end up challenging almost every item on the post, right down to the concept of God it presents. Progressively minded Christians, those who want the church to operate in the most current theo-logical paradigm, argue that leaders in the Christian Church have the responsibility to release the brakes—to apply critical reason-ing to whatever worldview the post declares as absolute truth. They demand that church leaders integrate what they know with what they say and do. They differentiate between what some-one chooses to believe and what they require that others believe. They are not about tearing down a faith system that is a com-fort and strength to anyone; they are not about tearing down the timeless values of compassion and justice; they are about tearing down items on the post that declare that a particular human construction has divine authority.

The disruptive challenge of progressive Christianity lumbers into every sanctuary, every pastor's office, and every gathering of parishioners for Bible study. Its shadow falls upon our church libraries, our national ecclesial magazines, our newsletters, our statements of faith. It stands patiently in every place that people gather to be spiritually nurtured, to learn about their Christian faith, and to hear the truth about what the church is, what it believes it is to do, and how it believes it is to do it. The elephant represents integrity in the church, and its presence confronts many of the church's leaders.

## Co-creators

It is time we acknowledge that we, the church—those of us who have written liturgy and those who have sung it, those who have led the prayers and those who have knelt to recite them, those who have painted the icons and those who have adored them—we have, all of us, created what it is that we call Christianity. We started by creating the concept of God. Then we created the concept of Christ. We created the image of Jesus the church has passed down through the ages. We created our doctrine and dogma, our traditions, and our holy stories. We created church. We created ecclesial authority, the argument over apostolic succession, and the rites that identify some as insiders and others as in schism. We created heaven and its opposite, hell. We created the ideas around what will or will not get you to one or the other. We created the free passes. We created the barriers. We created it all, and the elephant in the room silently bears witness to this fact. Many know it but do not want to admit it. We know the truth of what Christianity is, but we do not want to say that we know. Perhaps we are afraid of not knowing who we are, of declaring our insecurity in the world, of acknowledging our frailty. Perhaps it is the simple reality of fear that demands our silence in the shadow of the elephant we see so clearly.

The "offence" of progressive Christianity is not the elephant. It is the declaration that the elephant is real and that it threatens the future of the church. Speaking about its presence will bring it into sharper focus. As church leaders are faced with the constant pressure of progressive voices, as their integrity is seriously questioned, it will be more difficult for them to remain indifferent to it. Their negotiated coexistence with the beast will begin to crumble.

## Co-conspirators

Perhaps it is my sincere desire to hold my colleagues in the highest regard that demanded I name them earlier as co-conspirators who "cannot" acknowledge the elephants that share their space. However, the knowledge and understanding given to us by the findings of contemporary scholarship and the clarity with which it has been presented would suggest that sharing those findings is something my colleagues are certainly *able* to do. They have the information. They have the tools. Many of them have long since released the da Vinci logic brakes and thought their way through to a clear critique of the Christian worldview. That being the case, perhaps I should not have suggested they *could* not acknowledge the existence of the elephant but, rather, that it is something that many of them *refuse* to acknowledge. Ability is not the only issue. Sometimes intent is the issue, and too often it appears their intent is to feign ignorance.

There are also those who sit in pews who seek to destroy anyone who points out the elephant's features and calls his or her peers to attentiveness. Quick to pull out the heretic label, their dismissive tactics can be devastating to those whose livelihood is grounded in the church. Many clergy have been forced from pulpits and the ministry by those who were intolerant of any "modern" ideas questioning their faith. Often it begins as a simple conflict about some inconsequential matter. Then it grows to the matters of singing the old favourite hymns, the lack of "real" Bible study, and the sharing of communion at the sickbeds of the dying. Almost all of such points of contention rest upon illogical, superstitious Christian beliefs; and when clergy have thought themselves away from those beliefs, they are required either to live a life of dissonance at the level of their soul or to leave the church.

At a recent progressive Christian conference in Ottawa, a retired member of the clergy noted that in attendance at the conference there had been five, including himself, members of the theological class he had studied with in the mid-1960s. Only he had remained in the ministry after the first few years of congregational leadership. The open, progressive theology even then being taught in seminary was met with hostile anger when introduced to those in the pews. That hostility drove his classmates from the pulpit. It is a sad loss.

Over the past few years, however, I have met many clergy, in several denominations, who have made honest, courageous *attempts* to speak the truth to their congregations. Too many of them are now retired and have felt freedom to speak about their beliefs only in their retirement. The inability of clergy to speak openly and honestly is wrought by angry laity who refuse to allow their too-comfortable beliefs to be challenged. They threaten the livelihood of men and women who seek only to unfold a path of spiritual growth before their congregants. They raise challenges and charges within denominational hierarchies and have clergy either removed or emotionally destroyed by their bitterness. One retired minister in Newfoundland reminisced about a Good Friday service in which he preached about the probability that Jesus' body decomposed in exactly the same way his and those listening to him would. Within days, charges had been laid against him in his presbytery, and soon afterwards, he found himself in an administrative position within the church, one from which he never re-emerged.

We can no longer allow such abuse of clergy to continue. While fragmented myths leave only literary detritus, fragmented lives are a travesty and an insult to the human spirit. Perhaps this book and those like it will encourage leaders in congregations to band together, to share the burden of speaking the truth and name the fears of those who challenge them. We all have much to offer, much to share, and much to change.

If you are familiar with the family systems theory, you'll know it claims that it takes only one person in a family to disrupt its homeostasis. Once someone refuses to react as he or she has been patterned to do, uses a different conflict resolution technique, or argues for autonomy in a relationship, there is no telling when the system will gain back equilibrium. It is possible that others in the system will notice the change, honour the individual's new self-awareness, and adjust their patterns to respect him or her. That would bring it to a new level and once again into balance. But such inclusive action doesn't usually happen right off the bat. The more people have at risk when a system starts to change, the harder they will usually fight to bring it back to the homeostasis they enjoyed and which was the least painful and most palatable for them. If someone has had all the power in a relationship and the other person starts claiming some, there is much at stake. Generally, power is not offered up without some kind of fight.

It is no different in the church. The more people have to lose as the elephant comes into clear view, the more they will adamantly deny its presence, blame it for all the problems in the church, or seek to destroy those who are making it visible. We've seen all this happening already. Consider the 2003 papal encyclical on the Eucharist, *Ecclesia de Eucharistia*. It is a prime example of a faith community's initial reactionary response to change. Faced with the growing numbers of more liberal-thinking Roman Catholics who consider the Eucharist a welcoming banquet set out by a God who loves all people, Pope John Paul II undertook to correct their "perverted" understanding. He set out as clearly as possible the sacrificial underpinnings of the Eucharist's theological significance, argued strongly for perpetual adoration of the Lord's presence in the Blessed Sacrament, and spelled out the threat of any full sharing of the faith with the separated brethren that participating in ecumenical celebrations of the word or services of common prayer would constitute. The ordination of women as a possible way to respond to the shortage of priests was also dismissed as impossible by John Paul II in *Ordinatio Sacerdotalis*. Having a woman act as the bridegroom of the church, which is female, is simply unthinkable.

But it isn't unthinkable, is it? Taking a deep breath, letting the long pause sink in, and tilting one's head to the side, I am coached by my mother to set out these few truths. The whole concept of Jesus as the eternal sacrifice for our eternal sins was created by the church. Its origins, deeply rooted in the Jewish theologies of atonement, are woven into the writings of the early evangelists of the New Testament. From there the idea is argued, stretched, embellished, and justified. We can watch it develop through the interpretations and ecumenical councils of the first few centuries. We can read its unfolding in the catechisms and encyclicals through the history of the Roman Catholic Church. Wherever we come across the concept of eternal sacrifice, we can remind ourselves that it was imagined by human minds and recorded with humanly driven writing instruments. It is a *created* piece of ecclesial authority.

What then is at peril if we do not participate in this weekly ritual? Nothing. What is the threat to our faith of sharing it, should we want to, with excommunicated brethren? Nothing. And, incidentally, who has ever checked the sex of the church? No one. We've simply taken the Bible's word on that one. And, who wrote the Bible? We did.

The only thing that is actually at risk, should we keep asking these questions, is the authority of the Christian church and that of its popes, bishops, ministers, and priests. Gone is the whole system upon which their special privileges are based. Gone is the respect they are afforded by the community as a whole—a respect, I might add, that is dwindling. And so it is that we will see from those who have held power for more than two thousand years more and more clearer and louder calls to ignore the elephant in the room.

There are also those who will blame the elephant, or those who point to it, for the plethora of troubles that plagues the church. To them, the elephant and its seer are known by the name "Satan," whose sole purpose they understand to be the evil destruction of what the church calls "Truth." But the Greek root of the name Satan, *ha santanos*, means "the adversary," one who stands in opposition, one who questions "truth" incessantly. Satan is the one who disturbs and disrupts what, without question, might be mistaken for truth. By so skilfully condemning Satan, its own quality-assurance program, the church has too long been able to silence keen observations put forward by any adversary and present itself as a pristine vessel of truth when, in fact, it is a vessel that has managed merely to spare itself the corrosive possibilities of debate.

A gentler but no less manipulative condemnation has equated questioning with weakness or a lack of faith. Through the ages those who have examined their souls with fear and trembling as a result of such accusations have been innumerable—if only because we cannot know of those too afraid to speak openly or write about their lack of faith. Their self-recrimination will have taken place far from public eyes.

When those in authority use such tactics, they manage to turn the glare of examination away from themselves and toward those who ask the probing questions. Many of us recognize the bullying tactics from the schoolyards of our youth. They are used because of their enormous success. But embarrass the bully and you'll be swiftly put in your place. You need to be careful. You need to have friends.

If you are an Internet user, no doubt you will have received an email that tells a heartwarming story, a simple moral tale that underscores the depth and breadth of God's love. Sometimes at the end of the story a few lines looking something like these will appear with instructions: "If you are too embarrassed to send this to six hundred and thirty-four of your closest friends, remember, the Lord may deny you, too!" The admonition is scriptural. Jesus is purported to have rebuked his disciples and followers with these words: "Whoever acknowledges me before men, I will also acknowledge him before my Father in heaven. But whoever disowns me before men, I will disown him before my Father in heaven." (Matthew 10:32–33; Luke 12:8–9) No wonder the bullies have ruled the roost for so long.

And so it is that progressive voices are now being raised in the current church in that same way as my mother raised hers, pointing to the elephant we have long conspired to ignore, shaming those who have worked so hard to keep its presence out of conversation, and demanding that it be led from the room. And, like her, among our colleagues and peers, we, too, often meet silence: some is born of the embarrassment of having been wilfully complicit as leaders in the church; some, combined with utter incredulity, comes from those who have truly never considered the complications we introduce; and some comes as a visceral rejection of our depiction of what stands in our midst. Yet, beyond the adjournment of whatever gathering in which those voices are raised and hidden from the glare of others, colleagues both active and retired, furtively approach us, thank us for our words, acknowledge their concurrence, and sidle out of view. They say things like, "Well, after all, aren't we all non-theists?" or "I may not agree with everything you say, but I'm sure glad somebody's saying it," or "I don't want to call myself Christian," or "What does 'worship' mean, now? As a minister, I don't know what I'm supposed to do any more."

And sometimes, they weep.

And so do I.

There is much to be said and much more to be done. As the future demands voices that will speak with integrity and courage, more and more laypeople who are no longer content with the theological fare of their childhood will challenge those who try to feed it to them. More and more clergy will question the words they use and the assumptions inherent in them. More and more churches will require that their programs and their Sunday services reflect contemporary scholarship and so that any, *any* who might attend them will be able to participate as fully and completely as they desire.

We will be able, finally, to reach out and embrace that grey, lumbering giant, the call to integrity that stood so patiently in the middle of the room waiting for us to acknowledge how human our faith is and to honour the creative power that generated it. When we do, that power can be turned to its most urgent use—creating a future in which life, in its myriad forms, is holy.

# CONSTRUCTING CHRISTIANITY
## A BRIEF HISTORY OF BELIEFS

Everything outside of the natural world that we see, touch, and respond to—every person, every group, and every political movement; every system of thought, of education, of economics, every religious act—was created at some time by someone. It came out of someone's being, someone's creativity, someone's life force. Whether it be the family tradition of making your own Christmas crackers or your own private choice to walk in the nature conservancy each spring looking for signs of new life, the impetus for doing it came out of someone's ideas, energy, and passion. If you benefit from it, those benefits come straight from that creative impulse, whether your own or someone else's.

The idea of doing something such as making Christmas crackers or keeping an eye on local bird habitats is about doing something to bring about an effect. We make the crackers to connect us to our ancestral roots, provide a feeling of belonging, and make our table look festive; we are strengthening our family ties. Keeping track of bird habitats might be a decision to assist in the recording of changes to sensitive ecosystems, as a way to preserve species. It might be a spiritual discipline designed to increase attentiveness to the environment. It might be a chance to meet other ornithologists. The reasons are your own. Usually, there is a purpose woven into the things we do and our choices to do them. When we no longer have a reason, we stop.

It is important to remember that no matter how it is that we choose to express or explore our Christianity, we are either using something that someone else created or creating something new. And, as with everything else, when we think about practices and acts through which we express religious faith, we can be sure that there were reasons for creating them. What we might not be so sure of is what those reasons were.

We who engage in religious activities as part of our spiritual growth trajectory generally assume that those who created our spiritual rituals were also seeking spiritual awareness, growth, or connection with the sacred. We assume the things they developed—from contemporary evangelical Christian worship to confessional and petitionary prayer, to Taizé and Celtic rituals, labyrinths, and massive pipe organs—were developed in order to move those who would use them into a more spiritually awake and aware space in which they might come to a deeper relationship with what was, for them, the sacred. We who look for spiritual guidance will see these different practices and rituals as vehicles that can help us disentangle ourselves from the busyness of our lives and centre ourselves in the spirit, whatever it is we find that to be. We trust that these tools were created for this uplifting work.

That may or may not be so. It may be that the reason something we now think of as a spiritually uplifting practice was not created for that purpose at all. It may have been, but to say it was is to project our modern perspective on a history we do not know.

It is important that we think about *how* our beliefs, our rituals, our traditions came into being, that we ponder their beginnings and consider them from as many different perspectives as we can. It is possible that, uncovered even slightly, we might see things we have not seen before, expose considerations we have not formerly acknowledged, and change the way we understand and use the tools that have been handed down to us. Most particularly, it is important that we look at those things it took much longer than six days for us to create—the concept of god, the book we call the Bible, and the institution we know as the church.

## BIRTHING BELIEF

Before the concept of time had been conceived, something happened. None of us really know what it was. Oh, there are theories. There are ideas. There are people who claim to know, and there are others who claim to know something completely different. There are scatterings of evidence still in existence, but, try as we might, we can't yet decipher them accurately; indeed, we probably don't even know what they are. But we do know something happened. We know because, whether suddenly or gradually, gently or cataclysmically, somehow Everything came to be.

You may argue that knowing, itself, even what we believe to be real, is questionable. Philosophers have long clamoured after the truth of our existence, the reality of our perceptions of ourselves and everything else. As the proliferation of books written by scientists, mathematicians, philosophers, journalists and many others indicates, the quest will continue for some time. For our purposes, at least until the end of this chapter, let's suppose that what we can see and touch and taste is real. If you are one of the few reading this book for whom that will be a stretch, please skip to the next chapter.

So, back to Everything.

Everything that is, however, is not the same as the Everything that was. Things change. Even big things, such as continents. The world we inhabit is different than it was long ago. It's different now than it was not all that long ago. We can see from our maps and photographs that, even over the short time during which we have been recording things, geographical land masses, shorelines, and terrains have changed. It is logical for us to assume that these changes have been happening long before we began to notice. It's quite logical, even, for us to assume they've been happening since the beginning of Everything.

Think, for example, of the kid in your grade-five classroom who asked the question about whether South America ever fit into Africa. It wasn't just Al Gore's classmate who figured that one out.[1] The question probably surfaced not long after the first maps of the world were printed and the sheltering shape of Africa was compared with the long curve of South America. Only in the last century, however, have scientists developed the theory of plate tectonics to address that question, and, like Al Gore's classmate, many were laughed at, put down, or simply ignored when their creative minds recognized the possibilities in those massive curves.

Think now of what happens when things shift on a scale that changes the map of the world. We're talking *big* changes—cataclysmic changes. We've seen some of the effects of those changes over the last few years. The Lamont-Doherty Earth Observatory of the Earth Institute at Columbia University has posted an eerie recording on its website. You have to turn the volume up high to hear what sounds like the distant roar of a stadium crowd cheering their home team on to victory. As you listen, the sound grows, deepens, and then rolls its way to a full, threatening rumble, and you can feel its vibration in your feet, your gut, your heart. It subsides for a moment, then rises again and with it a sense of foreboding.[2]

The sound was recorded by underwater microphones at Diego Garcia, an atoll in the middle of the Indian Ocean. The microphones are part of a worldwide hydroacoustic system designed to pick up the telltale traces of an atomic blast. Sometimes, as in this instance, they record natural things happening—the snapping of an iceberg, the eruption of an underwater volcano, or the grinding of tectonic plates against one another. On December 26, 2004, from 1,700 kilometres away, they picked up the sound of 1,600 kilometres of the Indo-Australian tectonic plate shifting about 15 metres farther along the edge of the southeastern Eurasian plate. The rupture caused an earthquake that measured between 9.1 and 9.3 seismic moments in magnitude,[3] a tsunami that measured up to 30 metres in height, and a humanitarian disaster that measured close to 230,000 dead or missing and untold millions of lives affected. It was not just the sounds of a planet shifting recorded by those microphones; if we listen carefully, so carefully we might even be imagining it, we can hear the sounds of life being wrenched from whatever it knew as normal.

But it wasn't always that way. Before there was ever a mind that could conceive of a worldwide hydroacoustic microphone system, it was just the sounds of the earth. No sounds of life being changed. No sounds of catastrophe. Change happened devoid of the impact we now experience. It just was. That's all.

The earth has spewed its burning, viscous innards out into the atmosphere, wriggled its way from a single land mass to what are now seven separate continents, compelled colossal shelves of shale and rock to heave themselves into mountains, and thundered its way into its present form for millions of years. Coastlines have flooded, fertile valleys turned to dust, and breezes warmed and cooled the impossibly opposite ends of the orb since this planet first came into being. But remember—that was long before us. That was long before we ever cared about what it was doing— long before there was anyone who could reflect on the ferocity with which Earth hurled itself, seemingly intent on its own destruction.

Apparently, it was just birth pangs. I say "just" as though birth pangs are nothing—the trifling ripples of muscular activity that bring another being into existence. They aren't, but they do tend to mirror the previous paragraph's description of the earth's violent, rending shifts and changes and, ironically, with the same result. Whether the earth gives birth to itself or a woman gives birth to a child, the world is never the same, no matter what happens or how things end up.

What was being born was a planet capable of sustaining life as we know it. Bacteria, viruses, plants, animals—the whole shebang. Without the generative activity of this wild planet, it may just be that none of us would be here. But once we came into being, once we had pulled ourselves out of the primordial ooze, so to speak, all that activity wasn't just the indifferent rumblings of a turbulent planet. No. Once we were on site, it got personal.

## Help!

Imagine having a child back then, before we had managed to figure out everything we've figured out. Hold the *Men in Black* pen before your eyes and red-blink the memory of science, history, astronomy, genetics, medicine, health, biology, psychology, anthropology, and every other piece of modern understanding away. Gone. And there you are: stark naked in a world that wants to kill you—and you're holding a baby. Get into that feeling for even a moment and you begin to realize how essential it was to find something that would take care of you, something that would shelter you, something that would keep the reckless writhing of the world at bay.

Maybe I've been a bit too melodramatic. Life back then wasn't tsunamis every Saturday, of course. There were warm summer days and brilliant starlit nights. There were soft breezes and deep, cool pools of water. There were soft mossy riverbanks and sweet, succulent fruits. There were rainbows and flowers and pebbles and butterflies. (Well, I'm not sure about the butterflies.) There were lots of lovely things. The problem was you couldn't count on there not being the other stuff, too. Complicating matters were big animals that were seriously not into the whole house-hold-pet thing. In fact, an awful lot of them seemed to be intent on swallowing you either bit by bit or in one big piece. From your vantage point, neither was a pretty end.

So what did we do? What could possibly have helped us survive the anxiety and terror that such an existence offered us? How did we gain some sense of control, some way of moving into the next moment with confidence? How did we manage to make our way to the place where hydroacoustic microphones are a regular, if little known, part of someone's everyday experience?

We created belief.

Lodged between annihilation and another day is a tiny sliver of what we have long called "hope." It breaks through the impossible, shatters reality, and shines brilliantly in defiance of the most incredibly futile odds. Faced with a coughing, heaving planet infested with vile and ravenous beasts, from that hope we wove for ourselves a strand of silver-lining and created a garment of protection that has carried us thousands and thousands of years to where we now stand. It was our salvation. We called it many things, but mostly, we called it "God."

We will never know exactly how long it took for us to come up with the idea. Nor will we know what first triggered the thought that something beyond us might be in control, something with which we might have a little influence. It could have been that the dramatic and unpredictable behaviours caused by the female hormone system mirrored the erratic weather patterns and caused us to wonder if the earth itself wasn't a female with the same wild mood swings. Perhaps it was that someone wished for protection from a vicious predator at precisely the same moment that a protected shelter was discovered—a serendipitous event that, reflected upon, seemed to suggest something just a little too coincidental to be pure happenstance. Or maybe, when one family was away from the community, the whole tribe was killed by some inexplicable cause, leaving those who were spared to wonder why.

Was it the place they had visited? The objects they carried? The food they ate, or the food they avoided? Whatever the complex patterns or abstract thinking that went into the creation of a god or gods, the idea spread and took on a life of its own. Literally.

It is a fairly simple idea, actually. Once it came to life, stories of its power, anger, blessing, and curse could grow exponentially, each person adding their experiences to the mix. This family's hunt was successful because they were the ones who carried the spear that killed the venomous viper during the last full moon and saved the tribe's leader. The full moon becomes an omen, the spear a holy item. Or this family is cut off from the tribe because of illness, an illness brought upon them because they pitched their tents on the other side of the water. That area is banned, forbidden. That woman is barren because she mated before the onset of her menses. Mating before menses is prohibited. This woman is blessed with many children because she collects pretty blue stones and places them along the eastern side of her mat when she lies with her mate. Blue stones become the gods of fertility. The storms of last year will not return this year because this year we remembered to scar all male firstborns with the embers of the first fire of the new moon after their birth. Except that the storms came anyway, so we have to examine our lives again and find the fatal flaw.

Of course, I'm making this all up—at least the details, that is. Who knows what happened or how or when? We created deities who lived within, beneath, above, or beyond the world of our senses, and we tried to figure out what it was they wanted from us. To get to the monotheistic god of Christianity, it is generally accepted that we first had to work our way through the belief that animals, objects (such as the imaginary spear or blue stones), and people we knew and loved had supernatural powers, and then that multiple otherworldly gods had their divine hands in the mire of mortal matters. The emergence of the single, unified God of Judaism, Christianity, and Islam was a late development in the evolution of belief. And true to the nature of evolution, there is no reason to assume that the evolution of belief will not further refine the God we in the West have been raised to revere. (It is interesting to note that many are returning to a new manifestation of the animism of our ancestors as they place crystals in strategic locations in their homes and workplaces, drip flower essences onto their tongues, conjure love spells, and design their own altars to honour the spirits they believe are guiding them. An agnostic when it comes to many of these things, I remain open to the possibility that science may find proof for some of them, but I cannot and will not, in the absence of that proof, present any of them as true.)

## Staffing

Over the course of the evolution of our understanding of god(s), we sometimes managed to come up with an idea that seemed to prove itself over time, however slim, subjective, and anecdotal that proof may have been. When that happened, we regularized and ritualized it. We even made it the responsibility of the tribe to remember it. To reinforce its importance, we began to bring people together as a group and remind them what it was they needed to do in order to stay on the good side of the god(s)—offerings, eating ceremonies, planting rituals, whatever it took. Before you knew it, we had the makings of a worship service—bells, smells, perhaps a sacrifice or two, anything to create security in an absolutely insecure world.

And at the centre of the worship service, standing at its very core? Well, it wasn't God with a capital G. You couldn't get God to show up. You could get only something that represented God. Something that could tell you what God really wanted.

You guessed it: a priest(ess).

If you think about the scenario for even a very brief time, you'll realize that it is an unstable one, particularly for the priest(ess).

Leading a community in a series of rituals or practices that were intended to control the weather, wild animals, pestilence, and "Lady Luck" would undoubtedly place you, as the priest(ess), in a very precarious position. Reality unfolds as it will. The chances of your getting it right any more than roughly half the time were nil. It just wasn't going to happen. So recognizing what those odds truly were, you'd be standing in front of the whole community on a fairly regular basis with no one to blame but yourself for the raging of the planet, the onset of killing disease, food poisoning, birth defects, hailstorms, the infertility of a significant percentage of the women, and the periodic loss of children to wild beasts and quicksand. And your community would expect you to do a little more than just stand there and shrug.

There is no possible way that a priest(ess) could win in those days. You could point the finger only at so many places, and then people were going to demand some results. Something had to give. Belief was in desperate need of evolution, and evolution answered its fervent prayer.

## A Heavenly Idea

The shift wasn't quite a sleight of hand. It may not have been so intentional as that, but the transition was so smooth and so brilliant that we have been mesmerized by it ever since. Perhaps it evolved the moment that a single, clever, frantic priest was about to be killed for not being able to stave off, yet again (through the invocation of divine protection, of course), the destruction of the community's entire food reserve by an infestation of vermin. As he was about to be disembowelled, perhaps he cried out, in what he surely believed to be futile hope, that though some of them were going to die of starvation, the place they would go after death was a place of plenty, where the most succulent fruits awaited their feasting. Indeed, wasn't it true that mortal bodies shrivelled away after death, having no more need of physical food?

They were feasting in another place, in the presence of their god, and delighting in it! And the real culprits who had brought the calamity upon the community (only God knows their names, but they will surely be counted among the dead), weren't they headed for extreme punishment after their deaths, to be paid back in utterly devastating, grinding, never-ending starvation for the rest of time? What pure revenge for disaster! What a calming, beautiful, hope-filled image for the innocent! It might have been just the thing to save the priest's life, and, as the foods were rationed through to the next growing season, even as a portion of the community died of starvation, wouldn't it have helped them to see the wisdom in offering the priest the best of whatever there was to eat? After all, he was still helping them understand the ways and the will of their God.

It was a simple shift, but one that created an enormous change in the way we believed. Recognizing we could not ingratiate ourselves to the gods enough to avoid the wrath we attributed to them, we slipped God's response through the doorway of death and gave ourselves hope in eternity. God no longer had to answer our prayers or respond to our dances. We would be rewarded in the afterlife—a place beyond everything we know. It has been the most significant development in the history of religion. And, as it turns out, the most brutal, frightening, hope-filled, desired, and dangerous one we ever dreamt up.

## PRESERVING BELIEF

It isn't clear exactly when we slipped God's response to our choices into the ever after. If we read the Bible with the perspective that God is going to act in the here and now, that's what we'll see. If we read it with the perspective that we'll get what's coming to us in the afterlife; we'll find much there to support that claim.

In the century preceding the Common Era (CE), the Jewish community reflected the spectrum of beliefs typically in existence within any large religious group. The continuation of life beyond death was one of the issues debated among its various sects. Josephus, the first-century Jewish apologist and historian, notes in his *War of the Jews* the differences between two of the sects, the Pharisees and the Sadducees.

The Pharisees, who are considered the most accurate interpreters of the laws and who hold the position of the leading sect, attribute everything to Fate and to God; they hold that to act rightly or otherwise rests for the most part with men*, but that in each action Fate co-operates. Every soul, they maintain, is imperishable, but the soul of the good alone passes into another body while the souls of the wicked suffer eternal punishment.

The Sadducees, the second of the orders, do away with Fate altogether and remove God beyond not merely the commission but the very sight of evil. They maintain that a person has the free choice of good or evil, and that it rests with each person's will whether he or she follows the one or the other. As for the persistence of the soul after death, penalties in the underworld, and rewards, the Sadducees will have none of them.[4]

The Essenes, yet another Jewish sect active at the time, believed in the immortality of the soul, as did the Pharisees. Josephus also reports on their beliefs, noting them to be similar to the Ptolemaic separation of the body and the soul:

> For their doctrine is this: That bodies are corruptible, and that the matter they are made of is not permanent; but that the souls are immortal, and continue for ever; and that they come out of the most subtile air, and are united to their bodies as to prisons, into which they are drawn by a certain natural enticement; but that

---

*In the Greek concept that was being assimilated, this would likely have included women; in the Jewish interpretation, women would not have been included.

when they are set free from the bonds of the flesh, they then, as released from a long bondage, rejoice and mount upward. And this is like the opinions of the Greeks, that good souls have their habitations beyond the ocean, in a region that is neither oppressed with storms of rain or snow, or with intense heat, but that this place is such as is refreshed by the gentle breathing of a west wind, that is perpetually blowing from the ocean; while they allot to bad souls a dark and tempestuous den, full of never-ceasing punishments.[5]

Within Jewish tradition, concern has focussed primarily on appropriate actions and choices in the here and now. Each of the three groups in existence during the Jesus years had very clear regulations about what their followers should do on a day-to-day basis. Whether those activities would affect one in the near or distant future was a less important issue. What was important was that one act in accordance with God's will, thereby fulfilling one's duties as they applied to both God and one's fellow human beings. Such an emphasis allowed for a broad discussion of views regarding the continuation of the soul or life after death.

## The Next "What's Next"
The Christian additions to the Hebrew scriptures narrowed that discussion considerably. There is little to no room within the Christian texts to assume anything beyond death other than the continuation of life, for better or for worse. Whether there is a waiting period between life as we know it and life as we can expect to experience it in the hereafter is less clear, and consequently it continues to be the source of some debate. A friend remembers the interment of his father, an evangelical minister, over which two of his colleagues co-presided, one an evangelical minister, the other a priest from one of the sacramental churches. Following the latter's extemporaneous prayer assuring God that all present would endeavour to say regular prayers on behalf of

the deceased in order that the deceased might one day be made fit to be accepted into the presence of the Lord, the evangelical rose and gave thanks that this had already been accomplished through the acceptance of the Lord into the deceased's heart a long time before. No lineups in that hereafter! You see the confusion biblical interpretation can generate.

## Going in Circles

Although there is great discrepancy in the Bible regarding whether an afterlife exists, the assumption that God exists permeates the whole book. From the opening verse of Genesis to the final blessing of John's Revelation, God's presence is absolute. It may seem ridiculous even to point out that fact. Usually, we are unaware of the framework our belief system provides. If we fail to alert ourselves to the reality of it, we are unable to explore or study it. Oblivious to such a framework, the circuitous reasoning that so permeates conservative Christianity is possible.

It goes like this: How do we know God exists? Because it says so in the Bible. Of course, any self-respecting Christians will be ready for the question their response will no doubt elicit: How do we know the Bible is true? The answer, almost without fail, will be: Because God says so. So we move to the next question: How do we know God is telling the truth? And the final answer is: Because it says so in the Bible. A perfect circle.

Within the framework, these answers are sufficient. There are whole shelves of texts that use only biblical verses supporting other biblical verses to prove the Bible is true.[6] Inside the frame, they make perfect sense. The assumptions support and reinforce the assumptions. Once we realize we're looking at the question from within the frame though, we can explore beyond its periphery, even if we choose to remain within it. Essentially, we break the circle of reasoning because we realize the answer is not valid. There needs to be other support.

In the exploration of scripture that has enchanted biblical scholars for so many centuries, the question of what those scriptures were written *for* is often assumed. It is assumed that as the record of the history of the human race viewed through the lens of the people chosen to redeem it (the Jews), the purpose of the Bible is to bring people into right relationship with God. It is assumed that as the revelation of the power of God's active presence in the world, its purpose is to bring people into right relationship with God. It is assumed that as a presentation of how God prepared the world for the coming of Jesus, its light and its hope, its purpose is to bring people into right relationship with God. The reality of God is a straightforward assumption on every level.

Ancient texts brought together in the Hebrew canon in the second century CE are commonly said to contain the historical account of the Israelite community as it sought to live out its covenant with God. In fact, many of the books, passages, and stories it contains were not written to record events that happened as they happened, but were written long after those events, most likely in order to help the community understand them within the context of their relationship with God. If we raped and pillaged our way across new territory, it is because God told us to do so. If we, in turn, have been destroyed by others who have taken over our land, it is because we disobeyed God who is now teaching us a lesson. If we've been carried off into captivity, far from where we believe God resides, it is in order that we might learn that God cannot be contained in one place. If we . . .

The stories go on and on. Open the book anywhere, read a story, look up some contemporary scholarship relating to it, and you will find, every single time, that the reason why that story was written can be distilled to one purpose: reinforcing the belief that God was real, regardless of what actually happened. While the Hebrew scriptures were being written, most of the civilizations in existence understood their own worlds only inasmuch as they related to a deity or deities. The Hebrew people were no different.

## World with a View

By definition we don't usually think about our worldview. It operates below the level of our awareness in much the same way as do our feelings about our families of origin. We take those feelings for granted and don't tinker with them very much unless we really want to change them somehow. Then we bring them to a level of consciousness that allows us to explore them, and, perhaps with a great deal of effort, at least a modicum of emotional turmoil and often pain, we make the adjustments we set out to make. Worldviews are similar. They influence us greatly, yet we aren't really aware of the power they have in our lives until something stirs them up, brings them to our awareness, and we undertake the often difficult work of realigning them to accommodate new knowledge, experience, and understanding.

But we don't usually start tinkering with either our feelings about our families of origin or our worldview unless we have to. Often the reason we have to is that we've walked straight into a life experience that we simply can't contort our pre-existing, subliminal worldview to fit. Something's got to give.

We struggle to hold on to what we know. Our worldview is comfortable. It helps us make sense of our lives. Our choices, decisions, and lifestyle are made possible and reinforced by it. Our presuppositions about what is true, right, and good "pre-program" us to act accordingly without critically examining our beliefs, let alone our actions. Through the centuries, our worldviews have supported amazing acts of compassion and justice. But they have also been responsible for the subjugation of others according to their gender, race, or creed. We've been able to assert our domination over animals and the planet's resources. We've subscribed to ideologies that assist the powerful in maintaining their power, whether the power be held by an organized political party or underscored by an amorphous economic principle. We've seen ourselves as those with power or those without, all based on our worldview.

Our understanding of God permeates our worldview, yet we rarely pause to examine what that understanding is or how it influences our behaviour, politics, and choices. The Institute for Studies of Religion at Baylor University explored that link by examining the religious values, practices, and behaviours currently exhibited in America. Rather than organizing results in traditional denominations, the researchers sorted the data into new categories that described how believers see God: as authoritarian, benevolent, critical, or distant. The researchers argue that these groups will tell us much more about how someone will respond in different situations than former studies. Those who share a category, that is, a worldview, will act and make choices in a more similar way than will those who might share only denominational affiliation.[7] A person who is a devout Catholic and who believes in an authoritarian God is likely to have more in common with a devout Baptist who shares that view than a once-every-few-months Catholic who believes in a benevolent God whose main features are forgiveness and love.

Because our worldview so often reinforces our own particular preferences and privileges, when someone tries to change it, by whatever means, we find ourselves locked in what seems to be a life and death struggle. In truth, that is exactly what it is. Because our worldview is plastic, not elastic, it can stretch, but it cannot return to its former shape. So when someone or something has such an effect upon us that it changes our worldview, our consciousness is raised to a level from which it cannot return; as American author Oliver Wendell Holmes wrote, "Every now and then a man's [sic] mind is stretched by a new idea or sensation, and never shrinks back to its former dimensions."[8] We can't go back. Who we were and how we saw the world dies in the process. We are forced to find a new homeostasis—a new consciousness, a new us. In an effort to preserve what we have known and avoid the costs associated with consciousness-raising, we struggle—and hard. I've often thought that T-shirts with "Just leave my consciousness alone!" on them might find a very decent market.

## Can You Plan an Apocalypse?

As Christian groups were beginning to grow in the middle of the first century CE, the security of an established worldview was being threatened. The worldview presented by apocalyptic prophets during the years leading up to the destruction of the temple in 70 CE influenced how Christianity developed.

> Jewish apocalypticists maintained . . . that God would soon intervene and overthrow these forces of evil in a cataclysmic show of force, that he would destroy all that opposed him, including all the kingdoms that were causing his people to suffer, and that he would then bring in a new kingdom, in which there would be no more sin, suffering, evil, or death. These apocalypticists maintained that those who were suffering needed to hold on just a little while longer, for God would soon vindicate them and give them an eternal reward in his Kingdom.[9]

The socio-political situation—foreign rule, oppression, subsistence living, myriad religious observances and regulations—was considered by some to be salvageable only through the direct intervention of God. And that intervention would require the complete destruction of "what was" in order that "what should be" could be put in its place.

Some early Christian communities saw Jesus as the Messiah, the person sent by God to bring about the end of the "what was" and usher in the "what should be." Peter's sermon in Acts 2 linked

Jesus' death and resurrection to the prophetic claims of a Day of the Lord by quoting from the second chapter of the Book of Joel. The section quoted by Peter speaks of the response God will have when the people have repented and turned back to him, but all his hearers, all those for whom the sermon was written, would have been familiar with what preceded that passage. Day of the Lord theology unfolds in its typical fashion in Joel—God, made furious by the sinful ways of his people, rides dramatically into history to destroy unbelievers and everything for which they ever cared. It reads like the coming of the orcs in the *Lord of the Rings* movies, great waves of danger and horror, spreading like dawn with destruction. Peter deliberately claims that Jesus is the one sent by God to bring about that repentance. The people are moved to conversion by the power of their fears.

## Even the Best Laid Plans . . .

Those early communities had a problem though: Jesus had not fulfilled that mission in a way anyone had prophesied. There had been no apocalyptic destruction of the harvest, burning of whole forests, or drying up of wells and orchards. There had been no obliteration of cities by rival armies who had murdered all the men and raped all the women. There had been no swift turning again, en masse, to God for forgiveness, nothing that would have warranted God's blessing or change of heart.[10] Jesus, if he was Lord, had not succeeded in bringing about the Day of the Lord the way it had been expected.

So strong was the worldview that God's anointed servant in the person of Jesus would bring about the apocalyptic restoration of God's rule, and so strong was their opposition to any contrary evidence, that its preservation became paramount. That need, to preserve the worldview, superseded any evidence to the contrary. It was either that or do away with the worldview. Stripped of that promise, left an unchosen people in an occupied land with no evidence of God's favour, was incomprehensible. As an alternative, it didn't even merit consideration.

## Remains of the Day

So early Christian writers created the expectation of Jesus' imminent return. That's just what we do when we cannot, for whatever reason, incorporate new information into our worldview. We either alter the worldview or reinterpret the information. And when the worldview is so strong our very survival seems to count on it, it is much easier to manipulate the information. And so it is that Jesus, who had already sloughed off his mortal coil, was written in for a posthumous act.

In both the Hebrew and Christian scriptures, the predominant worldview posits a supernatural God with which the people had a significant, covenantal relationship. Contemporary biblical scholarship focuses on the manner in which these texts are written, applying a variety of interpretive tools to the task. Yet the underlying assumption, that God exists as described within those texts, is often not examined. To do so would be to launch an assault on the theism that frames not only the predominant Christian worldview but also that of Jews and Muslims. And as the following example shows, tampering with worldviews can be a very dangerous thing.

In the 2004 CBC Massey Lectures, *A Short History of Progress*, historian Ronald Wright describes both the effect of a predominant worldview and its subsequent destruction. The worldview he examined included an infallible belief in supernatural powers by the civilization of Easter Island, the Rapanui. Migrants from the Marquesas or Gambiers had settled the island in the fifth century CE, having arrived there in enormous catamarans. Farming the land with seeds they had brought with them, eating large rats that they had also brought, and enjoying the rich seafood stocks available helped the population grow to around ten thousand. As the civilization developed, clans and ranks were established, and groups began the practice of honouring their ancestors, the *moai*, with stone statues. Over time, competition between clans to create the biggest and best of these statues grew.

A key element of their religious practice involved moving the massive carved stones from where they were hewn to stands lined up along the shoreline. In order to get them there, the Rapanui used wood. Lots of wood. Eventually, the little sixty-four-acre island could not produce wood quickly enough to replace what was being used in the process of hauling these enormous statues into place. Wright chills us with the thought that even as the last tree was being cut down, the person cutting it would have known that it was, indeed, the very last one. No more wood would be available to haul the stones. No wood could be used to repair boats. No fibre from the trees would be available for weaving clothing or making rope. But the tree was cut down anyway.

For a generation or so, there was enough old lumber to haul the great stones and still keep a few canoes seaworthy for deep water. But the day came when the last good boat was gone. The people then knew there would be little seafood and—worse—no way of escape. The word for wood, *rakau*, became the dearest in their language. Wars broke out over ancient planks and worm-eaten bits of jetsam. They ate all their dogs and nearly all the nesting birds, and the unbearable stillness of the place deepened with animal silences. There was nothing left now but the *moai*, the stone giants who had devoured the land. And still these promised the return of plenty, if only the people would keep faith and honour them with increase. But how will we take you to the altars? asked the carvers, and the *moai* answered that when the time came, they would walk there on their own. So the sound of hammering still rang from the quarries, and the crater walls came alive with hundreds of new giants, growing even bigger now they had no need of human transport.[11]

When Dutch explorers found the island in the early eighteenth century, there was little left of the civilization that had survived there for more than a thousand years, its people reduced to a small remnant of what they had been. They were living in caves or rubble henhouses, hoarding from one another the small and limited source of protein that continued to exist. But the statues still stood, magnificent in size and stature, protecting the people and promising them a better future to come.

Perhaps it was the arrival of the Dutch, with their splendid food, boats, and wealth, that struck the sudden and killing blow to the worldview that had encouraged the Rapanui to entirely devastate their environment in deference to powers they believed lived in the great stones. By the time Captain Cook arrived on the island fifty years later, a vicious attack on the stones and the ancestors had begun. Statues were knocked over and destroyed, beheaded and cracked in what Wright suggests resulted from the recognition of the ancestors' betrayal:

> We do not know exactly what promises had been made by the demanding *moai* to the people, but it seems likely that the arrival of an outside world might have exposed certain illusions of the statue cult, replacing compulsive belief with equally compulsive disenchantment. Whatever its animus, the destruction on Rapa Nui raged for at least seventy years. Each foreign ship saw fewer upright statues, until not one giant was left standing on its altar. The work of demolition must have been extremely arduous for the few descendants of the builders. Its thoroughness and deliberation speak of something deeper than clan warfare: of a people angry at their reckless fathers, of a revolt against the dead.[12]

Our worldviews are primal. We tie them to our existence and cannot interpret our lives without them. If they are challenged, we fight tooth and nail to preserve them. We are fighting for our lives as we know them. As Wright shows, however, those lives might be our undoing. I believe, painful though it will most definitely be, that it is time we live our way through the pain in order that we might arrive at a worldview that will help us be creative forces in the world's ecosystems rather than destructive ones.

Recognizing that God's existence is only an assumption that in Christianity is supported and reinforced by the Bible allows us to get outside our frame of reference and speculate on the view from other corners of the vast universe of thought. From various points, the reasons for writing the stories and poetry included in the Bible could look very different from what we might expect. Perhaps the idea of being in right relationship with God wasn't the motivating factor for the authors. Perhaps they were seeking to insert the concept of a single god into cultural situations that were more disposed toward a multiplicity of deities. Perhaps they were hoping to reinforce a system of governance that gave power, authority, and the inherent privileges associated with those things to a small group of people who were believed to "have God's ear." Perhaps they were, as new stories were added, employed in the task of shifting human accountability to an afterlife, thus reinforcing a system built on fear and obedience. I know, it sounds a bit like a conspiracy theory, but it reads like one, too. At least, it does once you're outside the frame looking in. But then, of course, to be perfectly fair, I must concede that should someone choose a different point in that universe of thought from which to take a peek, they, too, might see it in an entirely different way.

The Bible, through the process of being written, compiled, and legitimized, built the worldview through which Christianity came to the position of power and privilege it has enjoyed for the past couple of millennia. But that worldview has not always had an easy go of it. On its own, the Bible might not have been strong enough to stave off the thousands of years of questions regarding its authority. Fortunately it wasn't complete before that need became apparent. The protector it required could be, well, written right into its holy and authoritative pages.

Enter: the church.

## REINFORCING BELIEF

Controversial theologian and author John Shelby Spong often remarks that what people need more than anything is a sense of security. You can fiddle with whatever you like, tinker here, shift there, redefine somewhere else, but if you start chipping away at people's security, you're going to be in for a rough ride. Spong has been challenging what the church has held sacred for the better part of his ministry, first as parish priest and finally as Episcopal bishop, and his challenges have been experienced by much of the laity as direct assaults on their security.

I doubt that Spong is the first to articulate the connection between the need for security and the work of the church. The Christian Church, after all, is one of the world's many self-appointed arbiters of religious existential security, so it is very likely that the connection has been made before, though perhaps in hushed tones or behind doors. Spong brings the church's role in creating security to the fore, despite the reality that doing so chips away at the cozy feeling it has given us.

### Early Church Security

Looking back again at the first century, it was all too easy for detractors of the early Christian movement to prove that Jesus had failed to bring about the prophesied Day of the Lord. (He was dead, remember?) For those whose security rested on the claim of his being the Messiah, the promise of his posthumous return mitigated the risk of losing that hope and became the dangerous promise that helped his status as a still-living Divine

Intercessor (and so many other things, too numerous to mention) strengthen and grow. Left scribbled on a few papyrus scrolls or shared orally among friends, however, the promise most surely would have drifted into the annals of antiquity with little notice if it hadn't been for the creation of the means to preserve and promote it. In the same way that any special interest group forms as a vehicle to disseminate information about its issue, the church was created to be the vehicle of what was, for its proponents, a vital message.

Many believe, as they have been taught, that the church was born on Pentecost, that dramatic day recorded in the second chapter of the Book of Acts, when the Holy Spirit fell on a gathered crowd in tongues of flame and wind and allowed all to understand one another despite their various cultural origins. The word *Pentecost* means fifty days and is celebrated, through only a slight manipulation of the figures, that many days after Easter.

In liturgical calendars, Pentecost falls at the same time as the Jewish festival of Shavuot, which is calculated to be celebrated seven weeks (or fifty days) after Passover. Perhaps initially a grain festival recognizing the seven-week harvest period, Shavuot is also associated with the sighting of the first rainbow following the flood and the giving of the Torah to Moses on Sinai. The latter two events mark the making of the Jewish people into a covenantal people, deeply related to and loved by God.

By giving the Spirit to the gathered people in the Book of Acts and following it up with a passionate sermon by Peter in which he points a finger at the "men of Israel" and blames them for Jesus' crucifixion, the authors were thumbing their noses at the Jewish covenant and instating *themselves* as God's chosen people. It could only have been a calculated choice designed to counter those in the Israelite community who did not support Jesus' messianic status. It sought to create security for a small group within a larger tradition that was hostile to its claims. In so doing, it did not negate the claims of Jewish law or prophets but sought, rather, to incorporate them into their own body of belief. By making Christianity the next logical step, they could effectively undermine the security of the Jewish people and take it for their own.

But what was the nature of the security that those who fought for the privileged place in God's books were claiming? Was it merely their desire for that privileged place, or was it more than that? Our worldview provides us with the ability to interpret the challenges life throws at us. In the midst of almost any crisis, a theistic worldview allows that we will be able to figure out just what it is God wants from us. If we concede that whatever we are experiencing nullifies our worldview, we have to give up all the answers we have had for difficult situations in the past and all the comfort we would have had for those challenges we have not yet realized. Like the Rapanui of Easter Island, our worldview refuses to allow for inconsistencies. We either have to make more statues and fortify the worldview or accept that whatever it is we thought was in control really isn't. And like those who set the first upright stone in the ground and worshipped it, long before the Rapanui, we're desperately afraid of being alone and powerless in the face of life's catastrophic possibilities.

For a growing group of Jesus' followers, the author of the Book of Acts wrested the privileged position of the Israelites out of the hands of the Jewish elite and offered it to this new community. Taken with the implications of this power, the evangelists continued to pull together the many stories that had collected about their deceased Messiah in order to roll them over the Jewish liturgical calendar. The effect, carefully exposed in Spong's *Liberating the Gospels*, was to connect the dots between the covenant with the Israelites and the life and death of Jesus, to eventually replace one with the other. In so doing, the authors of the Book of Acts reinforced not only the belief that Jesus was God's divine son and the Messiah but that God himself existed. If Pentecost is the birthday of the church, the celebration must also be recognized as the strategic championing of one privileged relationship over another.

In contrast to the security early Christianity was weaving for itself, beliefs the Romans had rooted in their collection of gods were being increasingly threatened by the vocal groups of Christians who were becoming regular participants in the many different levels of Roman society. The persecutions by the Romans on the early Christians were the result of that threat. Called atheists, or equally derisively, Christians, the promulgation of their monotheistic religion to the exclusion of all other gods was seen to displease the Roman gods. Dr. Robert Doran, Catholic theologian and professor of systematic theology at Regis College in Toronto, makes the connection between the persecutions of the Christians and the threat—existential perhaps but certainly political—that Christians posed to the Roman Empire:

Decius had come to the throne at a particularly crucial time. Rome had just celebrated its one thousandth year of rule in 247, but the Goths had attacked Rome in 248. Decius had forced the Goths out of the Danube provinces and in return had been hailed emperor by his troops (he would die fighting the Goths in June 251). In the midst of this crisis, Decius appealed to the gods of the empire for help in restoring it. Forces that interfered with a harmonious relationship between the Romans and the gods were to be eliminated. That meant the Christians. Although the persecution did not last long, it was the first general persecution of the Christians by Roman authorities and was to be repeated again under the Emperor Valerian in 257–260 and under Diocletian with the great persecution, which began on February 23, 303. We must not neglect the religious motives of the persecutors: The empire was constantly under threat in the latter part of the third century. Few emperors died peacefully; most died on the battlefield. In this atmosphere of crisis, the emperors asked for help from their traditional benefactors, the gods, and sought to remove anything or anyone who might displease them.[13]

Constantine's legendary conversion, at the battle of Milvian Bridge, was precipitated by his desire to seek security for his life and his troops. His proclamation of Christianity as the official religion of the Roman Empire reinforced the entire picture being presented to the world by Christians, including the story of Pentecost and its inherent attack on Judaism. Persecutions of the Christians, by both threatened parties, the Romans and the Jews, was ordered illegal. Christianity became the repository for the security of the Roman Empire, the stronghold for the proof that a single God was protecting it and promising it victory.

As one of monotheism's repositories, it became essential for the church to reinforce its own importance. Writing itself into the story of Jesus' life and death was a brilliant first step. Because the Gospels were still being told, amended, and recorded, it was easily achievable. In the Book of Matthew, one of the later Gospels, the evangelist authorizes the church's existence by none other than Jesus himself, who gives the concept his imprimatur* when he changes Simon's name to Peter, meaning rock, and says that he will build his church upon that rock. The creation of the papacy, its power and influence, and its ongoing disdain of contemporary scholarship that comes from anywhere other than the "one true church of Christ," all rest upon that "solid" foundation to this day.[14]

## The Cost of Security

Western culture dominates the developed countries of the world. Some who make references to the rise of European power through-

---

*The word *imprimatur* means to authorize something to be done, said, or printed. It is generally reserved nowadays for works sanctioned by the Roman Catholic Church. I doubt Jesus would have liked the concept, but, in this instance, it very tidily gets the point across.

out the world and the subsequent cultural genocide that followed choose not to lay the blame at the feet of Christianity. Others are more bold. But we must consider what role the church has had in the annihilation of whole cultures that did not subscribe to the Christian story and the one God it championed. In the face of the very different beliefs of other cultures, the church's security, both existentially and as a significant power player in the world, would have been severely challenged. How much of the destruction of cultures has happened in order to defend that security?

Cultures that have been taken over, however, can bite back and hard. Having converted much of Africa to Christianity, those who believed they were doing God's work were surprised when their converts began using it against them. Archbishop Desmond Tutu often quotes Kenyan leader Jomo Kenyatta, who complained that "When the missionaries came to Africa they had the Bible and we had the land. They said 'Let us pray.' We closed our eyes. When we opened them we had the Bible and they had the land."[15] But in that Bible, Tutu found much that condemned colonialism, along with the courage and energy to respond. Apartheid, too, was challenged vehemently by Christian communities that held the government and its practices to account using the biblical stories of the government leaders' own faith to argue the rights of people of colour to the justice and freedom that comes with that faith.

The current climate of conflict within the Anglican Communion continues the example in the opposite direction. African Anglican clerics are fighting against North American cousins seeking to move the church into more socially progressive areas such as rights for GLBTs. It gets complicated when those responsible for presenting the Bible as the authoritative word of God for all time (TAWOGFAT) in order to convert nations to Christ then try to tell people that only parts of it are true. And, if only parts of it are true, or if some parts contradict others, who gets to pick which parts are really, really true? This has been the question for a very long time and, no doubt, will continue to prevail in the milieu of unrest in which the church fights for survival.

Indeed, the question was in existence when Constantine asserted Christianity as the empire's religion. If the church was going to be able to provide Constantine the security, political or otherwise, for which he was yearning, it was going to have to be a cohesive unit. Many different interpretations of the message Jesus had given were being lived out all over the empire, sometimes in mutually exclusive ways. Constantine needed to make the church one. In his attempts to do so, he managed to shift the nature of Christian society from being to believing.

## DEFINING OURSELVES BY WHAT WE BELIEVE

Since the time of Constantine, Christianity has defined itself essentially through what it believes. In its early years, communities seem to have grown up around different teachers who interpreted Jesus' message and sayings in different ways. Even after the particular books and writings that would eventually be called the canon became primary, what they meant was still up for grabs. Different communities believed different things.

Constantine didn't seem to have been aware of the many different understandings of Christianity that existed across the Empire's growing frontier. Believing the Christian faith to be of one fabric, unlike the multiplicity of pagan religions that confused daily and political life, he had taken the faith as his own in the early fourth century, perhaps primarily as a way to unify his vast empire. Hearing, shortly after his conversion, of a brewing controversy that suggested all was not as harmonious as he would have liked to believe, he was sorely distressed.[16]

At issue in that first great debate was the "Godhead." Although Western Christians seemed content with an understanding of the unity of the Godhead and the equality of the three persons in it—the Father, Son, and Holy Spirit—eastern Christians were struggling to clarify whether all three persons were equal or if Jesus had been created at a later date. Constantine called an ecumenical council, likely in the hopes that once clarity on this particular fact was achieved, unity would reign.

## Creeds Past

Things at the council didn't get off to a promising start. Then again, you might say it set the tone for theological debate for millennia to come. The council opened with a speech by the emperor urging harmony and an end to the dissension that was challenging the church. Not long into the discussion, however, Eusebius of Caesarea, having already been excommunicated by another gathering of bishops*, presented a creed that he and his church were already using. The result wasn't pretty. Eusebius was humiliated when significant changes had to be made to his proposal. Constantine stayed on to participate in the ensuing discussions, and records indicate that he, himself, offered the word now understood to address the crux of the unity issue—*homoousias*, meaning "of the same essence."[17] Arius, a priest from Alexandria who argued that Jesus was not of the same substance as God, was condemned as a heretic and exiled. At the end of the council, the Nicene Creed was established as the description of the true faith, and Jesus was declared as having been with God from the beginning—begotten, not created. We've been making decisions by committee ever since. Will we never learn?

---

*We must remember that, prior to Constantine's first council, there was no "official" church. Gatherings of bishops regularly excommunicated others they deemed heretical and were, in turn, often excommunicated by those they had sought to defame, since each group claimed God-given authority.

But the council was only the beginning of a long process of clarifying belief. The Nicene Creed, in fact, continued to be challenged and tweaked for the next fifty years, coming into its final form at the Council of Constantinople in 381. This version is still recited regularly in Roman Catholic and Eastern Orthodox services. The Apostle's Creed, thought to be contemporaneous, addresses many of the same issues, particularly those raised by Arius.

Creeds fulfilled a variety of purposes in the growth and development of the Christian Church. Early on, they became integral to the Christian worship life, being offered just prior to baptism as a confession of one's faith within the community and recited as a commitment to it thereafter. Their liturgical role grew and developed over the centuries, and they remain a regular part of the worship service in many Christian congregations; sacramental churches recite a creed weekly as part of the Eucharist, while mainline Protestants often recite one as a confession of faith integral to baptism or communion services. Many evangelical churches subscribe to what may have been the earliest creedal form of all, declaring simply, "Jesus is Lord."

In addition to being a mark of assent, creeds offered a list of Christianity's beliefs that could be used to explain its more central points. Encapsulating the basic tenets of the faith, they became important teaching tools for the early church. Indeed, as their teaching role became obvious, the creeds developed into a longer form known as a catechism, which continues to be used in many denominations today. Using the question and answer approach to the study of faith, these creedal forms made the difficult theological arguments of the church accessible to those being initiated into the faith.

Creeds and catechisms were an easy way to ascertain one's adherence to an orthodox understanding of Christianity. While members of the earliest communities had been identified and derided as Christians for the way they lived and the things they did, post-Nicea Christians could be identified by what they believed. To say a creed was to make a confession of faith. Over time, those who couldn't or wouldn't articulate the faith's basic beliefs became the focus of the church's attention.

It may be that the impetus for all great religious inquisitions is the salvation of souls. The techniques used to elicit confessions of heresy, admissions of one's belief in something other than the "true" faith, however, suggest that the altruism of the church was perhaps too easily sacrificed in the pursuit of doctrinal conformity. In attempts to reinforce the perception that the church really and truly had the individual's best interests at heart, it became customary at the public sentencing of heretics to begin with the commuting of the sentences of those previously punished. Heretics who had been imprisoned might be freed and required only to wear crosses. Those who had worn crosses might be allowed to set them aside. The implication was that the Church loved and cared even for those who had strayed down heretical corridors.[18]

In inquisitorial times, the teaching aspect of the creeds was reinforced during these sentencing services by the reading of lists of *culpe*, the errors in belief that the heretics had embraced. The converse of creeds, the *culpe* reinforced exactly what it was that constituted heretical thinking and thereby underscored what the true beliefs of the church were. At the end of a long day listening to sermons, commuted sentences, lists of *culpe*, and consequent sentencing, any who might not have known what the church required them to believe were certain to have had it clarified for them.[19] Even today, it is often easier for people to articulate what they don't believe than to say what they do.

## Creeds Present

It continues to this day that creeds and statements of faith are the litmus tests for leadership in the church. Ordination services in every denomination include that church's accepted beliefs set out in one form or another to which the candidate for ordination must assent. And long after ordination, the set of beliefs to which one subscribed during ordination can be held up to assure ongoing uniformity of belief within the ranks.

Statements of faith can be slippery things though, as Andrew Freeman noted in 1994 shortly after his removal from his position as an Episcopal priest in the Church of England. Dismissed following the publication of a book that laid out his theological beliefs, Freeman, in an effort to position his beliefs with those of the leadership in his church, consulted "The Nature of Christian Belief," a statement created by the Church of England House of Bishops in response to daring theological comments made by another priest several years before. The statement, however, did not set out exactly what it was the bishops believed about things referenced in the creeds, such as the virgin birth. Instead of making it easy for Freeman to make orthodox choices, the language in the statement seemed to intentionally obfuscate, protecting the bishops from ever having to state what they really believed on any specific theological topic. Freeman argued that if the bishops were going to be dismissing priests for not believing the proper things, those same bishops, as leaders in the church, should at the very least be willing to state publicly and clearly what it was they personally believed.[20]

In 1997, the Reverend Bill Phipps, newly elected moderator of The United Church of Canada, said in an interview reported in the *Ottawa Citizen* that he did not believe Jesus was God. His remarks led to disciplinary procedures being recommended at a meeting of his overseeing presbytery. That motion was tabled and no action was taken, but shortly afterwards Phipps offered a clarification of his beliefs on a segment of Vision TV's *Spirit Connection*. In that statement, Phipps did what most clergy do when faced with the ire of their constituents—he positioned his beliefs in a manner that sought to calm both sides of the debate.

Just to clarify, I believe with all my heart and soul that God was in Jesus, reconciling the world to God's self; that as much of God as was possible was revealed in Jesus of Nazareth. And therefore we can say with confidence that Jesus was the Son of God; that Jesus is the Word made Flesh; that Jesus is God Incarnate, and I feel that with all of my soul.[21]

Similarly, in 2005, following the publication of an article outlining my own personal beliefs in my denomination's magazine, the *Observer*, steps were taken by a colleague at a neighbouring church to have a committee of the Presbytery to which I am accountable hold a meeting to ask me formally if I was "in continuity with the faith of the church." That "faith of the church" would have been according to the Articles of Faith in The United Church of Canada's 1925 Basis of Union or the 1940 Statement of Faith. The motion to hold the meeting, referred to by John Shelby Spong as a "heresy trial," was defeated.

As attendance in mainline churches has continued to decline, forcing an increase in "worldly" concerns (often in the church referred to as "temporal" to distinguish them from "spiritual")— that is, rising costs, crumbling buildings, fewer volunteers to do the work, and so on—focus within congregations has necessarily shifted away from conformity of belief to these everyday concerns. Criteria for belief is less stringent when you need numbers. In 1968, as the death of God was being declared throughout Christendom, The United Church of Canada commissioned a short piece to be used as an affirmation of faith. The writing of it seemed to reflect the church's desire to have a softer, gentler version of the denomination's Statement of Faith, which was more than twenty-four hundred words. Through a mysterious process, including publication of it in the denomination's hymn book under an assumed title, the affirmation became known as A New Creed, lending it a credibility its writers may not have initially intended.

A New Creed allowed those in the church who were questioning some of the traditional beliefs of the Christian Church to remain within the embrace of the United Church.

Similar attempts seem to have been made by other denominations. The preamble to The Confession of 1967 of the Presbyterian Church (U.S.A.) identifies the challenges posed by the 1960s to more than just their own church. In approving The Confession of 1967, the Presbyterian Church (U.S.A.) adopted its first new confession of faith in three centuries. The turbulent 1960s challenged churches everywhere to restate their faith. While the Second Vatican Council was reformulating Roman Catholic thought and practice, Presbyterians were developing their new confession.[22] The ten-page document was followed by a two-page version a few years later. Presbyterians in New Zealand, however, went straight for the shorter version and published a single-page Statement of Faith in 1969. The radical challenge of critical biblical scholarship, while becoming significant enough to cause denominations the world over to rethink their creedal documents, was put in its place by what look to be, from several decades away, relatively tame changes.* Temporal concerns have continued to ensure that radical change remain, thus far, safely on the back burner.

Those same temporal concerns have also taken a toll on the work of social justice by denominations. At the 2005 United Church Annual Meeting of the Toronto Conference, one of the judicatory bodies within The United Church of Canada, Jim Wallis (evangelical Christian, social activist, and theme speaker at the conference), asked the delegates if people would know why they did the good deeds that they did. He assumed that this group of people, members of one of the most socially provocative denominations

---

*I write from the safety several decades of hindsight can offer. The changes appear timid only from this perspective, but at the time, in each denomination, the efforts to change more than likely created deep division among members. While it is easy to say the changes don't seem very significant now, I do not wish to mitigate the pain that some may have felt throughout the period during which those changes took place.

in the Christian Church, lived in concordance with their beliefs. He was asking them (leading them really) whether they were evangelistic about why they did what they did—did they let people know it was because they were Christians?

The meeting was silenced when Hal Llewellyn, former general secretary of the Church's Theology and Faith Committee, stood and noted that, as a body, the conference had done nothing at their annual meeting that would have been the result of a Christian set of principles or values at all. In contrast to the provocative position statements the body would have once made to governments and their leaders—letters about economic, sexual, and/or social justice, or about government actions or world concerns—this particular meeting had focused almost exclusively on administrative matters. After an embarrassed silence, another member of the conference rose and, seemingly oblivious to Llewellyn's remarks, used the opportunity to complain about a fifty-cent increase in denominational per capita dues. Llewellyn's point stood.

Challenged to update its own Statement of Faith, The United Church of Canada undertook a multi-year project that culminated in the acceptance of A Song of Faith in the summer of 2006. The project sought the participation of congregations and individuals across the country, provided initial study materials, circulated a draft statement, and held a symposium on that statement late in 2005. At that time, the committee responsible for crafting the final product had not yet determined whether their task was to update the theological concepts in the Statement of Faith or to merely contemporize the language in which that statement had been written in the later years of the 1930s. The final result has been embraced by many in the liberal denomination, perhaps because, wanting to engage its diverse membership, it deftly managed to avoid asserting any particular theological position. Its melodic obfuscation lulls many with its poetic beauty while its contemporary language gives it the appearance of being up-to-date. But the United Church had to work hard to miss what was certainly a golden opportunity to distinguish itself as the first denomination to actually affirm contemporary scholarship in its Statements of Faith.* In what appears to be a concession to the World Council of Churches, A Song of Faith included the requisite Trinitarian formula (Father, Son, and Holy Spirit), without which it would have been excluded from membership. Between the energy the church has in the past put into ensuring conformity of belief and the energy and resources it now puts into ecclesial survival in the most blatant sense, little is left for discussion of the life-enhancing values by which we must live if we are to achieve a world we can sustain, individually, socially, and environmentally.

## Creeds Future

Yet this is exactly where a possible and perhaps the most important future for the church lies. The world is seriously in need of clarity around what values will help us create a sustainable future and what values will compromise our ability to get there. In the early church, the values of love, forgiveness, and compassion drove the work and lives of those known as Christians. This is a legacy of the church, and it must once again become the agenda by which it chooses to live. Not what we believe. Not our institutional survival. Our focus must be what we can do to challenge, edify, and support individuals as they seek to live virtuous and responsible lives. It is vitally important that we stop fumbling the ball; that is, if it's not too late already.

Could this supportive role of the church also be the future for all religions? There are those who argue that religion must die if

---

*The United Church of Canada has a habit of adding to its Statements of Faith rather than replacing them, so the 1940 Statement of Faith augmented the 1925 Basis of Union, itself a statement of the faith of the newly formed denomination. The appendices to its new A Song of Faith clearly state that the 2006 expression does not replace the Articles of Faith in the Basis of Union, the 1940 Statement of Faith, or the much-loved 1968 New Creed.

we are going to survive as a species. Soaring on the top of the best-seller lists are authors such as Sam Harris (*The End of Faith* and *Letter to a Christian Nation*), Richard Dawkins (*The God Delusion*), Daniel Dennett (*Breaking the Spell: Religion as a Natural Phenomenon*), and Christopher Hitchens (*God Is Not Great*), who call themselves the Four Horsemen, with obvious reference to the apocalyptic Revelation of John.[23] Their diatribes are against the most heinous aspects of religion and rightly so. Most non-fundamentalist religious people, too, are eager to distance themselves from the horrifying aspects of their own faith traditions, but they are loath to let go of those elements of their religious practice that help make them feel safe in a chaotic world. The loss of religion as a whole, although it would rid the world of the negative aspects of supernatural faith, would also eliminate one of its most regularly accessed vehicles for presenting, upholding, and reinforcing the challenges that ethical living present in our complicated world.

There are far too few readily accessible sources by which individuals are influenced to become caring, altruistic, and respectful humans with interests that extend beyond that of their own bathroom mirrors or backyard pools. Popular culture exposes youth to an understanding of sex as entertainment; alcohol, drugs and tobacco as social prerequisites; violence as an urban norm; and the trappings of fleeting fashion trends as obligatory. Those who do not acquiesce are considered losers, nerds, or worse. In stark contrast, youth whose families are involved in the close communities of large evangelical Christian congregations find enormous support as they develop values counter to those of the social milieu in which their peers are drowning. Is it possible that religion can provide a values-based alternative to what popular culture provides but with neither the stigma of nerd-dom nor religious fundamentalism?

Adults who survive their adolescent years without succumbing entirely to the pressures of popular culture and who think about the "big" issues are considered to be and even see themselves as unusual. Exchanges in a chat room sponsored by the Canadian Centre for Progressive Christianity express the feelings of difference that those who explore difficult issues experience. Many find validation for their counter-cultural thinking in communities drawn together for religious purposes. Something or someone needs to apply constant pressure against the values that a consumer society sets as the most desirable. Religion, of any sort, could do this well if it could divest itself of its destructive, tribal, and dualistic requirements and excavate and promote the life-enhancing values that rest at its core.

New Zealand theologian Lloyd Geering suggests that secular society is exactly that—a positive and logical outcome of Christianity distilled of its religious trappings and tribal preconceptions.[24] Established at its core are values that are basic to Christianity: love, justice, respect, forgiveness, and tolerance. But the exclusively religious elements of Christianity, which comparative religion scholar Wilfred Cantwell Smith called "cumulative tradition,"[25] are not recognized by the centre of secular society as having validity except to a portion of its members. Once divested of these religious elements, the remaining values are found to be shared by many other world religions and ideologies. Distill each of them, leaving behind the residue of exclusive religious traditions, rituals, and beliefs, and we are left with a variety of core values. These then can be examined for what they might bring to the creation of a civil, values-based society. Secular society finds itself well equipped to begin the process of building a table at which all religious and philosophical ideologies might rightly be seated. It is at such a table that the work of developing the agreements and commitments that might bring about a sustainable future may evolve.

The task of those who care to salvage something of the Christian Church in order that it might undertake this important work will be to identify the values worthy of being upheld and celebrated within Christian congregations. There will always be a diversity of preference regarding how such values should be highlighted, what rituals have meaning for whom, what can be considered of such importance that it remains beyond a process of distilling, and what is never to be seen again. So, too, will the diverse explanations for their origins—supernatural, evolutionary, or other—be fought over. But what can and must bring us together as community is our agreement that these values are essential: they will then become what it is we say we *believe* in. Allowing those beliefs that divide to evaporate allows us to see the beliefs we hold in common, and they are many. It can be only these latter beliefs, those shared and celebrated widely within the world's community, that call us to humane and just living, that can help us create a world in which we live together with respect for one another, ourselves, and the planet. "Nothing more is needed, but nothing less will do . . ."[26]

3

# CHALLENGING CHRISTIANITY
## THE DILEMMA OF NEW UNDERSTANDINGS

It seems almost incredible that, with the brilliant minds we have put to the task, we have not yet been able to adequately share progressive Christian scholarship with the wider church and, beyond it, the world. While I think much of the reason for that strange reality lies in the theological formation of church leaders, it must also be a significant factor that many in the pews show utter disdain for the insights gained over the past few centuries of study and discovery. Ensconced within worldviews that maintain a comfortable sense of divine privilege, who'd ever want to shake things up?

Our world is demanding that our worldviews change. As our tribal prejudices continue to be challenged by a shrinking globe and its shrinking resources, we're going to have to find another way. Exploring the roots of the problem is one way to begin finding a decent way out of it.

## ANATOMY OF A DISCONNECT

As noted briefly in a previous chapter, scholarship that questions the Bible as TAWOGFAT (the authoritative word of god for all time) has been available to those in academic institutions (by that I mean theological schools, many of which are attached to liberal arts universities) for decades. Beyond fear and a need to protect a vulnerable worldview, I believe there is another reason this scholarship hasn't made it to the pews. It's what happens when individuals are moulded for leadership inside the church. I call it "severing the corpus callosum."

## The Two-sided Brain

The corpus callosum is that broad thick band that runs between the left and right hemispheres of the brain. It provides for the necessary transfer of information between the sides, necessary because each side seems to have responsibility for separate kinds of mental activity.

The left side of the brain is where language resides. We house our learned speech and writing ability there. Rational thought finds its home there, too. And much of our mathematic and logic processes reside in the synaptic activity of the left lobe. Oddly, each hemisphere is linked to the movement of the opposite side of the body so the directions to the right hand, while writing, come from the left side of the brain, as does what is seen through the right eye.

The right side of the brain is where intuitive and creative impulses fire. Left-handed people are often found to be more artistic, their right hemispheres being dominant. Speech is not found here, nor is any kind of language skill. Verbal information that comes through the left eye, linked to the right side of the brain, is translated by quickly reaching into the left hemisphere via the corpus callosum and grabbing the information required.

So the left side of the brain is the place most exercised while we are learning academic information—facts, rational exploration of ideas, history, and languages. It is where information is stored and where new information, upon arrival, seeks out and replaces the old information—an update for your brain. (No wonder learning can be a struggle for people who are right-brain dominant and who think visually and not verbally!) The right brain is exercised when creative pursuits are undertaken and artistic imagery explored. Dance, painting, calligraphy, poetry, images, metaphor, and music—all these things are fired in the right hemisphere. Their connection to language slips easily to and from the left hemisphere so it is possible to use language to *describe* artwork, dance, and visual images, although such language is always subjective to some degree. It cannot be verified in the way that information on the left side can be. It is more intuitive and subject to the experiences of the individual making the description.

I'm wondering if theological training doesn't tamper with the corpus callosum. It is an educational process, of course, but the information being offered is so completely contradictory that I think theologues (theology students) survive only if they can neatly store it in separate parts of their brains. Even then the rapport between those two sides, when it comes to theology, needs to be highly controlled or, in the best interests of the church, prohibited. I've become convinced that throughout the process of theological education, my corpus callosum was severed.*

## Two-sided Education

Both sides of an individual's brain are exercised during theological training. The academics of biblical study, languages (the original languages of the Bible—Hebrew and Greek—are often prerequisites for divinity degrees), church history, and systematic theology all stretch and exercise the left side of the brain, while the worship acts stimulate and impress themselves upon the right side of the brain. And what a workout it is!

---

*My use of information on the corpus callosum is purely to create a working metaphor and, due to its general nature, while basically correct, it is not to be understood to be scientifically accurate. For further information, please consult your family physician.

At the beginning of my theological education, we were examined on our knowledge of the Bible in two tests—one on the Hebrew scriptures and the other on the New Testament scriptures. The results were laughable. Indeed, one of my fellow students so enjoyed being found out to be utterly ignorant about the Bible that he made a game of it, answering to the question "What is the significance of the town of Schechem?" that it was the only town where Moses cleared his throat! We were exposed to a Bible most of us had never bothered to read, a church history with intrigue no less fascinating or brutal than that of imperial England, and a critical systematic theology that put our brains (the left side) through gruelling contortions and experiential aspects of God we'd never before encountered.

That academic training kicked the knees out from under many of us, not only because we weren't used to reading from right to left as we had to do in Hebrew. The fact was that most of us had arrived at theological college with a fair number of presuppositions firmly in place. We thought we knew the Bible before we sat in front of those humbling tests. After all, for the most part, we'd been raised in the church, and, so we thought, the church had been teaching us what we needed to know about it. Hadn't it? Also, although there were pieces of the story we'd probably questioned, it had never occurred to many of us that the Bible wasn't a single piece of work. Discovering that it had been written by innumerable people and that significant additional writings had been eliminated through a puzzling process that often read more like politics and power struggles than theological clarification was beyond anything we might have speculated. The study of systematic theology tied the left side of our brains in knots as we tried to follow the thought processes of minds that were much better exercised than ours. To put it bluntly, we were slammed with academic information that staggered us and changed the parameters of our previously known worlds. It was a gruelling time in the left hemisphere.

It is possible that a couple of decades prior to my entering theological college, there may have been little found in those hallowed halls that would have excited the right side of any student's brain. After all, we in the Protestant tradition were the people of the Word. Exhortation of the texts was the most important part of a clergyperson's role in the church. Those who were the best at it were those with extensive filing systems in which tidbits of scholarly information on the meaning of words, the geography of the Holy Land, and cultural peculiarities and nuances of the world's peoples were set aside waiting for the time when they could be drawn out for use in an academic unravelling of a particularly tricky bit of scripture. While at school, we were even graded on our ability to create embryonic filing systems that would support our future preaching work.[1]

## One-sided (at a Time) Focus

But in the late 1980s when I attended seminary, there was another movement afoot that was stretching that other (until then practically unnecessary) part of a Protestant minister's brain—the right, creative, and artistic hemisphere. It was the rise of the liturgical renewal movement and the explosion of the sensual appreciation of God. Growing up in a traditional United Church congregation, I experienced liturgy* as a pretty static thing, and it remains so in many congregations, Protestant, Orthodox, or Roman Catholic. We opened with the processional hymn, the choir flowing in with their mortar boards and black gowns, followed by the minister in his academic regalia. Each proceeded to their appropriate places, and a few sentences were intoned, calling the gathered community to attention and asking God to

---

*No doubt, I use the term *liturgy* too broadly. I use the word to cover anything to do with the flow of a service of worship, one of the original meanings of the word. More recently it has become confined to meaning the prescribed services within more formal and sacramental churches.

grace us with his presence. The corporate prayer of confession followed, allowing those gathered to be purged of whatever it might be that had served to sully their souls and make them unfit for the hearing of God's word. The first scripture lesson would be read, the children welcomed at the front of the church for a brief object lesson, and then, as they filed out to their classes, the second lesson, also scripture, would be heard. Just as Ford's first cars could be ordered in any colour as long as it was black, the Sunday lessons could be anything as long as they were biblical. A hymn would follow, only identified by the number where the words could be found in the hymn book and the name of the tune to which we would sing it. The too-pedestrian title of the hymn would never appear in our very reverent service. The minister, during the last strains of music, would step into the grand pulpit and deliver his sermon from that exalted position, a somewhat longer item than that suffered by my sisters and brothers in the more sacramental churches whose liturgy needed to allow room for the Eucharist in each week's service—something we did only four times a year. The offering followed with the singing of the Doxology, a final hymn, and the Benediction. There you have it. For the most part, it remains unchanged to this day in many a Protestant congregation.

But late in the 1960s, following the debacle of the New Curriculum, which split our budding relationship with the Baptist Convention churches, we turned toward our sacramental sister, the Anglican Church, and began a series of conversations that seemed headed toward union. In the play *Maybe One*, written by Scott Douglas for The United Church of Canada's seventy-fifth anniversary in 2000, this bit of our history is brilliantly staged as a seductive dance between the two parties, a dance that, despite a series of provocative moves, ends when one dancer abandons the other on the dance floor.[2]

Now it may seem that my recitation of the history of the United

Church's entry into liturgical renewal is confined to the experience of a specific denomination confined to a specific region of North America and not, therefore, pertinent to the rest of the ecclesial world. I describe it, however, because I believe that what happened in the United Church happens wherever and whenever an ecclesial body begins, consciously or not, opting out of the discussion on the authority of scripture. In some of our evangelical sisters, the more liberal of their congregations are beginning to introduce liturgical seasons and the use of the lectionary into their worship life. I believe this emphasis on liturgy is often a last-ditch diversionary tactic, one that serves to save the denomination the challenge of addressing the difficult issue that lies at the base of so many other similarly contentious issues. If denominations would deal with the biggie first, the others would fall into place. Problem is, it's just too big.

The sacramental churches—Roman Catholic and Orthodox—and the more liturgical traditions within the Protestant Church have long since found meaning and purpose in the acts of worship. What clerics *do* has been given authority and power by the church. Therefore, liturgical acts hold the power within the structure of the worship service; the "Word" is less relevant. Ritualized confession is seen to actually cleanse the supplicant's soul when made before an ordained priest. The priest can then place those sins upon the elements of the Eucharist, turn them into the body and blood of Jesus, and sacrifice them, once again, to God, thereby achieving salvation for the said supplicant. To neglect confession bars one from the Eucharist. To be barred from the Eucharist resigns one's fate to the bowels of hell. It is the activity of the priest and the liturgical, ritual acts that are efficacious. Those things bring about salvation.

The discussion of the authority of scripture, then, is secondary, if not meaningless to them. The authority given to the *ecclesia*, the church, may rest in an interpretation of the Bible, but the thought is so remote as to be nonsensical to many within the church. The struggle of those in the Protestant traditions is seen as irrelevant to the liturgical traditions. And as long as the ecclesial authorities continue to wield the power they do, it is.

But for those in Protestant denominations that are seen to be confessional churches in contrast to their liturgical sister churches, the authority of scripture is a huge question. All of their teaching hinges on what the Bible says and how they interpret it. The continued chink, chink of the contemporary scholar's chisel against its heretofore impenetrable fortifications has begun to seriously threaten what the church is teaching. For the United Church, the New Curriculum had set the ground for the examination of the authority of scripture. Those in leadership positions at that time were some of the first to read Robinson's *Honest to God* and ponder Tillich's "Ground of All Being." They were thirsting for a new way of being real in the church and eagerly worked to bring about substantive change. But the fear that resided in the hierarchy and the pew was too great to be abated by their efforts.

Just in time to save the denomination from a discussion that would most definitely have sliced it into at least two, if not more, segments, we were swept out of harm's way by the sensual pleasures of those rich sacramental traditions in the form of union talks with the Anglican Church. It would have been ludicrous to be seen to be questioning the authority of scripture while in such discussions. Elements of the Anglican liturgical traditions that were new to the United Church—liturgical seasons, colours, vestments, and so on—became extremely attractive, perhaps because they were distracting. And those in the United Church were eager to be distracted.

And so it was that when I entered seminary, despite the fact that the United Church was no longer courting its Anglican brothers and sisters, the riches of the liturgical church were still being explored with vigour. Indeed, more and more ways of experiencing the divine were laid before my fellow theologians and I each day. We, who had only ever seen the black robes of the academy on our ministers, were introduced to albs, long flowing gowns that were wrapped at the waist with cinctures of different liturgical colours. Colours! The drab sanctuaries of our past were, for the first time decorated with a different colour for each season of the Christian calendar. Advent, Epiphany, Lent, Holy Week, the long six-week celebration of Easter, and the fire of Pentecost—every bit of it could be enhanced with chant, dance, candles, movement, evocative music, incense, silence, responsive readings, versicles,* and almost anything we could dream up that would deepen the experience of the sacred. We had never known such richness. We were seated before a banquet of sensual delicacies. And we feasted upon it. Well, the right side of our brains feasted upon it.

Long in Protestant hibernation, the sensory delights of the liturgical worship tradition came to us as an aesthetic, holy crucible. Our passion for the sacred could be purged of the coarse realities of the contemporary world, with all its harshness and cynicism, and refined into an arrestingly beautiful ritual of wonder. We were overwhelmed with the honour being bestowed upon us. Each sensuous avenue to the divine was emblazoned on that right hemisphere, untouchable, sacred, and holy. We were given the rights to it. (We came to see our leadership role in the denomination as "keepers of the vision.")

To preserve the pristine beauty of it though, we had to protect it from all that was being emblazoned, at exactly the same time, on the other side of our brains. Because the two things together just didn't make any sense. In three, maybe four, years of training, I believe we *all* managed to completely sever our theological corpora callosa.[3]

---

*A short verse spoken or sung by the worship leader and followed by a response from the congregation. For example, Leader: "The Very Word of God." Congregation: "Thanks be to God."

## Split Vision: The Cost

Those who suffer from the lack of an intact corpus callosum, whether through gestational dysfunction or surgical severance, look pretty normal. They can walk, talk, dance, and argue with the best of us. In fact, unless you did some testing of their abilities, or knew what to look for, you probably wouldn't even know they were different at all.

The test is an easy one. At your next dinner party, should you wish to determine who may not be "lobally" connected, here's what you can do. Write a word on a piece of paper and hold it out to the left of the person so that they are not able to see it with their right eye. If they cannot read the word but they can when you let their right eye see it, you have a bona fide disconnect.

The reason the individual can't read the word when viewed only with their left eye is that the left eye is governed by the right side of the brain, not the side where language skills reside. With the corpus callosum intact, the right lobe simply sends a message over to the left side and extracts the right word from where it is stored. Once that link is not available, it is impossible for the right lobe to find the word. The result is that the individual can see it, but they can't read it.

In a way, I imagine that trick exposes the way we have survived the enormous disconnect of our theological education. The information that has been established in the academically saturated left lobes of the theologically trained has been made inaccessible to the area of the brain that has been trained to create meaningful worship opportunities. It is as though all the contemporary scholarship we were taught has been written neatly on cards and held up to our left eye, confining its exposure to the decoding tools held by the right lobe. But there is nothing in the right lobe that can resonate with what is on the card. We are so deeply, viscerally connected to our worship rituals that we cannot see what is on that card, no matter how hard we try.

But the need has not gone away. The scholarship that fed the left lobe to the brim has now overflowed right into the pews, thanks to authors such as John Shelby Spong, Elaine Pagels, Marcus Borg, Karen Armstrong, and others. Such scholarship is no longer exclusive to the sermon-crafter's library shelves but has often been read by those who are listening attentively to the sermon. Good it is then that the right side of the brain can be taught to read. If its route to the left lobe's language stores is severed but its need to decipher language remains high, studies show it will develop the skills necessary to read and recognize words. (This phenomenon suggests that in the future it may be possible for split-brained people to read two books at the same time and retain information from each of them. The student's ultimate multi-tasking tool![4]) Faced with a self-educated laity, clergy have been scrambling to train the right sides of their brains to read what is on those cards, stuff their left lobes have long known. But they're having a hard time of it. The message becomes contorted.

Now, true enough, *contorted* is probably not a very nice way to describe turning something into a metaphor. By contorting the message, I mean that we just twist things a little to get them to mean what we'd like and then we call it a metaphor. There is nothing wrong with metaphor; we all use it. This whole chapter is based on a metaphor. It is our way of describing things that we have difficulty describing. It is the way we put into words all those experiences and feelings of the right lobe so that someone's left lobe might get the idea. You know, love is a rose. Someone who has only ever experienced the beauty and wonder of love will immediately resonate with the gorgeous image that appears in their mind's eye. Those who have felt the pain of lost or unrequited love will also create the image of a rose, but theirs will be brandishing daggerlike thorns. Each person connects the metaphor to his or her own experiences.

Here, though, when we're using metaphor to accommodate information we can't process, we're doing it in reverse. Information on the left side is clear—that isn't the problem. The difficulty lies in our loving what we stored on the right side so completely that we don't want to give it up. The information on the left, clear as a bell, can't sit with what the right side has made so important—the liturgy, the rituals of the worship service, all those meaningful things that have made people catch their breath for so many years. Rather than change to accommodate what's written on the cards, the right side of the brain decides that it will just accommodate what is on the cards. The right side calls it all metaphor, and everything remains nicely in place despite the conflict between what we know and what we say. For instance, if you know the Bible is a human construction, as we do, processing it at the beginning of a service, elevating, kissing, placing it in a position of honour—none of this makes any sense; yet we cling to those rituals and often defend them without even reflecting on what we're doing.

In his book *The Heart of Christianity*, Marcus Borg leads the reader to another of those sumptuous banquets of liturgy. There one finds that with just a little redefinition, every element of the worship service—interventionist prayer, the honouring of particular objects and people as "special," the recitation of the creed, the use of the word *Lord*—as it has stood for the past six hundred years (or more), can be made palatable again.

According to Borg, one of the primary purposes of worship—whether it be music, sacraments, the sermon, Bible readings, or liturgical words such as the Lord's Prayer, even the creed—is to become a thin place: "Thin places are places where the veil momentarily lifts, and we behold God, experience the one in whom we live, all around us and within us."[5] But note that focus on the meanings of specific words is secondary. Writing about the Lord's Prayer, Borg states that "the point is to let the drone of these words that we know by heart become a thin place." Similarly, in reference to the creed, "its primary purpose in worship is not propositional but sacramental; through these clunky words that stumble in the presence of Mystery, God is mediated."[6]

In a little etymological excavation, Borg tells his readers that *credo*, the word we translate as "believe" at the beginning of our creeds, was never meant to indicate that we agree with what follows. Rather, he suggests that its original meaning was "I give my heart to" what follows. With such an explanation, he imagines, we will no longer have to struggle with the theological and Christological content.[7]

Earlier, in his conversation with New Testament scholar N. T. Wright, published in *The Meaning of Jesus: Two Visions*, Borg similarly argued that Jesus' representation as the "Son of God" was merely another metaphor to be read alongside Jesus as the "true vine," "light of the world," "lamb of God," and many others, which are more clearly metaphorical. He suggests that the New Testament affirmations of Jesus as the "decisive revelation" of God, regardless of what they meant when they were written, do not now need to be understood to mean that Jesus is the only way to salvation.

> Instead, we might understand them (and similar Christian statements about Jesus being "the only way") as reflecting the joy of having found one's salvation through Jesus and the intensity of Christian devotion to Jesus. They should be understood as exclamations, not doctrines, and as "the poetry of devotion and the hyperbole of the heart." So *decisive* need not mean "only."[8]

Borg's message is clear. There is much to be said for tradition, but he knows the underlying stories upon which it is based can no longer be considered true in a factual way. To deal with that, we have to change what we believe about these stories, and we can easily do so by calling them myths and metaphor or changing how we mean them to be understood.[9] As such, we can use them to explore the mythic stories in our own lives and, in order to do so, accommodate all the religious ritual that has honoured them as true in the past—all we have to do is remember that they aren't.

Borg speaks to a generation of believers that are still in the church. They know its traditions and rituals, and some of them are willing to come to new understandings of them over time, as long as they do not have to give up their hymns, prayers, creeds, forms of baptism and Eucharistic liturgies, and their special ways of doing all those things. If they are predominantly closed communities with few new people coming in to see what is happening inside, they are free to do whatever they want with their traditions and their worship lives. There is no one else for whom it need be either comprehensible or relevant. If someone new does drop in, they can learn the language at a special class or meet with the pastor. Or they may not realize they have to learn a language and will take the words at their face value, assuming the things that are said are believed literally.

## Integrated Vision: The Challenge

The church I want, however, is not a closed community. I want a church that is open to whomever happens to show up, and, when they do, I want them to be able to understand everything being said and done. We can't change the definitions for all the words to which we've assigned deep theological meaning without publishing a glossary of terms and attaching it to each service bulletin given out on a Sunday morning. It would read like this:

Salvation: Previously understood to be the state of forgiveness and adoption as a child of God brought about by believing in Jesus' atoning sacrifice for sin, now understood to mean removing the causes of suffering in the world, new life.

Resurrection (as in "Jesus was resurrected on the third day" or "believers will all be resurrected"): Previously understood to be the spontaneous resuscitation of Jesus' body after he was crucified and kept in a tomb for an indefinite, though usually misrepresented as three days, duration, now meaning starting over, new chances.

Lord (as in "Jesus is Lord," or "Lord, have mercy"): Previously understood as the name for the one who is the supreme and perfect ruler over all creation, even by those who don't believe in him, now meaning that love shown as justice and compassion is supreme, and these concepts can be found in selected passages attributed to Jesus and God (passages asserting questionable concepts of love notwithstanding).

Communion (Eucharist): Previously understood to mean the act of coming before the priest and dipping a piece of bread (symbolizing the body of Jesus, or in some denominations understood to literally be the body of Jesus having been made so by the action of the priest) into a cup of wine (symbolizing the blood of Jesus) or having a wafer of bread placed on one's tongue by the priest and then eating it (symbolizing the eating of Jesus' body and blood, or in some denominations understood to literally be eating the body and blood of Jesus, those things having been made so by the action of the priest) as a way of making one a recipient of God's grace through Jesus' redeeming sacrifice, now understood to be an experiential way to accept the love of God and the power of forgiveness (or whatever the community has defined it to mean).

And so on. Without a glossary, those with a traditional understanding of the rituals of the church might inadvertently assume that they are still accepting God's grace through communion—not the message we may be trying to communicate. Furthermore, those who had come in with no previous knowledge of our traditions or liturgical rituals would still, no doubt, be confused.

If we say "Jesus is Lord" in the reading or song, we might explain it as not in fact meaning that the person Jesus is a Lord over us but rather that "his way is right." And what is his way? That of love, you say? (Well, selected teachings at least.) So "Jesus is Lord" really means "love is supreme." Well, then why not say "love is supreme"? All the world can understand that. They can embrace it regardless of their beliefs. If "Jesus is Lord" means "justice for all," then let's say that. Is it that we feel we need "theospeak," theological code words, to keep us connected to our heritage? They will surely do that but beware; "Jesus is Lord" is connected to our *entire* heritage, the full scope of proselytization, dogmatism, exclusivity, condemnation, and violence. It tells the world that our understanding is the best, when they can clearly see that in much of our history we were a long shot off the mark. The concepts of love, justice, and compassion are *also* connected to our heritage—the valuable part of it. So why don't we connect to *those* parts of our heritage and retain the supremacy of love and justice, just as they stand, independent of older dogma? When what we are trying to say is delivered in ordinary language, not code, it has the best chance of being understood and embraced by those outside of the church and, sometimes surprisingly so, by many on the inside as well.

The process of redefining, re-mythologizing, and reclaiming language as recommended by Borg might be fine if we had a few extra generations to figure it all out. We don't. The process of teaching the right lobe to read has already taken two generations too long, and the church doesn't have the time to allow another generation to ever-so-slowly pry its fingers off liturgical tools and the accompanying theospeak that ensures they remain beyond the reach of our understanding. We know that the stories those liturgical tools and rituals have stood upon for two thousand years are just that—stories, the best attempts that people could make to explain what was happening in their lives, fairly biased attempts at that. Rather than continuing the struggle to teach the right side to read in a way that allows it to keep all that it holds as sacred tradition, it is time for us to reconnect the corpus callosum, in whatever way possible, so that information housed in both sides of the brain can freely move back and forth. We have literally run out of time to waste.

## SUNDAY MORNING

If you've never been to a theological institution or Bible college or a seminary, chances are your corpus callosum continues to be operational and manages to flip information from one side to the other with nary a hitch. Even without benefit of magnetic resonance imaging (MRI), I think we can safely say that during your average Sunday morning experience, both sides of the brain are exercised, though perhaps at different times and to different degrees. In more sacramental churches where much of the service unfolds through liturgical ritual, the right side (home to symbol and drama) will get the better workout. In more reformed churches where the spoken word has more emphasis, synapses on the left side of the brain will be lighting up more frequently. It is also likely that, without benefit of an intentional pursuit of contemporary scholarship, those who attend worship services in many liberal or moderate congregations will have a fairly generic knowledge of basic Christianity. Those who have read and discussed the works of theologians (whether conservative, liberal, or progressive) will, of course, have a greater expanse or depth of understanding.

Because such a high percentage of the population holds beliefs in God and God's activity in their lives, even if they do not attend a religious institution with any regularity or at all, I think it is important for us to review some of the beliefs they may hold. If we are going to talk about reconstructing Christianity, it is imperative that we be at least somewhat aware of what is generally believed out there. You may or may not be the person I am describing, but I am going to use the word *you*. If you've done a lot of reading, you probably aren't. Think about who you were *before* you started to read. Think in general terms. Think about what someone who isn't Christian thinks a Christian believes. And remember, even here, I'm being generous. There are many whose beliefs are not *nearly* as well thought-out as are those I present here. Compared with the average non-churchgoer on the street, these are pretty sophisticated.

## In Attendance

Let's say you believe in God. But not that white-haired God who sits up on a throne in heaven. Not even the judgmental God of most of the Bible. In fact, were you pressed to explain God, you might describe something more like a feeling than a person, a presence than a being. Your words might speak of something far beyond comprehension, but, at the same time, something utterly familiar to you.

You believe in the Bible. It's been years since you read the parts you did manage to get through, but you believe in it. You don't believe it is TAWOGFAT though, more likely that it contains the word of God or at least that the people who wrote it were writing on behalf of God. Or something like that. In any case, you would agree that it is the most important book for Christians.

You believe in Jesus. He lived in the first century. You don't believe he was born of a virgin, and maybe even question the resurrection, but you believe that Christmas and Easter are important for reasons you can't articulate. You might believe Jesus died for your sins, but you aren't really sure what that means. When you think of God, you sometimes see that stained-glass picture of Jesus knocking on the door with no knob or the charcoal one of him laughing or the one that used to hang up in the Sunday school hall with the lambs and children all around. You don't think of him as *the* son of God, but believe that he contained more of God than you or I could ever manage. He was crucified. You know that much. Why is a bit fuzzy—something to do with the Jews or the Romans, maybe both. If you've read *The Jesus Mysteries* or *The Pagan Christ*, ignore the above; you believe he was a compilation of a bunch of stolen Egyptian myths.

You've heard the Father, Son, and Holy Spirit trilogy, but aren't quite sure where it came from, nor what it means. You've long since learned not to say "Father" when you're talking about God—not politically correct. You use the word *spirit* more than you used to, and you'd probably tell people you're spiritual before you'd tell them you're religious.

You believe in the power of prayer. You do not use it to ask God for ridiculous things such as a new Hummer or thicker hair, but you do turn to it when times are tough. You address your prayers to God, sometimes the Holy Spirit. You aren't sure how prayer works, but you can't believe that nothing happens either, so you participate in it when you need to, sometimes excusing what, deep down, you think others might call superstitious behaviour, by saying that we can't know everything.

If you have had a very powerful and inexplicable spiritual event happen in your life, you may have added angels and/or saints to your Christian belief repertoire. Whatever it was, it hasn't happened in the same significant way since, but when you talk about it sometimes others open up and share similar experiences with you.

If you don't go to church regularly, you feel a bit guilty but argue that you can be a good Christian without all that religious ceremony anyway. If you're married, you likely got married in a church (or at least considered it), and if you have kids, there was at least some pressure from the parents to get them baptized. Whether you did had a lot to do with timing or "belonging," rather than any sense that something bad would happen if you didn't. If you didn't have them baptized, it was because you were going to let them decide for themselves when they grew up. Your children never bothered to think about it again.

That pretty much wraps up the major points of the Christian faith and how they impact your life, though most theologians would be aghast at the brevity of the description. Remember, these are the beliefs that help us create the framework for how we see the world. When they are securely in place, everything we see comes to us through that framework. Knowing what they are is important. Believing that the universe is either unfolding as it should or that it is wildly off course will cause one to approach a situation in radically different ways—the first, perhaps, with calm, the latter with either fear or a need to impose control. Similarly, believing that there is either a benevolent being watching us from a distance or a judgmental one waiting to cast us into the fires of perdition will significantly affect our choices throughout the day.

## Assumptions of an Afterlife

The Bible, despite the fact that not all parts of it conform to a three-tiered pre-Copernican worldview, can be comfortably read by someone who holds one. Such a worldview consists of a heaven above us awaiting the saints, the earth upon which we live out our mortal lives, and a hell below in which we will writhe with pain for eternity if we don't believe or do certain things. Sometimes we think of them as not necessarily up there and down there but "out there," somewhere at a distance from us. And while liberal/moderate Christians are generally content to give up the concept of hell, holding on to the concept of heaven still has great appeal.

We often have difficulty with our beliefs framework, using

different ones for different days of the week; the worldview that exists on Sunday morning, for instance, being entirely inconsistent with the one held the rest of the time. Such inconsistency makes it difficult to rationalize beliefs, so most of the time we just don't bother. Members of the group we mingle with on Sunday morning are as unlikely to challenge the inconsistent worldviews we hold as we are to challenge theirs.

But that framework remains at work in a very big way all around the world, and our dismissing its significance is a dangerous thing. Despite the last five decades of decline in church attendance, it remains true that in thousands, if not millions, of churches across this continent someone climbs into the pulpit each and every Sunday and offers to those who sit in front of them (or in some contemporary settings a full 360 degrees around them) a fully operational model of how the world works. And whether that someone is speaking to the sixteen strong-hearted individuals in a tiny rural church on the Canadian prairie or the sixteen thousand arm-swinging evangelicals in the recently renovated arena in Houston, Texas, people are listening, beliefs are being expounded, and worldviews reinforced. And what those beliefs and worldviews might be is a very important matter indeed.

Whether the congregation is liberal, conservative, charismatic, sacramental, or evangelical, the purpose of the sermon is to teach, exhort, and edify the community of faith that comes to hear it. People gather after the week has taken its toll on them. They bring their burdens, they bring their joys, they bring their lives. Throughout the service they will be invited to examine each of those things and seek the renewal and healing that they need for the coming week. A good preacher knows the people in the pews well (though it remains a mystery to me how they do it in those arena-sized churches) and will speak to their particular needs. What she or he says will make a difference in individual lives throughout the coming week. At least it is supposed to.

But what is heard on any given Sunday morning in any given church varies widely depending upon what kind of church one is sitting in: liberal, conservative, charismatic, sacramental, or evangelical. The difference is based on the worldview that is being presented. Each grounded in a particular interpretation of the Bible, these worldviews are essentially mutually exclusive, yet they each begin with the acknowledgement of what is our greatest fear and perhaps the only truth upon which we will all ever agree: we are all going to die. The rest of it is commentary and looks something like this:

When you die, you will go to heaven and live forever:
1. if you believe that Jesus is the Son of God, that he came down from heaven to live among us, was crucified on the cross during which time he took all of our sins upon him, was rejected by God because of that stain of sin, died in that rejection but was raised by God on the third day, and lives forever with God.
2. if you believe in all of the above but know that Jesus couldn't have taken all the sins that hadn't happened yet upon him, his sacrifice is remade regularly so you can go and have your sins added to the list, and be cleansed, making you worthy for heaven.
3. because you already have God's Spirit living within you as evidenced by gifts, such as speaking in tongues.
4. if you are one of the elect who have been pre-chosen by God to live with God in heaven.
5. if you are a good person or probably even if you are bad because all of God's children are loved and forgiven.

There are no more; remember, we're talking about the worldview that determines what people will hear on a Sunday morning, not what they might believe about the afterlife . . . The Sunday sermon, even if it doesn't directly address it, is grounded in a worldview that isn't even about this world. It's about a world yet to come, which doesn't begin until after we die, and about which we know absolutely nothing.

If you aren't being forced to read this book, chances are you didn't blink when I pointed out how much we know about "the afterlife." If you've given it any thought (and who hasn't?), you probably think you've come to terms with the fact that the ideas presented in the Bible are, at best, only the same kind of guesswork you'd be forced to make up were you pressed on the subject. Even when people can rationally express that they don't know what will happen after death, there seems to be a deep desire to believe in a Bible-styled heaven, a place where we will be ultimately reunited, for better or worse, with our first two husbands and their subsequent wives. (Well, Jesus did say that for those raised up after death, there would be no such thing as marriage [Matthew 23:24ff], but that hasn't stopped us from all kinds of wishful thinking, now has it?)

Preaching on a passage from John in which the author draws a picture of the afterlife in the image of a mansion with many rooms, I once suggested that the picture was only one person's best guess at what might or might not be beyond the lintel that marks the place between life and death. I spoke of the delight we might have in creating our own images, ones that rang true for each of us and that would honour our struggle to live with integrity in this lifetime. My personal struggle was deepened a few short minutes later when one of the members of the congregation stood and asked me to pray that I might come to a better understanding of heaven as described in the Bible, the word of God. It was one of those moments when verbal callisthenics come in very handy.

Religious belief fast-forwards our vision beyond any time frame that we can know into one that we can only imagine. Its focus on the hereafter has such power that, in addition to its rather pedestrian use in framing the Sunday morning sermon, it has often been a critical factor in determining how we have treated one another on a world scale. Even today's political challenges can be set within worldviews that rely heavily upon afterlife scenarios.

Suppose that you believe in an afterlife in which you are going to live peacefully without want. With such a belief system firmly in place, a life this side of the grave that is filled with an inordinate amount of lack would be much more tolerable. Suppose that you believe in an afterlife in which you are going to get back twelve times the pain and injury you inflict on anyone in this life. You'd probably be much more careful about what you do to whom and how you do it while you're still on this side of the great abyss. Suppose you believe in reincarnation and that your subsequent form will be influenced by what you learn in this lifetime: you learn much, you come back more highly evolved and with fewer temporal challenges; you don't learn much, and you come back less highly evolved and with more temporal challenges. Chances are you'll want to turn your brain into a sponge and load it with everything it can possibly hold. Suppose you believe, absolutely and fervently believe, that there is something you can do, say, or eat that will save you the inconveniences of a bad next incarnation or twelve times the intensity of pain. No doubt, you're going to follow the instructions to the letter, even if it means cramming for finals or saying you believe something you don't.

Now suppose that you are leading an organization or a government that wants to act in a certain way and have its people support its actions. Changing their belief system is the single most effective way to have that kind of control in any situation. For instance, if we want the wealth of a certain geographical area, we make certain that the people there believe in an afterlife of peace and plenty; then they won't care if they have little in this life. (Remember the Kenyatta quotation that Desmond Tutu made famous!) If we want our people to be non-violent, even in the face of our own violence, we ensure that their picture of the afterlife gives them their just rewards, many times over. If we want people to be responsible for their own behaviour, independent of ours, we might instill some cyclical payback experiences, firmly planted in the next life for their own personal discovery. If you'd like them a little more alert to their responsibilities, you might speed up the expected payback time by suggesting that everything that happens to them is the result of something they have already done; they'll spend half their lives looking for reasons and the other half trying not to create them. If we want them to purchase a pain-free afterlife from us, we might help them believe that we have what is needed to cleanse their souls and squeak them in the back door to bliss.

You see where I'm going. The sad thing is, I'm not even scratching the surface. What religious belief in the afterlife has caused us to do, and continues to cause us to do to the earth, to ourselves, and to one another, has ranged from helpful, through harmful, all the way to heinous. And every Sunday morning some preacher somewhere is hammering the message home yet again.

Of course, it is easy for liberals to distance ourselves from the evangelicals we think are doing that, those we put down by suggesting they are merely plying the afterlife trade. We bolster our confidence having long since replaced claims of personal salvation with our interests in this world and the responsibility we take for its transformation (note that this, too, is based on what we think is going to happen when we die—it's all going to work out for the best, just you wait and see). Preachers in our churches don't even talk about salvation without using the word metaphorically (you know, salvation is when you get your life back together after divorce or the street kid makes her way home or the congregation sponsors a refugee family—that kind of salvation—clean, this-worldly, and nothing to do with blood!). And when our preachers talk about heaven, it certainly isn't a place where only some people go—all things are possible with our God, and we're pretty sure everyone is going to be loved just as much as we are. (You've no doubt heard the joke about having to be quiet when tiptoeing past the room in heaven where the evangelicals are because they think they're the only ones there.) We are a gentle, forgiving people. A belief in an afterlife that includes everyone, the guilty and the innocent alike, helps us at least pretend to a very tolerant Sunday morning experience.

Avoiding the shameful aspects of our religious heritage also comes relatively easily. After all, it has been some six or seven hundred years since Christians got really excited about heading off on crusades and at least two hundred since the last witch was burned in an effort to save her soul.[10] We assign labels that neutralize the religious nature of many of the world's ongoing conflicts, calling them "civil unrest," identifying "political factions," and naming nationalities long before we will identify the religions backing those warring factions. We are all too aware that the victims of the Holocaust were a particular religious group, but we carefully skirt the issue of the religious beliefs of its perpetrators. The Aboriginal residential schools scandals that exposed abuse in the government—organized, church-run institutions—rocked the United and Anglican denominations in Canada and opened our eyes to some of our most recent arrogance.[11] Our litanies of remorse, the financial obligations, and the healing circles we've entered into serve as healthy purgatives to our guilt. The terrible acts perpetrated in the name of Christianity are left to weigh significantly less than heavily on our collective conscience, if they weigh on us at all.

Most of us would describe ourselves as tolerant of others' religious beliefs and supportive of their right to hold those beliefs, whatever they might be. Should it become necessary, we might even fight for the right for others to hold beliefs that differ from ours, even those that differ critically. We might not choose to be seated next to an overly evangelical Christian at a dinner party, but we'd certainly not attempt to disabuse them of beliefs that we believe they have a right to hold. Rather, we would very likely smile, perhaps defend our right to call ourselves "Christian," and change the subject at the first possible moment.

Our beliefs in an afterlife that will include all people make us pacifists in the face of religious debate. We don't want to argue with those who have an exclusivist perspective on that final homeland. So we do not challenge them on their beliefs. In fact, we can't. The only legitimate tool with which we could do that, in their eyes, would be the Bible, and, as we all know, they have a better grasp on it than we do.

They sure do.

## Wholly Holy?

In the mid-1960s, an ecumenical group made up of representatives from many mainline North American denominations met to discuss the development of an agreed upon set of liturgical texts that could be common to all. Over time the lectionary, as it is called, was developed, setting out a biblical reading from each of the Hebrew scriptures, Psalms, Epistles, and Gospels for each Sunday in a three-year cycle of the Christian yearly calendar.

The use of the lectionary spread rapidly throughout the major denominations. Were one to worship in a Lutheran, Presbyterian, or Polish National Catholic Church on any given Sunday, chances are the scripture readings could be the same. Hailed as an extraordinary disciplinary tool that forced preachers beyond their favourite Bible passages, it quickly became essential to worship leadership. Preachers who had previously struggled over the choice of scripture passages each week soon became dependent upon the lectionary's weekly offerings and the plethora of books and websites devoted to supporting them, complete with background information, suggested sermon topics, humour, useful anecdotes, ready-made prayers, and hymn suggestions all linked to the readings for the day.

The selections provided in the lectionary cover all the major themes of the Bible during its three-year cycle. But they do not cover everything in the Bible. The texts chosen have been chosen for reasons that are not disclosed to those who use it, nor to those who hear it. They must be intuited from the texts. Preachers in more conservative congregations will spend their time discerning "God's word for today" from texts that are thousands of years old. Preachers in more liberal congregations will spend an inordinate amount of time putting the passages in context—clarifying the political realities of the day, who they were being written for, what those people believed, and what they needed to hear in the reading—in order that they can make sense of these ancient passages for their own congregations. Once done, there is little left to say, for many of the passages don't have much they can offer those who live in today's complex world.

The lectionary has anaesthetized us to the power of the Bible, which continues to sit, unabridged, in places of honour in our sanctuaries, and is referred to, in its entirety, as the Word of God or the Holy Book. In mainline churches where the lectionary is used, we have been hearing, for almost two generations now, a cut-and-paste version of the Bible that has removed much of its ferocity from the realm of our everyday. Few of us read it. Even those in more conservative and evangelical traditions often read it piecemeal, taking snippets here and there and making a theme of them. Once, it was a book that was familiar to many; now few in mainline denominations actually know what it says.

Our ignorance is not only unwise, it is dangerous. It's like signing a note your fifteen-year-old puts in front of you without reading it. When we present a book as holy, its texts as sacred, even authoritative, we must know exactly what it says because we are not only reserving it a special time slot on Sunday morning, we are *endorsing* what it says. And what it says is often frightening.

Episcopal bishop John Shelby Spong, in his recent book *The Sins of Scripture*, highlights some of the contents that are offensive to our modern-day sensibilities and points out the ways in which the Bible has been used to defend all sorts of abuses "in the name of God." But while reading through *Sins* might point out some of the major challenges you'll encounter in the Bible, nothing can replace the impact of its words taken head on. Forget the soft, friendly tones in which it is delivered by the weekly lay reader. It can get downright ugly.

Take a look. Here are some sample verses from the Revised Standard Version. If you like, look them up in context. From the Hebrew Scriptures:

> And my wrath will burn, and I will kill you with the sword and your wives shall become widows, and your children fatherless. (Exodus 22:24)

> For every one who curses his father or his mother must be put to death. (Leviticus 20:9)

> For no one who has a blemish shall draw near, a man blind or lame, or one who has a mutilated face or a limb too long, ... or a hunchback, or a dwarf, or a man with a defect in his sight or an itching disease or scabs or crushed testicles. No man of the descendants of Aaron the priest who has a blemish shall come near to offer the bread of his God. (Leviticus 21:18, 20–21)

> You may also buy from among the strangers who sojourn with you and their families who are with you, who have been born in your land; and they may be your property. (Leviticus 25:45)

And the people complained in the hearing of the Lord about their misfortunes; and when the Lord heard it, his anger was kindled, and the fire of the Lord burned among them, and consumed some outlying parts of the camp. (Numbers 11:1)

If you hear in one of your cities, which the Lord your God gives you to dwell there, that certain base fellows have gone out among you and have drawn away the inhabitants of the city saying, "Let us go and serve other gods," which you have not known, then you shall inquire and make search and ask diligently; and behold, if it be true and certain that such an abominable thing has been done among you, you shall surely put the inhabitants of that city to the sword, destroying it utterly, all who are in it and its cattle, with the edge of the sword. You shall gather all its spoil into the midst of its open square, and burn the city and all its spoil with fire, as a whole burnt offering to the Lord your God; it shall be a heap forever, it shall not be built again. (Deuteronomy 13:12–16)

And the people of Israel again did what was evil in the sight of the Lord; and the Lord gave them into the hand of the Philistines for forty years. (Judges 13:1)

Thus says the Lord, "Behold, I will raise up evil against you out of your own house; and I will take your wives and give them to your neighbour and he shall lie with your wives in the sight of this sun." (2 Samuel 12:11)

And at the beginning of their dwelling there, they did not fear the Lord; therefore the Lord sent lions among them, which killed some of them. (2 Kings 17:25)

The Lord, the God of their fathers, sent persistently to them by his messengers, because he had compassion on his people and on his dwelling place; but they kept mocking the messengers of God, despising his words, and scoffing at his prophets, till the wrath of the Lord rose against his people, till there was no remedy. Therefore he brought up against them the king of the Chaldeans, who slew their young men with the sword in the house of their sanctuary, and had no compassion on young man or virgin, old man or aged; he gave them all into his hand. (2 Chronicles 36:15–17)

But God will shatter the heads of his enemies,
the hairy crown of him who walks in his guilty ways.
The Lord said, "I will bring them back from Bashan;
I will bring them back from the depths of the sea,
that you may bathe your feet in blood,
that the tongues of your dogs may have their portion from
the foe."
(Psalm 68:21–23)

His [the Lord's] breath is like an overflowing stream that reaches
up to the neck;
to sift the nations with the sieve of destruction,
and to place on the jaws of the peoples a bridle that leads astray.
(Isaiah 30:28)

Samaria shall bear her guilt,
because she has rebelled against her God.
They shall fall by the sword;
their little ones shall be dashed in pieces,
and their pregnant women ripped open. (Hosea 13:16)

(If you've got your Bible open, why not check out Ezekiel 4:4–17 for a brief glimpse into the twisted mind of some ancient biblical scribe.)
From the Gospels we have the following:

I tell you, many will come from east and west and sit at table with Abraham, Isaac, and Jacob in the kingdom of heaven, while the sons of the kingdom will be thrown into the outer darkness; there men will weep and gnash their teeth. (Matthew 8:11–12)

Do not think that I have come to bring peace on earth; I have not come to bring peace, but a sword. For I have come to set a man against his father, and a daughter against her mother ... he who loves his son or daughter more than me is not worthy of me. (Matthew 10:34–35a, 37b)

And whoever says a word against the Son of man will be forgiven; but whoever speaks against the Holy Spirit will not be forgiven, either in this age or in the age to come. (Matthew 12:32)

He [Jesus] said, "To you it has been given to know the secrets of the kingdom of God but to others in parables; that seeing they might not see, and hearing they might not understand." (Luke 8:10)

John [the Baptist] answered, "He who believes in the Son has eternal life; he who does not obey the Son shall not see life, but the wrath of God rests upon him." (John 3:27a, 36)

Jesus said to them, "Truly, truly, I say to you, he who hears my word and believes him who sent me, has eternal life; he does not come into judgment, but has passed from death to life." (John 5:19a, 24)

He [Jesus] said to them [the Jews] "You are from below; I am from above; you are of this world; I am not of this world. I told you that you would die in your sins, for you will die in your sins unless you believe that I am he." (John 8:23–24)

And from the rest of the New Testament:

So then he [God] has mercy upon whomever he wills, and he hardens the heart of whomever he wills. (Romans 9:18)

If anyone has no love for the Lord, let him be accursed. (1 Corinthians 16:22a)

But even if we, or an angel from heaven, should preach to you a gospel contrary to that which we preached to you, let him be accursed. (Galatians 1:8)

When the Lord Jesus is revealed from heaven with his mighty angels in flaming fire, inflicting vengeance upon those who do not know God and upon those who do not obey the gospel of our Lord Jesus. They shall suffer the punishment of eternal destruction and exclusion from the presence of the Lord and from the glory of his might. (Thessalonians 2:7a-9)

Indeed under the law almost everything is purified with blood, and without the shedding of blood there is no forgiveness of sins. (Hebrews 9:22)

As long as millions of people are still calling this book "The Authoritative Word of God for All Time" (TAWOGFAT), as long as others continue to refer to it as wholly "inspired" by God, as long as anyone holds it up uncritically as the text that is relevant for everyone forever, it will continue not only to declare a message of exclusive salvation for believers and sure condemnation for non-believers, but also, as it was in the Dark Ages, to deny freedoms that we have now established as right and good, many of which are not supported by its passages. It is time we who call ourselves moderate, liberal, or progressive Christians take responsibility for countering these harmful and dangerous messages.

## That's More Like It

Of course, there is much in the Bible that is worth keeping. In many stories and accounts of the people of Israel and the earliest communities that grew up following the death of Jesus, there is a constant cry for justice for those who are least able to care for themselves in that ancient society, the *anawim*, the "little ones." "And when you reap the harvest of your land, you shall not reap your field to its very border, nor shall you gather the gleanings after your harvest; you shall leave them for the poor and for the stranger: I am the Lord your God." (Leviticus 23:22) Exodus 22:22, in fact, is a direct demand from God in that regard, "You shall not afflict any widow or an orphan." Anyone who does so gets the punishment highlighted in the first example noted above: "I will kill you with the sword and your wives shall become widows and your children fatherless." Other passages, too, place concern for those society marginalizes at the centre of the religious life of the community. "Religion that is pure and unbridled before God and the Father is this: to visit orphans and widows in their affliction, and to keep oneself unstained from the world." (James 1:27) "If you really fulfil the royal law, according to the scripture, 'You shall love your neighbour as yourself,' you do well. But if you show partiality, you commit sin, and are convicted by the law as transgressors." (James 2:8, 9) The Good Samaritan (Luke 10:25–37), the Sermon on the Mount (Matthew 5:1–12), the good parts of the sheep and the goats story (Matthew 25:31–40), these all draw out a command to love one another with a radically inclusive love. Liberal Christians know those stories. Liberal theology and its offshoots, liberation theology, feminist theology, womanist theology, are built upon a God of justice and compassion.

However...

It is former evangelical Christians who have an easier time seeing my point. The theology they once embraced was built upon passages that separate Christians from the rest of the world, that speak of a special status acquired through belief, and of the torment that will be suffered by those who do not accept the faith. These are the very passages that are often overlooked or contextualized by mainline interpretations. Evangelicals animate their faith by the Great Commission:

> Go therefore and make disciples of all nations, baptizing them in the name of the Father and of the Son and of the Holy Spirit, teaching them to observe all that I have commanded you. (Matthew 28:19, 20a)

and by the promise to Nicodemus, reasserted at football games across the nation:

> For God so loved the world that he gave his only Son, that whoever believes in him should not perish but have eternal life. For God sent the Son into the world, not to condemn the world, but that the world might be saved through him. He who believes in him is not condemned; he who does not believe is condemned already, because he has not believed in the name of the only Son of God. (John 3:16–18)

Other well-loved passages clarify the distinction Christians are expected to understand exists between themselves and unbelievers.

> But now the righteousness of God has been manifested apart from law, although the law and the prophets bear witness to it,

the righteousness of God through faith in Jesus Christ for all who believe. For there is no distinction; since all have sinned and fall short of the glory of God, they are justified by his grace as a gift, through the redemption which is in Christ Jesus, whom God put forward as an expiation by his blood, to be received by faith. (Romans 3:21–25)

Since, therefore, we are now justified by his blood, much more shall we be saved by him from the wrath of God. (Romans 5:9)

For by grace you have been saved through faith; and this not your own doing, it is the strength of God—not because of works, lest any man should boast. (Ephesians 2:8)

For in him all the fullness of God was pleased to dwell, and through him to reconcile to himself all things, whether on earth or in heaven, making peace by the blood of his cross. (Colossians 1:19-20)

And, of course, the other half of the sheep and the goats story, which mainline Christians generally tend to avoid:

Then he will say to those at his left hand, "Depart from me, you cursed, into the eternal fire prepared for the devil and his angels; for I was hungry and you gave me no food, I was thirsty and you gave me no drink, I was a stranger and you did not welcome me, naked and you did not clothe me, sick and in prison and you did not visit me." (Matthew 25:41–43)

Anyone who has read Spong's *Sins of Scripture*, or *Rescuing the Bible from Fundamentalism*, Pagels' *The Gnostic Gospels*, or *Beyond Belief*, Borg's *Meeting Jesus Again for the First Time*, or the Jesus Seminar's *Five Gospels* will be familiar with arguments that take into account the audience for whom the evangelist wrote, the communities out of which the writing was being created, the state of the early church and its relationship to the Jewish tradition from which it was differentiating itself. They will know that these passages can be attributed to the later perspectives of the authors by whom they were written. They can dismiss them as additions and therefore not at all accurate reflections of what Jesus expected or wanted; they can turn them into metaphors; they can frame them with whatever perspective they like that will temper the ferocity of the words as they stand. But anyone who hasn't read one of those, or any number of other books of liberal biblical criticism, anyone whose sole experience of the Bible is confined to Sunday morning or media presentations of it, anyone who does not know the context in which those words were written or the metaphors in which they have been plaited will *only be able to read what the text says*. That's the problem. The text condemns itself.

If you haven't caught the importance of this point yet, it may be that you have been steeped in the liberal perspective for a long time and aren't aware of the strength of that anaesthetizing effect. Take note of the length of time you have been connected to a liberal congregation, imagine what effect that number of years might have had on you and, if you can, try to erase it (no small feat if it's anything over, say, a year or two). Now, imagine yourself walking into a traditional Sunday service in a fairly liberal denomination (you're a bit late, not being familiar with the schedule), and the congregation is just getting set to hear the day's readings. Here we go.

They start with Psalm 124:

If it had not been the Lord who was on our side,
let Israel now say—
if it had not been the Lord who was on our side,
when men rose up against us,

then they would have swallowed us up alive,

when their anger was kindled against us;

then the flood would have swept us away,

the torrent would have gone over us;

then over us would have gone the raging waters.


Blessed be the Lord,

who has not given us

as prey to their teeth!

We have escaped as a bird

from the snare of the fowlers;

the snare is broken,

and we have escaped!


Our help is in the name of the Lord

who made heaven and earth.


The second reading (unbeknownst to you, they skipped the Hebrew scripture reading—it was about Moses in the bulrushes) is from Romans 12:1–8:

I appeal to you therefore, brethren, by the mercies of God, to present your bodies as a living sacrifice, holy and acceptable to God, which is your spiritual worship. Do not be conformed to this world but be transformed by the renewal of your mind, that you may prove what is the will of God, what is good and acceptable and perfect.

For by the grace given to me I bid every one among you not to think of himself more highly than he ought to think, but to think with sober judgment, each according to the measure of faith which God has assigned him. For as in one body we have many members, and all the members do not have the same function, so we, though many, are one body in Christ, and individually members one of another. Having gifts that differ according to the grace given to us, let us use them: if prophecy, in proportion to our faith; if service, in our serving; he who teaches, in his teaching; he who exhorts, in his exhortation; he who contributes, in liberality; he who gives aid, with zeal; he who does acts of mercy, with cheerfulness.

The Gospel reading is Matthew 16:13–20:

When Jesus came into the district of Caesarea Philippi, he asked his disciples, "Who do men say that the Son of Man is?" And they said, "Some say John the Baptist, others say Elijah, and still others, Jeremiah or one of the prophets." He said to them, "But who do you say that I am?" Simon Peter replied, "You are the Christ, the Son of the living God." And Jesus answered him, "Blessed are you, Simon Bar-Jona! For flesh and blood has not revealed this to you, but by my Father who is in heaven. And I tell you, you are Peter, and on this rock I will build my church, and the powers of death shall not prevail against it. I will give you the keys of the kingdom of heaven and whatever you bind on earth shall be bound in heaven, and whatever you loose on earth shall be loosed in heaven." Then he strictly charged the disciples to tell no one that he was the Christ.

After that, the reader says something like, "The Word of the Lord," and everyone else says, "Thanks be to God." Next you stand up and sing. (This hymn is one of the suggestions for the week found in The United Church of Canada's hymn book, *Voices United*, considered by some to be the most progressive hymn book in the world. The first suggestion was in French and the second, "A Mighty Fortress is Our God," uses too much exclusive language for many liberal congregations. I went with the third.)

There's a wideness in God's mercy like the wideness of the sea;
there's a kindness in God's justice which is more than liberty.

There is no place where earth's sorrows are more felt than up in
heaven;
there is no place where earth's failings have such gracious judgment given.

There is plentiful redemption in the blood that Christ has shed;
there is joy for all the members in the sorrows of the Head.

Troubled souls, why will you scatter like a crowd of frightened
sheep?
Foolish hearts, why will you wander from a love so true and
deep?

For the love of God is broader than the measures of the mind,
and the heart of the Eternal is most wonderfully kind.[12]

Kind, indeed. Read carefully. God is kind as long as you are on
God's team. The kindness of God's justice, according to the biblical witness of the psalmist, weighs perhaps more heavily on the
enemy who attacked like wild animals and would have killed all of
Israel had God not been on the psalmist's side. Sing Faber's hymn,
accept the redemptive blood of Christ, and the kindness is yours.

That is, unless you heard the Matthew reading as meaning that
one person, or his authorized personnel, would be the final arbiters of who had access to that kindness. In the day's gospel lections,
tribal distinctions remain and deepen as Jesus apparently hands all
the power of heaven to a single person, a decision that undergirds
two thousand years of ecclesial authority and power.

The reading from Romans, while it could be the beginnings
of a good motivational speech—be all you can be but no more—

remains confusing to me yet. What does it mean to offer one's body as a sacrifice to God? What is sensible about that? What if I've been trying to let God change the way I've been thinking, and I still think like the people of this world and haven't a clue how to do everything that is good and pleasing to God? Do I just keep trying? Won't I feel a little inadequate? How am I supposed to be all I can be if I feel so inadequate? (You might recall what happened the last time you took your prophecy gifts seriously, too.)

I know, I know. There is a sermon coming and it's going to help it all make sense. The sermon, however, often touches on only one of the readings for the day. (The callisthenics required to get all of them into one sermon is paralleled only by Steve Martin in his role as a faith healer in the comedy film *Leap of Faith*, when he wins the bet that he can work the words *aluminum siding* into his evening sermon.) It leaves the rest of the biblical passages read to the individual to work out for himself or herself. Over the course of a few years of Sundays and their requisite sermons (each taking the weekly readings apart bit by bit and explaining how it doesn't really mean what it says by explaining the author's context), developing scriptural images as metaphor and recasting the stories within a modern framework, you will have developed a classic liberal nonchalance about the Word of the Lord. Thanks be to God.

Now, you may say that the readings identified above aren't particularly troublesome to you and that I'm just itching for a fight. In fact, I was trying to be fair. Here are a few other passages that the lectionary throws at you, often without the benefit of an explanation from the pulpit. Jesus says in one of them,

It was also said, "Whoever divorces his wife, let him give her a certificate of divorce." But I say to you that every one who divorces his wife, except on the ground of unchastity, makes her an adulteress; and whoever marries a divorced woman commits adultery. (Matthew 5:31–32, Lectionary Year A, Epiphany 6)

This has something to say about many of our neighbours:

> But godless men are all like thorns that are thrown away;
> for they cannot be taken with the hand;
> but the man who touches them arms himself with iron and the
> shaft of a spear,
> and they are utterly consumed with fire.
> (2 Samuel 23:6–7, Lectionary Year B, Reign of Christ Sunday)

Zephaniah offers this drastic passage at the end of Year A:

> Be silent before the Lord God!
> For the day of the Lord is at hand;
> the Lord has prepared a sacrifice and consecrated his guests.
> At that time I will search Jerusalem with lamps,
> and I will punish the men
> who are thickening upon their lees,
> those who say in their hearts,
> "The Lord will not do good,
> nor will he do ill."
> Their goods shall be plundered,
> and their houses laid waste.
> Though they build houses,
> they shall not inhabit them;
> though they plant vineyards,
> they shall not drink wine from them.
> The great day of the Lord is near,
> near and hastening fast;
> the sound of the day of the Lord is bitter,
> the mighty man cries aloud there.
> A day of wrath is that day,
> a day of distress and anguish,
> a day of ruin and devastation,

a day of darkness and gloom,

a day of clouds and thick darkness,

a day of trumpet blast and battle cry

against the fortified cities

and against the lofty battlements.

I will bring distress on men,

so that they shall walk like the blind,

because thy have sinned against the Lord;

their blood shall be poured out like dust,

and their flesh like dung.

Neither their silver nor their gold shall be able to deliver them

on the day of the wrath of the Lord.

In the fire of his jealous wrath,

all the earth shall be consumed;

for a full, yea, sudden end

he will make of all the inhabitants of the earth.

(Zephaniah 1:7, 12–18)


I'll leave you on your own to find the very ugly little story about a vineyard, starring Ahab and Jezebel. It's due to be read Year C, sometime in June (1 Kings 21:1–21a).

Finally, on the fifth Sunday of Easter* in Year B, a well-known favourite. Read it carefully. To the very end.


I am the true vine, and my Father is the vinedresser. Every branch of mine that bears no fruit, he takes away, and every branch that does bear fruit he prunes, that it may bear more fruit. You are already made clean by the word which I have spoken to you. Abide in me, and I in you. As the branch cannot bear fruit by itself, unless it abides in the vine, neither can you, unless you abide in me. I am the vine, you are the branches. He who abides in me, and I in

---

*Easter, as a Christian season, is actually counted as the seven weeks following Easter Sunday.

him, he it is that bears much fruit, for apart from me you can do nothing. If a man does not abide in me, he is cast forth as a branch and withers; and the branches are gathered, thrown into the fire and burned.

Of course, there are those who just pick up the Bible randomly, who don't get the liberal explanation of it or any explanation at all because they don't go to church and, after reading a few pages, don't have any idea why anyone would want to.

It is extremely important to note that it is not just the Bible that needs to be demoted from its exalted position as the Word of God. Every religious tradition has holy books of some kind. Most of those books are read as having been written, inspired, or revealed by God. That's why they're called "holy." And too many of them are understood, as has been the Bible, as TAWOGFAT, the authoritative word of God for all time, and, I should add, for all people, too.

This TAWOGFAT thing would be fine if each of the various versions were all telling us to live in peace and harmony. Or if they were teaching us some revolutionary methods for personal growth and spiritual evolution. It might be helpful if one of them was God's *Compleat Herbal.* Not only might we be able to cure any number of cancers, we'd revere the natural world enough not to herbicide the plants that might one day be key elements in the biosphere's delicate balance. Sooner or later, however, it would be discovered that God hadn't actually written the *Herbal* and several, if not most, of its remedies didn't work. What then?

The question is really "What now?" We are in the position of having vast resources of scientific, philosophic, anthropologic, and astronomic information at hand. Any one person can sit down at a computer hooked up to the Internet and research any of those disciplines, coming up with sites that will give him or her both the latest information and the latest quack ideas about any of it. How do we sift through this information and responsibly bring it to our religious ideas and beliefs?

## The Tribe

In his book *The End of Faith*, author Sam Harris draws the picture of a fourteenth-century Christian brought into the contemporary world and quizzed on a number of issues. We quickly see that what he knows about the many disciplines we might question him about would be laughable, if it weren't so sad; all, that is, but that of religion. When queried about matters of faith, the fourteenth-century Christian would be as well versed, perhaps even better, than the twenty-first-century Christian. Questions pertaining to faith can be answered today in exactly the same way that they could be answered in the fourteenth century as those in no other discipline can.[13] This peculiar honour is bestowed on faith because it, by its very nature, is beyond question. Why? Because our holy books tell us so.

But we have learned much since the fourteenth century not only in science and anthropology, medicine and astronomy but in our understanding of relationships and our responsibilities for one another. We feel the need to care for others as our understanding of them as beings of inherent worth, independent of our needs, grows. In the first century, we cared for those within our own tribe, and then, by extension, our nation. Within that tribal sphere our responsibilities reached different levels dependent upon the perception of "humanity" attributed to different subjects within that sphere: in diminishing order, men, firstborn males, other male children, virgin daughters, wives, girls, widows, orphans, concubines, slaves. As our consciousness regarding a particular group of people or things (the environment, for instance) has grown, our sphere of responsibility has widened.

There are many Christians who suggest that Jesus may have been one of the many voices trying to increase personal ethical responsibility both within and beyond that tribal sphere. Others within his tradition had done it before, and many have since.[14] Whether due to their influence or the general progression of our consciousness, our sphere of responsibility has grown. We no longer have to be made to think twice about our second-born children. They are as loved and as entitled as are our first-borns. Over time, many would say too long a time, most of us developed a distaste for the enslavement of other humans, and we set aside our penchant for concubines. For the most part, we have come to value girls and boys equally.[15]

But tribal prejudice is reinforced, not eliminated, by religion. On a global scale, we have remained tragically stunted in our understanding of the worth of those outside of our tribe or nationality. The connectedness and responsibility that needs to be engendered within us if we ever hope to achieve a peaceful world is not even on the horizon for whole groups of people. Religion is much of the problem. If Jesus had been attempting to break down tribal barriers, he failed or, rather, religion brought him down.

Religion, by its very nature, is divisive. Its rituals, traditions, the things it calls sacred become tools that work to identify tribe and distinguish clan. Every religion in the world has practices and beliefs that distinguish it from others around them. The biblical witness sets off a certain religious group as the route to the sacred. Both the Hebrew and Christian scriptures have been used to name who is acceptable and who is not, to identify privilege and, without sensitivity to the inherent worth of others, prejudice. Christian theology has further reinforced that tribal distinction with its emphasis on the scripture verses that describe salvation as exclusively achieved through belief in Jesus Christ, or on the church traditions that dispense salvation through sacraments.

The progressive elements within the church are those that are able to assist the church to relinquish its hold on the Bible as TAWOGFAT. If the Bible is the baby that so many are afraid will go out with the bathwater, they need have no fear. It is not the Bible that must go; rather, it is the Word of God that must go. We do not, any of us—whether Christian, Muslim, Jew, Baha'i, Confucian, Jain, *any of us*—have a corner on what the word of God is, on what religious beliefs are universally authoritative for humankind. This we must confess. Those who recognize the Bible's claim to be the word of God as the monster in the tub with the baby are those who must whisk it out before it does any further damage.

When the Bible is no longer seen as the authoritative word of God, it takes on a completely different aura. We are freed to see it as it is. In that light, some of it can be seen as poetry and studied, memorized, and assessed as such. Some can be seen as inspirational. Some will be seen to give support to our struggles, to live according to life-enhancing values we have named as important. Some will be anthropologically significant, reflections of life in a time long since past. Some can be seen as the utterances of a fearful or angry or violent people. So, too, will other pieces of holy scripture, other sacred texts belonging to other faiths, be freed for such purposes. It will be up to us—those of us who have called it holy in the past—to name what is worthy of being welcomed into our places of worship and what will need to be left behind in the historical record as a document once, but no longer, believed to be "holy" and the word of God.

# 4

# LIBERATING CHRISTIANITY

## A WAY FORWARD

When we allow the progressive scholarship of the past centuries to challenge us to reconsider the foundations of our faith, we find ourselves left with an enormous task: constructing something viable to replace what we find to be no longer working. Well, that is our task if we see the endeavour worthwhile. We could just leave everything lying there in a messy muddle and walk away. Many have done that before us and many yet will.

Isn't that always the question? No matter what it might be that we are reconsidering, if we find it in need of an overhaul, we have to decide if it is worth our time and energy to tackle the problems and try to right them. Whether it is an old car, a long-term relationship, or a system of accounting, if we take a long look and see it's not working, we have to decide what we're going to do about it. If we undertake to set about righting things, we need the tools and the know-how to do the job well. Progressive thinking is not everyone's cup of tea, but it is the only tool that will possibly pull us through to the next stage of the church's development. Lucky for us, it's been tried many times before, albeit in other disciplines, with some wonderful results.

If we take a few moments and think about what the world was like when our parents or, better yet, our grandparents were born, we will each be imagining a world radically different than the one we now inhabit. In the early years of the twentieth century, while my grandmother was coming of age, the concept of progress was a powerful one. Humanity ("Man," back then) was coming into its own, as evidenced by sweeping advances in almost every discipline. Modernism was fast conquering the Western world. In 1893, the Chicago World Fair presented a beautiful vision of utopia achievable through a virtual wonder of technological advances (and a not-so-pretty picture of religious disharmony, as attempts to gather leaders of the world's religions around the ethic of the Golden Rule were stumped by divisive squabbling over incompatible beliefs). Wealth and glory were tangible in every sector. Inventors raced to beat one another to the patent office and entrepreneurs to have their pick of the most promising inventions. Growth, for many, was not only an option; it was a promise.

Creeping into this explosion of technological and cultural advancement was the work of a young scholar named Albert Schweitzer. Having grown up ruminating over the discrepancies and gaps in the biblical record of Jesus' life, Schweitzer's best known theological work examined the attempts of previous scholars who had sought to wrestle with the challenges that record presented. It was a book that would shake the underpinnings of New Testament scholarship. With chapter titles such as "Further Imaginative Lives of Jesus," *The Quest of the Historical Jesus*, published in 1904, exposed the works of theologians and philosophers who had ventured the quest before him—Reimarus, Schleiermacher, Strauss, Renan, and others—as their authors' own autobiographical projections. His final conclusion was that any inquiry into the life of the historical Jesus could only ever result in revealing the truth that the first-century Jew had little to say to the ethical and moral struggles of the contemporary world. Influenced by his own discoveries, Schweitzer left his ecclesial career, studied medicine, and moved to Africa.

But his work served as a foghorn on the sea of faith. In Christendom's hallowed academic halls, the book halted explorations into who Jesus had really been and what the truth behind that question meant for the church. Rather than absorb its provocative and challenging insights, the church seemed to log the position it intoned and skilfully calculate another course. It would be easier to ride the gentle swells of the personal experience of Jesus—the only way we could ever know him, according to Schweitzer—than to head into the iconoclastic seas of historical *dis*covery. And so they did.

Schweitzer's closing remarks in *The Quest* provided the new course for the church, even as it moved on without reference to them. Holding close to the world-negation Schweitzer argued was the core value in the sayings of Jesus, liberal denominations rode effortlessly on the wave of the social gospel, casting aside concerns about the historicity of the Bible and the man it upheld as the saviour of the world and reaching into the sympathetic hearts and experiences of their followers. Each of us could have our own experience of Jesus and follow our conscience as that experience directed us.

That personal experience could be exponentially powerful, and it proved to be so. Personal experience is, if you'll excuse the redundancy, a very personal thing. There isn't much one can say to negate someone else's experience of something. Even in the middle of an argument with one's spouse, it is often prudent to acknowledge that his or her perspective or experience of you is different than what you may have wished to project, thereby conceding that it may, at least for them, be accurate.

Personal experience has the ability to shelter us from the examination of what we know. It has the power to place a very high validity and a very large "off limits" sign on anything we identify as our personal experience of Jesus. And personal experience can be extremely rich and diverse, allowing for intricate investigations of what is not concrete but still understood to be equally real: thoughts, feelings, and perceptions. Theology provides the perfect language with which to explore such nebulous things and, in a sense, further protect them from examination. It was the better part of the century later that Northrop Frye conquered the exploration of this terrain in *The Great Code*, using literary tools to wrestle new meaning from the Bible. Frye's clarification of the different kinds of language we employ to access different levels of our existence—concrete, conceptual, persuasive, mythic, and literary—further endorsed the use of the esoteric language with which theologians maintained the heavenly mists that shrouded the historical development of the faith tradition.[1] Having stifled the concrete search for the historical Jesus, long before Frye identified the pattern, our language in the church had flowed naturally and smoothly past Frye's first three categories and lodged itself securely within the realm of the mythic or literary. It was a very safe place in which to entrench the tradition.

By the time Frye spelled out what we were doing, however, the pursuit of the historical Jesus was, once again, coming to the fore. Perhaps it was that the heavenly mists were found to be too damp and close. Perhaps scholars, tired of the obfuscation inherent in the language of their discipline, sought more concrete stuff, something against which they could work up a sweat. Several generations after the attempts Schweitzer had made, the territory appeared to be new, though close examination proves that many of its paths are well worn.

Spurred on by the same extremes Schweitzer had noted in the scholars he reviewed, either admiration or disdain of the man known as Jesus, and including arguments against his existence at all, the effect of recent scholarship has been much the same as it was a century ago. There is little we can definitively say about the man that allows the teachings attributed to him to address the issues of our times with any incisiveness. Indeed, if we in the twenty-first century were to insist upon adopting whatever world-view he was found to have, it would be so extreme that we would have to reject completely the way of life we have assumed.

But much of that way of life must be challenged. Because we cannot simply lift a first-century worldview from the cryptic passages that describe not it but Jesus' purported reaction to it, and impose it on ourselves, we can only consider the values presented in the text and determine whether they are relevant for our time. Disdain for and denial of those who do not agree with our perspective seems to be highly regarded by Jesus (Mark 3:34), but I suggest that we now hold dialogue, diversity, and community as higher values. Succumbing to the unjust treatment of others is also highly recommended (Matthew 5:39, 18:21–22), but I believe we now value justice and its pursuit more highly than submission. Recommending that we live without care for the future (Luke 12:22–29) reinforced one's dependence upon the community and a benevolent deity. But we now recognize that it is we who are responsible for one another and the earth. We cannot afford to be reckless about the future. Nor can we strip ourselves of our resources and be able to positively affect the world. Placing all one's assets in common with everyone else's, giving everything we have to the poor (Matthew 19:21), or lending to our enemies with no expectation of repayment (Luke 6:34) all rely upon a utopian model of human society that we have not achieved and very likely will not achieve. To act in these manners can serve to abdicate the responsibilities we have to one another. Conscientious, ethical oversight of our resources is a more prudent and potentially beneficial response. The values we choose to live by must set a radically ethical standard for our time, not by what seemed relevant to a vastly different world two thousand years ago.

It is impossible to lift an appropriate moral high ground out of Jesus' life, works, and sayings. As ground gets higher and higher, it eventually comes to a peak or a precipice. A peak, compared with the whole of the mountain, is a very small fraction. A precipice offers little consolation. What we need is a broad base that will help us wrestle with those difficult ethical issues. Jesus just isn't able to provide us that broad base—his vision is constrained by the context in which it was cast. A Christianity based on the belief in his divinity can't either.

The world has spun itself through aeons of progress since it came into being. In its most recent ages, humanity has had an enormous hand in that progress. Since my grandmother was born, we have leapt ahead exponentially. But we find that we are now standing at the precipice created by our own arrogance and desire for self-gratification. Pointing to Jesus and telling people that he is our salvation is just not going to work. His words are dead to many people. The world has changed. The words don't make sense any more, and shouldn't. In trying to capture exactly what he said so that it could be brought into our time, we have found, quite by accident, that what he said has little power. The liberal church, home to the scholarship that has disclosed these realities for us, needs to recognize that fact, assimilate it, and adjust itself. Because it does have something relevant and important to say, and the alternatives—a rejection of all that which is good or the continued tribal prejudices of fundamentalist Christianity, or fundamentalist anything—will create a world in which many would not wish to live.

Moving forward, in any discipline, is something that happens one step at a time. Sometimes those steps seem huge. Others seem so pathetically limited as to be of no use at all. Forward, however, is forward, and as Richard Dawkins, in *The God Delusion*, has so ably argued on behalf of evolution, half a wing can still keep one from ending up a blotch on the ground.

> Half a wing is indeed not as good as a whole wing, but it is certainly better than no wing at all. Half a wing could save your life by easing your fall from a tree of a certain height. And 51 per cent of a wing could save you if you fall from a slightly taller tree. Whatever fraction of a wing you have, there is a fall from which it will save your life where a slightly smaller winglet would not. The thought experiment of trees of different height, from which one might fall, is just one way to see . . . that there must be a smooth gradient of advantage all the way from 1 per cent of a wing to 100 per cent. The forests are replete with gliding or parachuting animals, illustrating, in practice, every step of the way up that particular slope of Mount Improbable.[2]

All over the world there are birds that can't fly any more than a barely decent hop. But their wings do what they need them to do. Where the evolution of the church might finally take it is, I hope, a full and marvellously effective wing away; but since I think we have incredible work yet to do, I have no interest in becoming that blotch on the ground. It's time to grow that half-a-wing and see where we can go from there.

The problem facing the church is the catching up it has to do. Had we read Schweitzer and made some effective changes in what we were saying and doing, instead of just veering to the left (or was it listing?), we'd be a hundred years ahead of where we are now as we grapple, once again, with the consequences of our research into the historical Jesus.

For progress to take place in any field, there are a variety of things that must be in place in order for it to happen and another few things that should be in place if it is to happen well. In other words, some of it is essential, and the rest is a wish list. Without the wish list, change can and does happen, but it does so under duress and often with force. Indeed, that seems to be our history, but it need not be the legacy we leave those who follow us. We can do this with care, honouring what has been without compromising our necessary choice to move forward.

It is interesting to note that many of those things required to move something forward have been present throughout the history of the church, but the forward movement has still not taken place. Oh, we've tinkered with this and that now and then, trying to make things clearer for everyone. The idea of icons; the translation of the Bible into English; printing it and making it available; the Catholic liturgy of 1501 and the consequent "Reformation" (which could have been called "the split"); the challenges about whether to sing or not to sing, to stand or not to stand; about who reads the Bible out loud in public worship; what we wear and where we sit; all those little details and so many more have been addressed at one time or another. We've worked out a lot of things, and, when we've pulled back from actually killing one another over them, we've generally agreed to disagree and gone our separate ways, sometimes with each side passionately sneering "Good riddance!" over its shoulders.

And so I note four initial elements that are essential in spawning progressive thought—an open mind, passion, creativity, and intellectual rigour. It is sadly true that one can have all these four elements, make great strides in a chosen discipline, pursue new vistas of thought, and create innovative ways of solving problems but, for want of the courage to speak honestly and to do so with respect and balance, fail to deliver the message to a world in need of it. And so, I also offer four subsequent characteristics of a progressive perspective. They, too, I believe are essential but only to those who are seeking to do something with what their progressive endeavour has brought them to know. Anyone can think themselves to new understandings if they work hard enough at it. Not everyone can make appropriate and life-giving use of those new understandings. We are in need of all eight characteristics if we are going to create a church able to have a positive effect on the future.

## The First Four Essentials
### An Open Mind

The first essential ingredient of any progressive perspective is the concept of the open mind. We like to think of ourselves as open-minded, but we are often this way only as long as the things we're invited to think about aren't things that require we change our worldview, opinions, or prejudices. Think, for instance, of your closest female friend dating someone half her age or your closest male friend dating someone twice his age. It may, of course, not be an issue for you, but many perfectly rational, compassionate, grown men and women simply can't get their heads around this one, and not for very rational reasons. And if it isn't an issue for you, and you haven't been forced to think through the issues already because of your own particular life circumstances, think of yourself doing it and talking it over with your kids or your parents. Feel any discomfort now?

Opening our minds is hard work. We live in an anaesthetizing culture. What we should think is flashed at us in a variety of media every minute of the day, and we are virtual sponges for it. A local radio station has been banned in my home and not because its disc jockeys regularly ridicule and show disdain toward women. We've already cleared that one up. It has been banned because they regularly ridicule and show disdain toward styles of music that aren't on that particular station's playlist and, by extension, to those who listen to those other styles of music. I don't want my child to assimilate a style of thinking that isn't open enough, big enough to imagine that people can and should appreciate different things than he does. Believe me, it can be a battle.

Having an open mind within the church has been rather unnecessary for most of Christendom. Everything we've ever needed to know has come to us through the "proper" channels, with a few breaks from the norm down through the ages. A quick scramble for the keys to the kingdom and their inherent power over determining just what it was that we needed to know took place in the church's early days. But there were so many different apologists, each of whom was cast by the others as heretics, that it was actually Constantine's councils, not Jesus, that finally granted those powerful keys to a group that eagerly claimed them. Since that time, the church, with amazing consistency, has masterfully engineered, managed, and controlled its doctrine. Given that it hasn't changed much since then, it has been what some would call an easy job.

With the church having been made the repository of the truth and claiming the right and authority to interpret the Bible in its pursuit of that truth, there was little anyone needed to think about. Where to take your burning questions* was very clear: if you dared, you went to those who, in the appropriate ecclesial garb, could answer them. And you believed every word they said.

If you didn't believe what they said, you could doubt. The faithful have always doubted. But you didn't say much about it, and you certainly didn't argue publicly against what the church said. To present or profess a different understanding could easily lead one to be excommunicated. In this day and age, particularly for those of us who are Protestants and have lived with the fact for centuries, excommunication from the church might not seem like a very big deal. For those within the Roman Catholic Church, however, it is still a very big deal, indeed.

---

*Sometimes "burning questions" were those which, if asked, ended with you tied to a stake on top of a burning pyre.

The Roman Catholic Church has taught for millennia that the soul is eternal and that beyond this life it has two possible places of everlasting repose, although the nice one, heaven, is usually accessible only after a purification process that takes place in "the condition" of purgatory.[3] (For a while there was a third, the non-doctrinal but very comforting "limbo," signed into the realms of those things the faithful can acceptably *not* believe by Pope Benedict XVI early in 2007.)[4] The other one, hell, could hardly be described as a repose. Excommunication means eternal banishment. Outside the Roman Catholic Church, so it claims, there is no hope of eternal peace.

For most of Christendom, outside the church there has been no mortal peace either. Heretics, those who would put forward a version of reality that was inconsistent with that presented by the church, could be disciplined, imprisoned, killed, or forced to recant heretical beliefs through any number of creative ways, some of which continue to be used to this day for political purposes.[5] Having an open mind within Christianity has, for much of its past, put one at a decided disadvantage.

Many church leaders today continue to thrive on the intellectual privilege with which the institution has vested them. I qualify that statement with the term *many* because there are undoubtedly leaders who do not allow their parishioners to presume they, the clergy, know everything. But I believe, compared to the number of clergy in total, it would be few. Clericalism is alive and well within the church today, and with the authority to speak on the Bible and matters of faith, our "God-given right," we have been careful to control our power. Many have used passages within the Bible to warn members that to venture beyond its teachings is a treacherous thing. Often, in the more conservative corners of Christianity, the young are taught to disparage higher education lest it lead one straight into the arms of the devil. Those who venture from the faith, in some instances, experience what is called disfellowshipping, a practice used by Jehovah's Witnesses to shun individuals who have rejected some or all of the doctrinal beliefs of their communities. Within mainline denominations, there is a smug security rampant among my peers, and it is reinforced by an entire faith tradition made up of unintelligible answers. How convenient it is when we ourselves don't understand what we are saying, that those to whom we are saying it think we are so wise.

If you are going to move forward though, you need to have an open mind, a mind that might end up in the evening with different stuff in it than was there when it awoke in the morning. New perspectives can come to you from any source, even one you revile. Perhaps the most difficult part of being open is the need to lower our estimation of our currently held beliefs enough that we are receptive to others, to be non-arrogant about what we know so that we can hear what others are bringing to the table. It will allow that our perspective can't have, nor provide, all the answers. An open mind will be eager to be understood to the point of being challenged. It is non-defensive and able to suspend judgment, holding ideas tentatively as they are assessed. It will be comfortable with complexity and ambiguity, not needing to have all the answers all at once. You need to be able to critique what you hold in your head. Ideas that have been offered to you are just that, ideas. They are malleable. They can be shifted around, stewed over, seen from different angles. They are mere food for thought. Your own thought. The church has worked very hard to hold on to their responsibility to do that for you. Take it back.

When my daughter was very young, she experienced convulsions. They were diagnosed as being febrile, related to a high fever. But on the occasions that she had a convulsion, her temperature had been normal. Furthermore, she had not shown any signs of illness. Nevertheless, she was placed on phenobarbital, a relatively strong anticonvulsant, and, in a few short hours, I lost the healthy, vibrant daughter I had known. She was replaced by a ghostly spectre that the doctors assured me would return to normal once she became used to the drug. She never did. At least not on their timeline.

About a year later, my sister recommended a holistic physician who, through a process I took to be entirely bunk, arrived at a list of items to which she advised me Hazel was "allergic." (I now use the word *intolerance* to describe what had been called an allergy.) I left the office and told my sister I would put up with such nonsense for three weeks and no more. Within three days of eliminating the offending food substances, the daughter I had missed, who had become a child that oscillated between horrific screaming tantrums and head-on-the-table lethargy, was back. She was healthy; the colour had returned to her cheeks; and, best of all, the moods that had so viciously gripped her were gone.

I relay this story for the punchline only. When I went to Hazel's pediatrician and said that I was taking her off the phenobarbital, he warned me against it. He said food allergies were so non-existent that no one was even studying them. Not only that, he argued that *I* didn't need to take the *responsibility* for her life when *he* was willing to do so. And there it is. We can hand the responsibility for our lives over to the professionals. They are the experts. They'll make the diagnosis. They'll take on the liability and all the risks. We have nothing to do but trust them.

Hazel came off the medication. It is time those in the pews did, too.

## Passion

So here we are interested in those realms of theological discourse that have so long been off limits to the mildly curious. When one gets beyond the "closed" barrier, moves into "open" territory, and is able to hear and engage with challenging theological and spiritual concepts, my experience has been that mild curiosity rarely stays that way. People quickly become passionate about the subject and for various reasons.

For some, they are astounded to learn that others have been thinking, for just as long, the same things they have. Over and again, when in groups being exposed to the concepts of progressive Christianity for the first time, participants often linger afterwards to tell me that they had no idea anyone thought such a way. With the glee of a child who has just made friends with the new kid next door, they are eager to exchange ideas, talk about their beliefs, and share with me every question they have ever worked through to a conclusion they believe wouldn't be accepted by the church because it was outside the church's professed doctrine. They ask me direct questions that go a little further than the conversation in the group went, disclosing more and more with each question about what they really do believe and how far out of the box they really are.

The stories, as I've noted before, are stories of isolation even when the individual hasn't actually experienced it as such. They have not been able to completely share an integral part of who they are with another living being. It is absolutely heart-wrenching. While I am moved by the isolation in their stories and honoured that they feel they are able to connect with me, their passion and my sadness kindles my anger at the reality of the situation. In truth, they have been preached at, pastored to, and prayed with by clergy, many of whom, themselves, have definitely thought "such a way," many of whom have long since given up ideas of an interventionist God or a salvific Jesus, who don't believe that the Bible is authoritative, who struggle with their Easter sermons because they can't explain what happened either, and, if given a choice, would quickly give up the concept of a bodily resurrection. Yet with the person standing in front of me who is excitedly wanting to connect on every possible detail of faith in the few moments I have to share with them, they have remained utterly silent. It is a travesty of unknowable proportion.

These individuals have also shared pews, potluck suppers, Bible studies, and homes with friends and family members who also thought "such a way." But the church has not given them the tools with which to speak together about them. Afraid, perhaps, of giving away the keys to the shop, the church has kept them focused on ancient texts from which they are to draw life's complex meanings, has used such esoteric language that it befuddles even many theologically trained minds, and has secured the discussion of matters of life and death within its own boundaries. It has so skilfully created an almost impenetrable barrier to spiritual conversation that, on this basis alone, one could wonder at it being called spiritual at all.

A secondary sadness comes over me when people share their stories of isolated discovery and rumination. Much of their excitement is predicated on my being clergy. They cling to my words because those words are still coming from one of those who "knows." In my words, they are hearing permission to speak, read, and learn more. I wish I could reject the word *permission*. It assumes an authority I believe the church and those in its leadership don't have. However, for millennia, we have acted as though we did, we have told the world that we do, and we have hammered it home as truth. It is, therefore, our responsibility to intentionally divest ourselves of it. In order to do so, however, we need to use it, finally, for what will be its most vital purpose—that of assuring people, one at a time if need be, that we no longer and never did hold that authority, that each person is responsible for his or her own seeking, learning, exploring, interacting with whatever it is she or he finds holy, and for naming that specific quest, that unique journey, as valid. No one, certainly not the church, can do that for them. But we must take the responsibility of telling them that.

There are many outside the church—those who were never part of it, or who left it for these very reasons—who have spoken about matters of faith, about belief, and about doctrinal issues. They've written on ideas about God, the Bible, and the values that are important in contemporary society, despite what the church has said. We've taken interest in what they have said but have been reluctant to apply it to what the church says. We have not credited these outside voices with power in our conversations on faith issues. It is as if within the church their words have fallen on deaf ears. They have had much to say both to the church and to its people. We must turn up the volume so that those many important voices can be heard.

When others move into that "open-mind" space and become passionate about the church, it is betrayal that fuels their passion. They hear new ideas about God, Jesus, and the church that are in direct opposition to what they have been taught as true in the past, and they have good reason to be unhappy about it. Years and years of self-loathing, scorn, and hostility—much of which has been built upon a worldview that presented God as judgmental and authoritarian, conceived normal human impulses and realities as evil and abominable, and foretold consequences that included eternal damnation—are suddenly seen to have been worse than wasted. The destructive effects of that worldview, if not irreparable, can fall into the "lifetime-to-repair" category. It is a purgative process, and we all know how messy purgative processes can be.

The enmity which had been focused by church doctrine on the individual finds a new target as it turns on the powers that have directed it in the first place. Engaged in what might be perceived as a life and death struggle for ownership of one's own spiritual health, individuals consume book after book by authors whose works question what the church has always said was true. Their intuitive spirituality (by which I mean that part of us that offers sustenance to our relationships, to our quest for meaning, that helps us develop and continually assess our values) spurs them on for it finally finds resonance in what others are saying about these essential elements of their nature. Many, with or without tears, often utter the words, "I feel like I'm home for the first time."

Passion is the second necessary element in a progressive perspective. Whether it be beekeeping or millinery, you aren't going to move the discipline forward if you don't care a whit about it. You're not even likely to make much of a difference if you care only a little bit. Lots of us care little bits about whole lists of different things, but we're unlikely to make any real changes in them because we don't care quite enough to change our schedules or get involved in a really concrete way. If you're headed to make progress in an area, you'll know it. You'll find you're engaged in it more; you've rolled up your sleeves; you feel the stuff of it oozing between your fingers. In fact, you feel it taking possession of you. That's when progress is ready to happen.

## Creativity

But, even with passion, progress can't happen without creativity. Without creativity, nothing changes. Life, for me, is a great creative force on its own. We can choose to ignore it or we can become its midwives. So predisposed are we to the latter that much of our creative work seems perfectly natural to us. Fashioning love out of nothing is an enormously creative act, yet it is enthusiastically undertaken by almost every human on the planet. We are, each of us, creators in that respect.

For many, the energy used in partnering, parenting, and building meaningful relationships is creative expression enough. There are among us, however, those for whom creativity is a particular gift. They see things differently. They have a way of turning stuff upside down, figuring out how it works, taking it apart, and putting it back together in a better way, often with parts left over. They seem to have little homing devices that present them with a constant supply of things that could use "a little improvement." Interest them in beekeeping, and they'll have the most advanced apiaries ever seen; in millinery, and they'll sport outrageously unique creations and still, just barely, be able to call them hats. They thrive on the imperfections in the world, for in those very imperfections they find their reason for being.

Alongside them are those whose creativity is not so much a response to the shortcomings they find in the world as it is an outpouring of spirit into life's great empty chasms, of giving substance to something that, before, had none. Writers, poets, artists, composers all bring into being what previously didn't exist. For sculptors, as well, for though their medium may be solid, what stands finished at the end of their work is certainly not what stood there prior to the creative impulse. Those who set out upon this sort of inspired undertaking have to have more than a passing interest in the subject. In addition to their passion, the creative impulse seems to well up from some unknown place, some intuitive reality within.

Creativity is like that. Something nascent grows and grows, ideas swell, visions become more focused, reality begins to pale in comparison with the urgency of what is inside, one becomes almost fixated on it, and then something has to give. It has to come out, to be born, released into its own.

We are often awed by what comes to be in those sacred moments of birth. The wrestled beauty of a Bach concerto stands as testimony to the immense worth of the labour rooted in such creative tension. The creative, visceral passion out of which it grew must have seemed almost crushing in its power. We are the benefactors of that creativity, that passion.

## Intellectual Rigour

The fourth prerequisite for a progressive perspective is intellectual rigour. This seems like a no-brainer (sorry, couldn't resist), but it often isn't treated as one.

Think, for a moment, about your physician. The last thing you want in a physician is one who believes that studying days are over at graduation. You want someone whose leisure reading includes *The Lancet* and who has BioMedWorld as the homepage on her laptop. Actually, if you think about all the ongoing research and publication of the subsequent results, you'll probably decide you want your doctor in the office only half the day so he or she can spend the rest of the time reading up on just what might be wrong with you.

The reality is that no one could stay entirely on top of the findings of medical research. Your family doctor certainly can't. That's why, when you hear on *Oprah* or read in *GQ* about something that sounds a lot like something you've been trying to cope with for a while, your doctor isn't likely to deal with it directly. Bring him or her the information, and before you leave the office, you'll have the name of the specialist to whom you're being referred. There's just too much information out there for a family physician to take in. The faster they acknowledge that, the better off you'll be.

We're comfortable leaving the details of our X-rays and MRIs with technicians who know how to read them and the Latin names of our medications with our pharmacists. But sometimes, the specialized language doesn't seem quite so necessary. It gets into that "job security" category; as long as those in the profession know what they're talking about, you're not likely to try to figure it out yourself—especially when the subject area is deemed to be so far beyond the intellectual capacity of most of us mere mortals that we'll avoid it like the plague.

Richard Dawkins opens a chapter in *A Devil's Chaplain* with the following query:

Suppose you are an intellectual impostor with nothing to say, but with strong ambitions to succeed in academic life, collect a coterie of reverent disciples and have students around the world anoint your pages with respectful yellow highlighter. What kind of literary style would you cultivate? Not a lucid one, surely, for clarity would expose your lack of content.[6]

The chapter is devoted to exposing the gobbledegook employed among the academic elite, a deliberate use of jargon that, because it is so oblique, often doesn't ever get questioned.

Language holds power, incredible power. Those who control language control power. It's as simple as that. In 1996, Newt Gingrich put together, as part of the training program for Republican Americans seeking public office, a list of "Optimistic Positive Governing Words" to use when speaking about oneself and "Contrasting Words" to use when speaking about one's opponent. The reason? Language is recognized as "a key mechanism of control."[7] For Gingrich and his compatriots, even simple, straightforward words such as *initiative* or *excuses* can be used to manipulate our minds. They don't seek to confuse as much as to derail our thought processes. Being led by a speech as carefully crafted as one Gingrich might put together, without taking responsibility for getting the facts behind the stories, is exactly what such a careful and powerful use of language is meant to do.

It is important for us to remember that preachers are specialists when it comes to language. We don't usually think of them as using words to control people or to retain power; they are our pastors, our teachers, our leaders. But we need to listen as carefully as we (now) would to a political speech and be prepared to seek out facts and deeper understanding, to be intentional about trying to figure out where the speech is headed, and, if they use big theological terms, we need to talk to them, find out what they mean, and let them know we want to grapple with the ideas they are trying to express but that their language is getting in the way. Be wary of big words. One of the most difficult questions I was ever asked was at the end of a baptismal service. A visitor asked me, "What did you just do to that baby?" My responses were all terribly weak. Eventually I had to admit nothing, but it was the first time I'd really thought about it as more than just something I was supposed to do.

When developing The United Church of Canada's new Statement of Faith, a symposium was held in October 2005 to look at the initial draft. Those who presented papers used language that I, fifteen years out of theological college, could no longer understand. My brain was rusty. To me, its twists and turns seemed, and perhaps were, circuitous, providing no clear route to what the presenter was really trying to say.

One of the few laypeople present stood up and honoured those who had presented for being so much smarter than he, as he had not understood anything either. It raised an important question: just what was the purpose of the Statement of Faith being written? Clearly, if it was to help people inside and outside of the denomination achieve an idea of who we were and what we believed, it was missing the mark by far. But, as was stated later, perhaps that was exactly the point. Likened by one participant to football (or some other male-dominated sport, I can't remember exactly), the speaker argued that Christianity, too, should have an initiating language; there should be a learning curve for membership that would serve to separate those who believe from those who don't. He urged the committee responsible for writing the new statement, in response to arguments I had made for clarity, not to "dumb-down" the language. Perish the thought that any fool might know what it meant!

So get in there. Get to know your subject. Find all the cutting-edge stuff, and consume it piece by jagged piece until you've ingested the whole damned thing. Read, listen, ask questions, demand clarity, and ask some more. Stay on top of the "game" as at least one cleric would have it portrayed. Know everything you need to know, and then start asking more questions. Without intellectual rigour, there's no getting ahead.

## The Other Four Essentials
### Honesty

It should go without saying that in order to move forward in a discipline, those responsible for speaking about it must be honest about what they know. In contemporary society, however, we spend so much time trying to fudge the facts that I'm not at all certain that the desire to be honest can be considered an expected norm any longer.

The cosmetics industry spends gazillions of dollars every year in advertising. As part of their latest target market (female, North American, aging skin), I am particularly susceptible to their claims, which are generally quite fantastic and very alluring. But you don't have to be a Marshall McLuhan devotee to figure out that whatever it is the products can really do, it isn't reverse the effects of gravity. At best, you might get to *look* for a few hours like your face has not succumbed to it, but if you read very carefully, you'll see no miracle results are ever *really* promised; they only seem to be. While the content of the claims may be technically true, it is presented in a manner that suggests something other than what is being said. Skim anything these days and you're as likely to be misled as not.

If you complain that you don't see any results, chances are you'll be expected to look a little harder (can't you see a difference? I see a difference!), use the products more consistently (you know you don't!), or pay a little more money for something that will enhance the products you're already using (I promise, you'll love this!). Our entire culture serves to underscore the promises of the cosmetics industry and makes our need to believe in its claims all the more urgent.

It is perhaps unfair of me to take aim only at the cosmetics industry. Almost every marketer in the world twists/bends/stretches the truth to make people believe claims that aren't really being made at all. Furthermore, what is being sold is often not the product itself, but, rather, the *feeling* associated with it. Exactly what is the core product of a cosmetics company? It isn't a cream that will reverse the aging process and give you younger skin. It is the belief that you have control over the aging process. That belief is just sold in a bottle.

We have to examine the church in the same way, seeing through its hyperbole to the real core product. They would have you think it is salvation—a virtual freedom from trauma, tragedy, and turmoil in this life and an absolute freedom from eternal death and torment in the next. But can it actually produce that product? No, not any more than the cosmetics industry can yet (but I keep hoping!) produce an age-reversing skin cream. So the church's core product must be something else.

The church, it turns out, is in the same business as the cosmetics industry. It's core product is belief. Belief that you are safe and secure in a universe ruled by a benevolent deity. It markets that belief in a variety of products, any one or combination of which will help you think you are able to abate the trauma, tragedy, and turmoil of this life and become worthy of a beautiful by-and-by*. Because it keeps you focused on the promise, the church, like the cosmetics trade, never actually has to produce the goods.

And, like the cosmetics industry, we have been expected to

---

*"There's a land that is fairer than day,
And by faith we can see it afar;
For the Father waits over the way
To prepare a dwelling place there.
In the sweet by-and-by,
We shall meet on that beautiful shore . . ."
Sanford F. Bennett, 1868

accept any of the shortcomings as though we are the ones on the short end of the bargain. For Christians who have suggested that they're getting short shrift in life, the church has been quick to denounce their doubt, blame them for things that have gone wrong, and diligently assure them that the program is still in place. They haven't prayed properly or hard enough, tithed regularly (for those of you who've forgotten, that means giving 10 per cent of your income, pre-tax, to the church. If you don't do it pre-tax, well, there's your problem), or given enough credit where credit is due (you could have been killed in that accident, just thank God that your injuries were only . . . ).

Grade four, for my daughter, was a traumatic year. We had moved away from a very strong and supportive family system and all of her friends. The French immersion school in which we enrolled her was in a distant neighbourhood. Commuting, she didn't have much opportunity to connect with the other children, many of whom were in well-established cliques that could be quite cruel (inviting the whole class except two children home for lunch, that sort of thing). Her classroom teacher was generally indifferent to our concerns and was unable to support Hazel through this difficult transition.

When grade five arrived, Hazel came home dazzled by her new teacher, a young, energetic, and, we learned, beautiful woman. We were overjoyed. She was excited about school again and glad to be reconnected with the friends she had made. We looked forward to a better year, pleased that she finally felt happy.

It didn't last. In the third week of September, Hazel's teacher took ill. Later, the children were told she had been diagnosed with a brain tumour. Week after week, we waited to hear how she was. News was scarce. It was several months later that Hazel came home, devastated. Her class had been told of her teacher's death. Hazel's anger was abrupt and swift. Screaming at me, she demanded to know why God hadn't answered her prayers. She had prayed every single day that her teacher would get better and come back to the school. She had done what I'd taught her to do. She'd done it the way I'd taught her. But it hadn't worked.

I remembered a children's time I'd led at church with Hazel in attendance in which I had taken a cup of water and threatened to pour it into a bowl. I had asked if anything could stop the water from reaching the bowl. Quickly, the children assured me, and demonstrated, that all they had to do was stick their hands in it as it poured from the cup and they could make it go all over the place. They loved it.

I then told them the water was like their prayers. "When we pray, we're asking God to do something for us. If we don't get what we want, we assume God has said 'No.' But what really happens," I said, "is more like the water trying to get into the bowl. Too often we stick something like our attitude in the way—we are angry at someone else, or we haven't been kind to someone, or the reason we want what we're asking for is a selfish reason rather than the right reason. Our prayers just don't get to God. Like the water, if something gets in the way, it can't get into the bowl."

Remembering that story, I could barely look into Hazel's streaming wet and furious eyes. In her understanding, something she had done was the reason for her prayers not being heard. It was either that, or God just didn't care. Which was it? Her pain deserved an answer. I didn't have it.

Now, I wouldn't suggest there was a bowl or any kind of direct access to it. Now, I wouldn't set up a scenario that, when it was carefully examined, placed the responsibility for someone's life on the shoulders of a ten-year-old. Now, I wouldn't present a product—security, comfort, a positive outcome—because there is no way I could promise it would happen. Now I know enough to say I just don't know.

## Courage

Naïveté, brutality, courage—three basic motivations for honesty. Which of these is likely to effectively change the church?

Naïveté breeds a simple and sometimes devastating honesty. We are honest because it doesn't occur to us that there will be consequences for being so. Before we are taught honesty etiquette as children (a lesson usually precipitated by our first ingenuous remarks about someone of whom our parents have spoken too freely in our presence), naïve honesty innocently opens for scrutiny the realities with which we all live, and it can, if we're ready for it, provide opportunity for rich and rewarding conversations at levels we may not have previously allowed.

A second type of honesty is, by its nature, much more intentional and, therefore, exponentially more dangerous. This is where one chooses to be honest knowing that there will be consequences and sometimes pretty nasty ones.

You and your partner are preparing to go out for the evening. It's a significant social event and there is a bit of anxiety in the air about looking good for it. Your partner zips and turns to you with that heart-stopping question—"Does this look good on me?" Now, if you chose to answer that question with "No, love, that outfit looks awful on you," you certainly couldn't plead naïveté. You know exactly what is going to happen! There would have had to be some reason in your decision to spin that particular evening in that particular direction.

Indeed, there are two.

I used to have a fortune cookie insert taped to my kitchen doorway that can shed some light on the first of those reasons: "Those who like to be brutally honest get more out of the brutality than they do out of the honesty." To choose to be honest in order to hurt someone leaves the victim drowning in the consequences of your nasty choice—the intentional decision is to forget all those whispered instructions in honesty etiquette you received from an embarrassed mother and to go for the jugular—the softest, most vulnerable, and exposed point. To be sure, it is honest, but it is a devastating, ruthless honesty, and one often used to maintain power and control in a relationship. Such honesty targets those who live trying to meet the ruthless criteria others have set for what is worthy in life—job, looks, wardrobe. They exist on the knife-point of that brutal honesty, ever vulnerable to someone's barbed and cruel assessment.

But it might not have been that at all. Perhaps your honesty is based in courage. Perhaps you take the wardrobe opportunity presented to introduce some of your concerns about your partner's perception of himself or herself. Perhaps you've tried other, more subtle ways to raise the topic only to have them neatly sidestepped. Perhaps it is important enough that you are willing to risk your partner's hysterical refusal to venture beyond the bathroom door or spending several nights on the couch yourself. Perhaps you worry that your partner's anorexia or obesity could be life-threatening. Honesty, here, is not seeking to maim, hurt, or destroy, but to challenge, change, and heal. Honesty based in courage may sound the same as that based in brutality, but its purpose is entirely different.

I ask again which of these will change the church: naïveté, brutality, or courage?

Until now, many questions have been posed by naïveté, but the church has ignored the importance of them. Children like my daughter have been noticing that their prayers aren't answered even when they said them the way they were taught. When they have turned to us and asked why, we have failed to respond to the truth exposed in their queries and have instead dismissed the questioners themselves as unable to understand. We have taught them—in their homes, religious institutions, and schools—what they are "supposed" to think on the matter. They have been given angels to pray with them and Jesus to comfort them when their prayers aren't answered. And, perhaps worst of all, we have tormented them with the kind of teaching that suggests they were too sinful or self-absorbed to be worthy of God's ear. Their naïveté has been forced to go the way of most naïveté—into the abyss of adult superiority. Their honesty has had no effect on the church. We have made sure of that. No, it will not be through naïveté that the church will progress.

Now, think through the implications of telling a congregation full of individuals, for whom, to some extent or another, prayer is a significant part of what helps them get through the day, that the benevolent deity to whom they pray and from whom they hope to receive some comfort or respite has not yet managed an impressive batting record. Let brutality take a swing at it.

The challenge to be honest has been neatly avoided in the past by those who see honesty solely as brutality in sheep's clothing. Many times a parishioner "in the know" has been told by their minister/priest/pastor that the reason they don't share what they really believe is that people wouldn't be able to cope with it. They have a point. For many in the church, in varying degrees, prayer is part of what helps them make sense of their lives, make seemingly impossible situations bearable. Telling them that there is no interventionist God, no divine being that is going to swoop down every time they're in trouble and yank them up again, has the potential to be earth-shattering. It will certainly be worldview-shattering. The problem is exacerbated by the reality that there is nothing to put in the place of that God that will reassure them of their security. Nothing. You're putting them in a very precarious position, psychologically, emotionally, and spiritually. Many are going to be devastated. So was your partner when you were honest about that outfit.

That doesn't mean you didn't need to challenge your partner about their eating habits. And it doesn't mean that you can alleviate your responsibility for being honest by calling on your responsibility to be nice. Honesty etiquette only hampers progress. The courage to be honest propels it.

But what of those who have tried to bring about change in their congregations and been treated dreadfully for doing so? What of those clergy who have spoken honestly from the pulpit, shared what they know of contemporary scholarship, risked speaking truthfully in front of their congregations, but who have faced an angry and hostile crowd as the result of their efforts? They have chosen to take the road that is abysmally less travelled and therefore all the more treacherous. I honour the courage they have shown. It will give them the strength to face the charges that will be made against them, and they will stand strong in the face of the chaos that their honesty opens up in their congregations, in the calls for their resignation, and in the threats of dismissal and investigation. If they can avoid the temptation toward brutality, they will do well.

If, however, it was not courage, but rather naïveté, a lack of awareness of the implications, that led them to be honest, then I encourage them to find strength in the words of this book, and in the faces, no matter how few, of those in their congregation, among their peers, and in their families who recognize and honour their integrity.

Perhaps, in fact, it was you. You will have found yourself on that abysmally less travelled road quite by accident. But you are not there alone. Seek out support. Find those who honour honesty, and be healed by their en-*coeur*-agement, the wrapping of their hearts around your efforts. Find your courage wherever you can find it. Build it up. It will not be easy. Soon, however, you will be called on to share it with another. And then another. And then another. Be ready when that call comes. Mark the road where you have passed so that another might know the way and, by you, come to be en-*coeur*-aged.

## Respect

No one wants to be told they are stupid, and, luckily, for the most part we aren't. We are, however, every one of us, ignorant of most things, in the true sense of the word. No one can possibly know everything there is to know about everything. Even the most intelligent people in the world must pick and choose their areas of expertise from among the plethora of subjects in which they might be interested. If they don't, all they can hope to become are dilettantes amassing little bits of knowledge from a broad field of topics. So it is that engineers are often ignorant when it comes to beekeeping and figure skaters when it comes to millinery. It doesn't mean that either is stupid; they are merely, and quite naturally, ignorant of the intricacies of a discipline about which they know nothing.

There are beekeepers out there, however, who will make you feel like an idiot for not knowing why bees spend all their time making honey, how they do it, what different kinds of bees there are, or why orange blossom honey is different from clover honey (they all taste the same to me!). And there are milliners out there who would scoff at your favourite hat should you make the mistake of wearing it into their shop, despite its having faithfully done its job of keeping you warm or brightening up your bad hair days for six or seven years now. You may, when confronted with either of these sneering individuals, find the grace within your heart to engage them in their topic and come away feeling like you'd made the best of it and learned something. Good for you. The rest of us, however, had likely long since fled in embarrassment and its usual cohort, anger.

The art of making someone else feel small is so regularly displayed by adolescents and teenagers that one might argue it is encoded in our DNA to erupt into action at around the age of fourteen. It is then that they perfect the art of inflection and, with a slight emphasis on the last word in their sentences, manage to silently punctuate almost everything they say with the word *Stupid*: "Gnarls Barclay isn't a person, it's a *band*, (Stupid)." "It's not cotton, it's *hemp*, (Stupid)." "I did my homework at *school*, (Stupid)." Perfectly placed, subtle inflection is imperative, and the result is almost always an escalation of tempers.

Most of us, fortunately, mature out of that stage in our lives. Or we at least learn to use that tone more sparingly than we did as youths, reserving it for those really dreadful relationship spars when it seems vitally important that we display all of our very worst attributes. We learn, instead, the art of conversation, sharing perspectives with openness to learning, even our own conversion. Arrogance, in such conversations, is only a barrier.

Knowledge is power, so the old adage goes. And so it is that, whether factual or theoretical, those who have it find themselves in the position of having to choose how to use it. If their intent is to disseminate it as widely as possible, there will be a simple grace to their sharing of it. What one has come to know will be offered with respect for all the learning, struggle, and wisdom that has disclosed and upheld previous truths while inviting the hearer to reconsider those truths in light of new insights, to set them aside so that new understandings can be explored and, if all goes well, assimilated. It is a gentle process.

Alas, too often we share newfound insights with the glee of the adolescent who is finally right about something and can't wait to inflect a perfect, silent "Stupid!" at the end of his or her outburst. We assume, incorrectly, that to have figured it out, whatever "it" is, makes us somehow smarter than everyone else, and we revel in our temporary superiority. Too many who have the insight and skill to help us move beyond the previous confines of Christianity fall into this tempting space. We feel we have been duped, and, to make things right, we too often feel compelled to humiliate and denigrate those we believe have duped us.

Scholars who write and lecture on contemporary biblical scholarship are too often still in the anger stage. Their vitriol scars the lessons they have to give us and undermines their attempts to develop a Christianity that can be relevant in both today's and tomorrow's worlds. Referring to "f—ing fundamentalists" or denigrating other scholars does little to invite consideration of concepts that are worthy of being considered. Oh, it is true that many, coddled alongside what is often seen to be a brilliant and acerbic wit, may find it humorous and enjoy the show. But those who do so, for the most part, already share in the perspectives being presented. There is little new territory gained and few enlightened by the scholarship offered.

We need progress. And so it is that respect becomes essential for our purposes. It is imperative that we remember this important truth: all the perspectives that have come before ours have had their purpose, have brought meaning to whole generations of believers and continue to do so. Such knowledge must be honoured even as it is set aside.

We can take no credit for the knowledge we hold. We are not smarter than anyone else because we happen to have assimilated it before they did. We are not better because we read the book before the person next door. Even if we wrote it, we are not made superior for having done so. We are mere vessels for ideas that are, perhaps through us, now available to the world. Although we can control it and, for periods of time, perhaps, feel strong because of our control, knowledge itself belongs to a wider audience, and should we wish its influence to be felt in the world, we must relinquish our control of it. If knowledge is worthy of being heard and considered, it is most certainly our responsibility to share it respectfully in order that it might be accorded that honour. To do so, we are obliged to present it with a deep and twofold respect; one that simultaneously honours both the truth we bring and the truth it may ultimately displace.

### Balance—Patience, Perseverance, and Pace

Scott Campbell, author of *5-D Leadership* and consultant on change in the workplace, illustrates his points on the sluggish rate of change within organizations using a simple diagram. Beginning with a rectangle lying on its long side, he swipes a diagonal line from the lower left corner to the far upper right corner.

"This," he says, indicating the left side of the rectangle, "is the way things are. And this," indicating the right side of the rectangle, "is the way you want things to be." He points to the dot where he began drawing the line. "You're here. You've got to convince everyone to join you if you're going to make it to the other side, if the change is going to work. The problem," he then says, "is that the length of this box is about fifteen years."[8] At that point in his presentation, everyone either groans or breaks into that thin just-about-to-have-a-nervous-breakdown kind of laughter. It's no wonder. We want change to happen the moment we think we know how.

Fortunately, for most of us, the changes for which we opt, from the barely noteworthy choice of new drapery to the more significant decision to become parents, have limited repercussions. They affect our own personal space and life, but have little impact on the community or, more broadly, the world (ecological footprint notwithstanding). Usually, the time it takes to assimilate such changes is much less than Campbell's fifteen years.

But remember, Campbell wasn't talking about personal change. He was talking about changing worldviews and beliefs, the things that inform social and corporate culture; those things do take time. Ideas that dispute what people have always believed, even when proffered with respect and all the back-up documentation necessary, are rarely met with a ticker-tape parade. Quite the contrary. It is often derision, argument, anger, fear, or hostility that rises up to meet them.

For good reason. Life is hard enough as it is. Just managing to get through the day with the challenges that are placed before us by our relationships, jobs, lists of things to do, the weather, aging parents, sassy teenagers, the perception of rising crime rates, food preparation, oil changes, cancer, and failing immune systems. People are not interested in having more stress added to their lives. They live stress from the moment they wake up through to the moment they fall exhausted back into sleep. Come roaring up the front walk at them with a new idea that's going to shake some of their preconceived notions up a bit, make them have to double think their decisions, and you're not likely to get a foot inside the front door.

If you want to get your progressive ideas across, you're going to need two kinds of strategies. Campbell's little diagram warns us of the first: coping with the reality that change doesn't happen overnight, no matter how excited or passionate we are about it. It has been for much longer than fifteen years that proponents of global warming trends have been trying to get their message across. Government committees presented with the research have, for decades, politely thanked the scientists for their work, passed the tomes of documentation to another committee or level of bureaucracy, and cleared the room for their next scheduled meeting. Whatever screams of frustration may have reverberated in the halls as scientists and activists left the premises were muffled long before the public could ever hear them. Spin, the art of controlling difficult political situations, flew into high gear. So it is that, forty years or so after the trends were first noted, we find ourselves smashed up against the end of a too-short timeline with paralyzingly few options available to us. But, given all the current realities we see, we still want to scoff and call Al Gore, savvy messenger that he is, a limelight seeker in order that we might yet avert our need to change.

Think about it. Those scientists were talking about the end of the world as we know it. One wonders how high the stakes actually have to be in order to have the need for change acknowledged and acted upon.

Patience. Perseverance. More patience. More perseverance. Find out how to keep up that regimen and you'll have developed the first strategy you will require when presenting a progressive perspective. Without patience, it is impossible to endure the length of time between our first fervent desire to change the world and any real action. We go mad facing the intransigence of bureaucracy, of society, of people. And we simply give up. Patience without perseverance is festered time. It slides into arrogance and from there into irritability, sarcasm, and disrespect. Perseverance without patience locks us into the same chasm of anger. We end up merely discrediting our ideas and limiting, if not denying, whatever impact we might have had.

The second strategy is also related to that diagonal line in Campbell's box: the process of walking with a group of people, however slowly, toward the future as it has been envisioned. Remember, for the most part, they are not willingly along for the walk. Change is not a welcome program. One would think it comforting, however, to suppose that a progressive perspective in the realm of spiritual matters would be far less likely to evoke the sort of anger and fear that instigated the campaigns raised to discredit global warming alarmists. It is an argument in the realm of ideas, is it not? Such arguments are best settled around a civilized dinner table or on the floor of a presbytery. After all, we're not even talking about the real world.

Think again. The understanding of God, of our relationship to "it," of the balance of good and evil in the world, of our assured salvation, of an eternity of security and peace—these are not trifling issues. God, or whatever we deem to be sacred, is understood to be *very* real, and toying with what it is and how we relate to it can bring out the worst in people. Bishop John Shelby Spong, for challenging the church to demote the Bible's claims in regard to homosexuality from "divine command" to mere ancient (and not-so-ancient) human prejudice, has been the recipient of serious death threats. Letters to editors of newspapers and magazines around the world, in response to progressive religious voices, are swift and angry. Passions around beliefs run very high. People hold fast and furiously to their ideas. In William Safire's *No Uncertain Terms*, the *New York Times*' "word maven" exposes the anger he aroused by merely entertaining the suggestion that the standard usage of BC (Before Christ) be changed to the more broadly accepted BCE (Before Common Era). Even on such a seemingly innocuous issue as this, response was acidic. "'It is one thing to deny the divinity of Christ,' observed Michael McGonnigal of Silver Spring, Maryland. 'It is quite another to deny His historical existence, which is what is implied by the superfluous switch from the traditional BC to the PC BCE.'"[9] Safire goes on to tell that the journal *Biblical Archaeology Review* had so many angry letters as a result of the dating nomenclature controversy that they published a paperback, *Cancel My Subscription!*, filled with the letters.[10]

There is no moving forward that does not necessitate a letting go of what was held in the past. Whether one is eager to embrace the new or fearful of leaving what they have known, the same holds true. A ninety-six-year-old member of my congregation, Les Spurrier, grew up on the Canadian prairie. As the motorcar began to rise in popularity, Les' father was delighted. He marvelled at the new technology and celebrated its increasing use in their community. But he was a harness-maker. Despite his enthusiasm for the motorcar, it would destroy his trade and leave him and his family destitute during the Great Depression of the 1930s. The family scattered, Les hopping a boxcar for Toronto when there were no prospects left on the prairie. Balance is everything.

It is the responsibility of the individual or group presenting a progressive perspective to anticipate as many of the challenges it will present as is possible. As they are identified, it is then our responsibility to act to mitigate negative effects. To eliminate them would be impossible, and it is ridiculous to suggest that we could. But finding ways to lessen the burden of change, to make the new terrain more habitable, to honour what has gone before even while pointing out its inadequacies, is a responsibility that progressive thinkers hold. Learning how to anticipate the problems and creating a positive environment for change is essential—strategy two.

Howard Gardner examines the processes implemented to bring about change in a variety of settings in his book *Changing Minds*. He develops a theory of mind-changing that can be utilized in shifting cultural belief systems within both homogeneous and diverse groups. Underlying the factors Gardner identifies as present in situations where minds are changing, lives a story. Gardner notes the importance of the story particularly for diverse groups headed for change. Presenting a story that resonates with the audience is one of the most significant factors in mind-changing. Margaret Thatcher, whose politics and personality are often far from the hearts of common people, was yet able to bring about sweeping changes in Britain, composed of a broadly diverse group, by framing them in terms of story. Hers, that Britain had lost its way and needed to reclaim its entrepreneurial spirit, and through that spirit its greatness, was presented through astute management of the factors Gardner identifies as crucial. The simplicity with which it was presented and the resonance it bred within the British public allowed a dramatic mind-shift to take place that might otherwise have been impossible.[11]

The population to whom we would speak of theological shifts is also very diverse, despite the probability that all are members of a single faith tradition. Resistance to a new story will be strong. The old story of redemption and acceptance is arrestingly simple and enormously powerful. Any new story that would replace it must be clear, simple, evocative, and, as did Thatcher's, seek to replace the security of the old with the security of the new.

This presents us with a difficult problem. Thatcher's Britain saw tough times for many who had relied upon the social safety net of the previous decades; in the midst of their plight, however, Thatcher handed them the rock-solid belief that things would improve. Whenever and wherever she was able to deliver the goods, she held it up as proof and encouragement. We don't have such rock-solid hope. Our story leaves the fate of the world in too-human hands, and our confidence in such a future, given what we know of ourselves, of one another, is slight. How can we tell a story that shatters the God-given security with which the Christian world has wrapped itself for two thousand years, in a manner that cares for those who, divested of that security blanket, stand afraid and shivering in the harsh light of reality? Is it even a loving thing to do?

We have merely to reflect on the significance of the religious perspective in matters of choice that affect humanity and the planet to realize that there truly is no alternative. The dangers inherent in fundamentalist religious perspectives are well known. They often revel in the devastations brought about by an over-heated planet or peacekeeping efforts gone awry, and see them as the foretold preparations for God's final judgment. (The Satanic forces in the ultra-conservative Christian video game *Eternal Forces*, based on the popular Left Behind novel series by Tim Laflage and Jerry Jenkins, are called the "Global Community Peacekeepers.") Liberal religious perspectives, heavily built upon relativist arguments that demand any religious perspective be tolerated, are complicit in the escalation of the danger. Patience and perseverance are our allies. Ignorance and the *false* security of the old story are not. The way forward must be taken with care.

The most compelling facet of the old story is its security. The most compelling facet of the new story is its seeking after truth. As the story is heard, considered, and assimilated, people are called out of their security and challenged to live in the face of that discomforting truth. Pastoral skill, the stuff the church claims to be full of, is deeply needed. Whether or not the church itself can get beyond its own need for security will determine whether or not the new story will prevail.

## VALUES, THE ROOTS OF OUR TRADITION

### Belonging

As the decline in mainline church attendance has continued, the appearance of Christian symbolism in contemporary culture has been on the rise right alongside the growth in conservative megachurches. Right-wing conservative Christianity seems to be the it-product of the new millennium. Religious greeting cards, once a tiny portion of the industry, are now a growing market product. Pop stars begin the tributes on their CD liner notes with appreciation to their Lord, the one who made sure they got the gifts they needed to get where they are. Gold crosses are obligatory fashion items for many in both the music and movie industry.

The rituals, language, laws, and behaviours that define a particular religion, nationality, or group serve to distinguish its followers from all the other tribes and peoples among whom they might live. In a cosmopolitan culture, where the "risk" of integration is great, peculiarities of behaviour, dress, and ritual may be more carefully attended to in order to strengthen tribal or religious affiliation. A recent Canadian study showed that when cultural and national distinctions are maintained by new immigrants, they experience a greater sense of security in their new surroundings, and youth more easily become confident. It shouldn't come as a surprise that when youth can avoid the loss of belonging that often occurs when they attempt to assimilate into "melting-pot" cultures, they maintain their confidence and security. Belonging is a major human need. People with whom you belong are people you can trust. In unfamiliar surroundings, knowing your tribe is extremely important.

Gang behaviour in North America is another example. Large urban centres have become more and more impersonal and less and less caring as they have grown. Desirable distinctions are often unattainable. The popular song "Rock Star" identifies sought-after status symbols as a house big enough to attract the attention of the MTV show *Cribs*; easy access to drugs and alcohol; plentiful, pretty Playboy-bunny blondes; a personal jet; anorexia; and limitless credit. Distinguishing oneself against an impersonal backdrop, within which excess is considered the ultimate asset, takes some doing. But status can also be acquired by acceptance into a revered group, a gang. Belonging is reinforced within the gang with unique religious-style language, signs, tags, tattoos, gestures, code words, and distinctive dress. Gangs use these "laws" in exactly the same way Jewish circumcision laws, Christian Trinitarian language, and Hindu bindis have long been used—to identify who belongs to what group, what their status is, and the group privileges to which that person has access.

While Hindu women continue to paint bindis on their foreheads, some progressive Muslim women return to the practice of wearing hijabs in order to raise awareness of Islam within secular society, and orthodox Jews wear distinctive dress. The evangelical Christian world has been peaking out the sales market with WWJD bracelets, handbags embossed with little fish, and T-shirts with "A Blood Donor Saved My Life" printed alongside a red cross—a Christian one, that is, not a Red Cross red cross. On the back, a stylized cross is created using the words of Matthew 16:19: "This is my blood of the covenant, which is poured out for many for the forgiveness of sins." Roman Catholics have always had crucifixes (crosses with the body of Jesus still hanging on them). But liberal Christians, well, there just isn't much out there. Make Poverty History bracelets are worn by just about anybody these days. Liberal Christians just don't stand out in a crowd, if you know what I mean.

## Foundational Shifts and Liberal Losses

Perhaps this lack of differentiation outside of the church is responsible for the strength of the bond some liberals have to the use of exclusively Christian language inside the church. There are those who are happy to assert agreement with the scholarship that clearly exposes the Bible, Christianity, the concept of Christ, Jesus' divinity, and so on as human constructs, yet who demand clergy remain committed to language that claims otherwise. Faced with the choice between oral integrity and a continued presentation of Christian concepts in which they no longer believe, they will choose the latter.

Clergy have great difficulty reckoning with this seemingly irrational contradiction. We are, in part, to blame for the difficulties of the current situation. Laypeople in the liberal church (and many in other forms of church) have always wondered about Christian "truths." They have doubted the virgin birth, the resurrection, the promise of heaven, and the dread of hell. Their life experience, more than likely, didn't do much to reinforce the church's claims. But even in the depths of their deepest doubt, even if they scoffed at what the church said, even if they swore they had no use for it whatsoever, there has existed always, at the back of their minds, the confidence placed there by someone they *really* believed, a parent, a spouse, a teacher. If that person wasn't a minister, pastor, or priest, chances are one of them was the second in line. The God-guy was the specialist with the training and learning and all the faith, hope, and belief anyone would ever need. As long as the pastor believed, everyone was safe.

But now, as clergy begin to reveal the truth about their own faith, hopes, and beliefs, those laypersons who always had a sure foundation upon which to stand as they flaunted their disbelief feel that foundation slipping. For them, acknowledged clergy disbelief is completely disorienting. Clergy who don't have the answers can't reassure liberals with doubts. Even if no one believes the words or understands them, they tie us to a tradition that has defined us and helped us know who we were. As much as bloggers and the next generation continue to rail against the application of labels, our psychological health depends on our being able to identify ourselves over and against our environment. We need to belong to something. When people feel that something with which they have long identified is no longer a significant part of how they see themselves, it can be as disorienting as the death of a parent or the beginning of a new life stage. It is so extremely unsettling for some that, on occasion, they've pleaded with me to "just" say from the pulpit what it is they want to hear, even when we both know that neither of us believed it any more.

It is difficult to be either laity or clergy in a milieu in which theological, Christological, and ecclesial language—theospeak—is *de rigueur* and deliberately choose not to use it. When one does, a challenge to one's "Christian" status is sure to follow. After all, if you stop saying that you believe in such things as the resurrection of Jesus, his assumption of the title Christ, his atoning sacrifice, and his coexistence with God, how can you say you are Christian? If you start saying, instead, that you celebrate the cyclical renewal of life, seeing it as a symbol for so much that we experience, or that you see yourself and your choices as the incarnation (whoops, a little theospeak there!) of what you believe, or that you experience a sense of the most sacred aspects of life when you gather with others and see them as embodied shards of whatever it is you might call the divine, well, you are certainly going to be considered undeserving of the Christian handle. You will be labelled a humanist or a Unitarian or an atheist or a heretic or whatever supposed "insult"* might occur to your accuser. Without being willing to claim the terminology, you will be hard pressed to claim the category, even though those things you say may exactly reflect the metaphorical understandings of the Christian terms used by those who refuse to share the moniker with you.

## Roots of the Tradition

The argument that progressives have a right to the name "Christian" is rooted in what we perceive as the original purpose of the movement, rather than what it has come to mean. Whether or not someone named Jesus ever lived, the stories that describe his ministry have a particular focus, and that focus is not the man

---

*These are not insults.

The Humanist Manifesto is a document that many would benefit from reading. Written in 1933 and updated forty years later, it promotes such thoughts as these worthy reflections on the individual. "The preciousness and dignity of the individual person is a central humanist value. Individuals should be encouraged to realize their own creative talents and desires. We reject all religious, ideological, or moral codes that denigrate the individual, suppress freedom, dull intellect, dehumanize personality. We believe in maximum individual autonomy consonant with social responsibility. Although science can account for the causes of behavior, the possibilities of individual freedom of choice exist in human life and should be increased."

The tenets outlined in the Principles of Unitarianism are, as well, admirable. They affirm and promote: the inherent worth and dignity of every person; justice, equity and compassion in human relations; acceptance of one another and encouragement to spiritual growth in our congregations; a free and responsible search for truth and meaning; the right of conscience and the use of the democratic process within our congregations and in society at large; the goal of world community with peace, liberty, and justice for all; respect for the interdependent web of all existence of which we are a part.

Atheists don't actually have a manifesto or principles of their own as a group. As Sam Harris has pointed out, there really shouldn't be such a thing as an atheist just as there shouldn't be such a thing as an a-astrologer or an anti-racist. See "The Problem with Atheism" (lecture, Atheist Alliance conference, Washington, D.C., September 2007, http://newsweek.washingtonpost.com/onfaith/sam_harris/2007/10/the_problem_with_atheism.html (October 8, 2007). One should not have to declare oneself as someone who does not believe in something else, even if that something else has been set up as a norm.

A heretic is someone who does not ascribe to what is considered the accepted norm. Every instance of progress in human history has been the result of heretical thinking. Think about it.

called Jesus. That focus is on how to live. Much of the teaching attributed to him was common knowledge among his contemporaries. With aphorisms and parables (graphic picture stories that without proper contextualization make little sense in the twenty-first century), the Jesus written down for us spelled out that focus to a following that was being told something completely different by the religious right of Jesus' day—the Pharisees. They argued that the law they presented was the best way for people to live. He argued they were wrong.

The Pharisees were interpreters of the law. Out of what we know as the first five books of the Bible, called the Torah, they gleaned codes of conduct that they believed kept the Israelites in proper relationship with God. If any of those codes were broken, the whole community was out of right relationship. But it was easy for them to see that even the voluminous legal requisites set within the Torah were insufficient to respond to the needs of a changing society. Some things had to go and others had to be added. The Pharisees clarified the laws with interpretation and augmentation. During Jesus' lifetime, these laws were extensive and covered many of the everyday activities of the Israelites.

Jesus is presented as being in almost constant conflict with the Pharisees, challenging the ritualized nature of the laws and arguing that they diminished human experience. In Mark, the earliest Gospel, Jesus, through his reminder to the Pharisees that the Sabbath was made for humans, not the other way around, is presented as having a *relationship* with the law, not a responsibility to it. He is portrayed as understanding it as something offered for the benefit of those who embrace it, not for the mastery of them (Mark 2:23–27). Later, Jesus entangles the Pharisees in the intricate weaving of their own religious interpretation, noting that the "traditions of the elders" they hold so sacred allow for some of the laws of the Torah to be set aside. In doing so, Jesus is not saying that the law of the Torah prevails but that attempts to fulfill the whole system distract from its original purpose, which, he is quick to point out, is helping people live ethical lives. His list of the things that prevent ethical living follows immediately upon his interaction with the Pharisees and includes evil thoughts, sexual immorality, theft, murder, adultery, greed, malice, deceit, lewdness, envy, slander, arrogance, and folly (Mark 7:1–23). He is saying, "If you wipe out religious ceremony, you're still going to have people who live ugly lives. If you wipe out the things on this list, the world will immediately be richer and more beautiful—and not just for some, for everyone." His interest, as it is reported in Mark, certainly seems to have been less in what we would call religion and more in what we would call spirituality—the challenge to live a radically ethical life.

## From Spiritual to Religious

Philosopher Ken Wilber notes that there are at least a dozen different meanings for the words *religious* and *spiritual*. As we talk about these two terms, we tend to fall into one or another category of understanding. We can think of religions as "immortality projects," as "regressive or infantile," or as important "mechanisms of social cohesion." Without clarifying which definition we are using, he argues, our talk cannot be entirely comprehensible.

Wilber notes that many of us, of late, have actually begun separating the two terms, religious and spiritual, identifying that which is religious as being rote, ritualistic, devoid of spirit, and dead, and that which is spiritual as being intensely personal, having great depth of meaning and value for us each in unique and individual ways. In fact, he points out that we're starting to speak as though religion is what spiritual becomes once it is handed over to someone else or passed on to the next generation.[12] And, indeed, that is just what I find myself doing.

In March 2004, Jesus Seminar scholar John Dominic Crossan, at the conclusion of a lecture in Niagara Falls, Ontario, was asked who God was for him. In his response, which came after a moment of deep silence, he neatly avoided a direct answer by stating that he believes all humans to be hard-wired to seek out some form of ultimacy in their lives and that once they have found that which holds such meaning for them, they name it and can then relate to it. In other words, Crossan makes the point that we are individually responsible for seeking out our own sense of ultimacy. This wiring would be the equivalent of what Wilber says we are now calling our "spiritual quest."

I think Crossan only begins to tell the tale. While on the quest for spiritual ultimacy, individuals explore and undertake a variety of tools or practices. Should we find a tool or practice to be enlightening, uplifting, or of some other spiritual value, we share it with another and another and another. Eventually it can become adopted by an entire group. Somewhere in that process, it slips from a spiritual practice to a religious practice. It becomes an *established* religion when a group of people (usually men) decide that a particular set of ways that were once meaningful and valid for one or more individuals is the way for all. The leaders of the group identify that which is ultimate, name it, and then tell their followers how they can relate to it.

This process is what the Pharisees were about. Having had the ultimacy named long before, their job was to define and clarify the proper religious practice for the whole tribe. Jesus, as I see him written, didn't like it. His protests against the legalistic practices that encrusted the Jewish relationship with God were courageously progressive.

## From Religious to Spiritual

Challenging legalistic practices is not to say that there is no purpose or meaning in the continued use of sacred objects, reading of special texts, or following of sacred traditions. These items and activities, stripped of the authority given to them by the religious establishment, can be, once again, part of one's personal spiritual quest, perhaps in a way similar to that in which they began. The power of the article or act is not and has never been in the actual item or practice. It resides in the relationship created with it by the individual employing it. Saying rote prayers is a highly effective ethical practice for some. It leaves others empty. The practice of reciting prayer is not, in and of itself, efficacious. Yet it can have a profound effect on an individual *for whom it has meaning*. Similarly, walking a labyrinth may be a very helpful spiritual discipline for an individual that will allow her or him to focus on a particular issue or question, freed from the distractions that the mind might otherwise use to block such intense examination. But the same tool may be seen by the next person as too much walking around and getting nowhere. Claims that a labyrinth's geometry and placement create a spiritual force that will affect any properly prepared individual who walks it simply cannot be substantiated. Any effect an individual experiences when walking the labyrinth does not come from the labyrinth. *It comes from the walker.* Religious institutions would do well to offer their followers a variety of tools that individuals might use to follow their own spiritual paths, rather than arguing for the primacy of certain rituals and activities that are effective only for a select few.

Those who wrote about Jesus, rather than attempting to create a new institution that would have control over spiritual, and consequently religious, expression, were pushing for a return to a covenantal spirituality that bound individuals to God and that called for them to live radically spiritual lives. His was a life that tore through the religious dogma of the time, past the written directives of the Torah, past the oral analyses of the Pharisees, into the way people lived their lives. It presented a Kingdom of God that was about real people trying to live intensely ethical lives, regardless of the religious or social context in which they found themselves. He himself embodied the principles that demanded right relationship, and the early church, with its scrabbled foundations, asked its members to embody those same principles. Not because *Jesus* said they were right. Simply because *they were*. Jesus looked at the systems that made ethical living practically impossible in his day and age and named them wrong. To embody the spirit of that impulse then would be for us to look at the systems that make ethical living practically impossible in our day and age and name them wrong.

## Why Heretics Can Still Call Themselves Christian (If They Want To)

To be Christian is not to say specific words, attend a particular church, believe in a certain set of doctrinal beliefs, or participate in a special ritual; indeed these things would be anathema to an individual who was trying to get people to see and live with deep respect for one another's humanity. To be Christian, for me, is to do whatever it takes to bind me to a life lived in a radically ethical way. Considering how difficult that is and will always be, I'll need all the help I can get. So will you.

Stripped of the authoritative power of its doctrine, symbols, rituals, and sacred objects, the crux of the Christian faith as I see it, those principles of radically ethical living, is found to be shared with other faith traditions and many non-religious, positive philosophical perspectives. Individuals who follow different spiritual paths often come together under the umbrella of interfaith dialogue. That dialogue rarely, if ever, allows for the human construction of all the different things people in the dialogue believe. Religious traditions continue to be held as "the" way, privately if not publicly. They are not seen or shared as "spiritual tools" that might or might not be helpful on the quest.

Were we to bring all that we have in common together and leave the religious detritus of our traditions behind us, we would have come a long way in our efforts to bypass tolerance, whereby we merely and stingily acknowledge someone else's right to hold a position different from ours and to practise rituals we privately believe have no purpose. With nothing "religious" remaining— that is, nothing imbued with an authoritative or sacred power vested in it by an institution, its founder, or its teachers—each tradition would have a rich store of "spiritual" tools it could make available to all. As my son, Izaak, fasts during Ramadan in solidarity with his Muslim friends, they are each enriched by sharing a spiritual discipline that has the potential to be a profound opportunity for reflection on their place in the world. His efforts cannot be considered insincere by his friends as theirs cannot be considered of more or less value than his. Each must determine for himself if the spiritual tool is helpful in his efforts to live according to what he believes is the essence of their spiritual undertaking.

If yoga or meditation or Gregorian chant or lying on the floor feeling the bass rhythms of a rock ensemble help to lift me out of my own myopic experience of life and into a transcendent understanding of our collective beingness, then they will strengthen my commitment to the other, to needs that extend beyond my own, and to a radically ethical life. They will be my spiritual practices and, for me, serve to strengthen my Christian witness. What any of them will do for you is yours to find out.

## ANALYZING FOR A CHANGE

In the opening decade of the twenty-first century, Christianity is vulnerable. Against the backdrop of non-stop scientific discovery, its claims read like the stuff of fantasy and magic. A distant deity creates the world and all its creatures in six days and rests, exhausted, on the seventh. He then parades the whole of the animal kingdom past his penultimate creation, a man, seeking a mate for him. Unable to find one that appeals to the man, the deity, in one version, puts the man to sleep and completes creation with a being fashioned from his rib. The earthling now has a partner. Beguiled by a serpent, however, they disobey the deity and their reverie is short-lived. The angry god casts them out of the idyllic garden in which they were created, and they are left to roam and populate the world without that deity's blessing.

Their offspring create a covenant with the deity following a dreadful flood sent by the god to pay back the earthlings for their wicked ways. The flood kills everyone and everything on Earth save a single family and a reproducing pair of each type of animal. Eventually the offspring of this family again multiply and grow into communities. They seek communion with the deity and attempt to build a tower that will let them do so. The deity, now known as "Lord," confers with others like him and determines that the ability to band together makes the earthlings too strong, so they confuse the earthlings' speech and make it impossible for them to ever work together as one community again. The generations that follow continue to try to placate the judgmental deity who finally, whether out of frustration or pity, makes provision for humanity to return to a state of grace. He sends his child to the earth to be sacrificed by the earthlings in atonement for their sins.

While on Earth, that child grows to be a miraculous healer. Not only can he cure the blind, the lame, and the leprous, he can raise the dead. In addition to his healing ministry, he walks on water, calms storms, and feeds thousands from meagre provisions. His gifts are supernatural. As the reader, we know these powers are possible only because he is divine.

Of course, those in the story with him don't have the perspective that we, the readers, do. They do not know he is divine. They do not know what their part in the divine tragi-comedy is, and, as its pawns, they participate willingly and ignorantly in the crucifixion of the divine child. At his death, the sky darkens, the temple curtain is torn, and the dead rise from their graves, go into the city of Jerusalem, and are seen by many.

It is only afterwards, when the healer's tomb is found empty, that they speculate upon and come to understand the cosmic plan. In the wonder of the days following his resurrection, they realize they had been in the presence of one who must have been God. He remains with them a short time, supporting their new understandings and then, with a brief but powerful promise, rises and disappears into the sky. Within the paradox of sadness and excitement that follows, they begin the process of creating communities dedicated to living out the wisdom of a man whose significance they only latterly came to understand. The holy spirit, promised in that last contact with their "Lord," comes down upon them in tongues of flames, and the whole community, diverse in its language, for a brief time overcomes the curse of language in a miracle of understanding.

We should be so lucky.

I do not know whether those who had sex with Aphrodite's temple priestesses in their ritual worship of that goddess believed or didn't believe that she had been born from sea foam after Uranus' testicles were tossed into it. Perhaps they did. I do know that we, who understand the basics of the reproductive process, do not believe that volleying severed testicles into the waves would result in the creation of either a human or a divine life. And we've also given up Aphrodite's requisite temple sex worship ritual, sad though some may have been to see it go. We approach the details of Aphrodite's birth and significance as a goddess as myth. If it was ever believed literally, at some point in time it transitioned from literal to mythological and, to this day, rests in the latter category. We do not approach Aphrodite, or any of her divine Greek or Roman compatriots, with any sense that she existed in historical time and participated in temporal-spatial reality.

Acknowledging Aphrodite as myth allows us to examine the

story in a variety of new ways. We can approach it from an anthropological perspective, exploring the context out of which the myth grew, to understand what it meant within that cultural place and time. Or we can lift it as an archetype and hold our own lives up against it regardless of the original meaning or intent of the story. Such an exploration might lead us to consider the concept of erotic love, embodied in Aphrodite as lust, over and against our more contemporary understandings of romantic love. We might find in her symbolic birthplace the ever-shifting, tidal power of love's manifestations, even as we acknowledge our projection of modern concepts into the past.

Myths are useful to us to make sense of our own experiences. Whether we are accurate in regard to the original intent is irrelevant. The relevance is purely subjective. You know where I'm going. Biblical accounts of anything and everything from creation through to John's Revelation are currently experiencing the same process through which Aphrodite's birth narrative has passed. Believed as true, for many centuries and by many people, they are now entering into the realm of myth where their application and relevance can become subjective. Loosed of the demand that they be believed literally, biblical stories become therapeutic in our search to understand ourselves and our place in the universe.

## Excavators

John Dominic Crossan, in his book *The Birth of Christianity*, remarks on the role of the gospel narratives:

> We have learned that the *gospels* are exactly what they openly and honestly claim they are. They are not history, though they contain history. They are not biography, though they contain biography. They are gospel—that is, good news. *Good* indicates that the news is seen from somebody's point of view—from, for example, the Christian rather than the imperial interpretation. *News* indicates

that a regular update is involved. . . . The gospels are written for faith, to faith, and from faith. . . . It is *our* problem if we wanted journalism. We received gospel instead.[13]

Crossan underscores the subjectivity with which the material was both created and meant to be used. He recognizes our penchant for facts and tells us it is folly.

In reality, we do not know whether the myth of Aphrodite or the biblical narrative were understood literally when they first came into being. Indeed, we could not, with any certainty, claim to know what "understood literally" may have meant. We only know that Aphrodite is now categorized as myth—non-literal truths that have the capacity to allow us to see ourselves reflected in them, no matter how far away we are from the original story. In time, I believe, we will all understand the Bible in the same manner.

Crossan is an amazing deconstructionist when it comes to the study of the historical Jesus.[14] He picks the assumptions out of the contemporary understandings and leaves little "heaps of possibilities" lying all over the place. Rather than come up with a comprehensive, definitive picture of the historical Jesus, the picture we're all looking for, he invites us to consider those little heaps and to develop our own wary attitude toward what is said to have transpired two thousand years ago. Indeed, reflecting on the fickle nature of our own memories, he suggests we should be wary of almost anything we've experienced ourselves any more than, say, a few months ago.[15]

Crossan's work serves as a perfect example of the sort of deconstruction work we need to attend to in the church as we learn to critique the theology, ecclesiology, Christology, liturgy, hymnody, and doctrine that has been handed down to us. He deconstructs history, something we usually accept as a given. Things happened the way they happened, didn't they? With startling clarity, he manages to throw into question most of what we have been taught was historical fact and much we have never considered, as documents and perspectives are brought to bear on the accumulated assumptions. We simply cannot, even in an area that might seem to be more concrete than theology, operate with assumptions. Crossan himself accepts the rebuke of another scholar, Amy-Jill Levine, who challenged his assumption that Jesus' intention in ignoring the ritual laws of Judaism was to subvert them. Levine suggested that "neither to attack nor to acknowledge may translate into taking something 'for granted,'" a perspective Crossan came to embrace.[16]

Deconstructionist philosopher Jacques Derrida said in 1997, "If by religion you mean a set of beliefs, dogmas, or institutions— the church, e.g.—then I would say that religion as such can be deconstructed, and not only can be but should be deconstructed, sometimes in the name of faith."[17] For Derrida, faith is something that is more primal than religion and so is encumbered by it. We have sought to express faith through religious ritual, in word and in song, all the while only ever managing rough approximations of what is inexpressible. In our attempts to critique Christianity, if we can see those things we assess as extensions of our faith, not its essence, as Derrida suggests, then we will be more able to be honest about whether a particular element brings us closer to what it is that we seek or pushes us further away from it. The pipe organ, to name one example, is not essential to our faith. For some, it may more closely express their experience of faith than anything else, but it is not faith itself. Similarly, other elements we have used to express the inexpressible, such as the Bible, are not faith either. Despite the personal experiences of the religious elements of our faith, we must assess them in this manner.

So exactly what is it that we do to deconstruct the traditions that have been handed to us in order that we might both relieve ourselves of carrying forward those things that are no longer relevant and find those things that are of lasting value to us? First, it is important to understand how those beliefs and practices, whether they be the songs we sing, the doctrine we uplift, or the buildings in which we worship, came to be and by whose authority they became part of our faith tradition.[18]

## Working Tools

Throughout the history of the Christian Church, and very likely every other religious system, people have worked out issues of faith—what they believed to be true and how they were to live out that truth—influenced by a number of different things. These influences include the theological or philosophical history of the community; its personal and shared experiences; contemporary perspectives on the theological or philosophical worldview of the community; growing knowledge in areas of import to the theological perspective, such as science; the personal needs and experiences of community members and their tests of the effectiveness of the belief system; and insights from neighbouring or transient cultures, religions, or worldviews that come into contact with the community. Each of those things would cause the community to incorporate or reject considered elements.

### *Theological History*

Whether a faith community is matriarchal, patriarchal, pantheist, theist, animist, or whatever else, the theological and philosophical beliefs deeply entrenched in that community have an enormous impact on whether a new concept will be accepted or rejected. If there is a congruency between what has been carried forward within the tradition and what is being considered within its development, the new is more likely to be assimilated. If the nature of that change is incongruent with the existing worldview, however, it will be more difficult to assume and easier to reject. John A.T. Robinson, in *Honest to God*, discusses the imperceptible shift we made as our understandings of astronomy required that we move from belief in a God "up" there to belief in a God "out" there. The nature of God didn't change during that shift, making it easier for Christians to accommodate.[19]

## Personal and Communal History

The personal histories within a family or tribe affect the way that community approaches new issues of faith. Most communities will incorporate those things that affirm their own experience. For example, in Crossan's work on the early evolution of the ritual meal shared by Christians, he helps us consider the root of that tradition in the community in which it developed. Crossan juxtaposes his own life experience of food as being ever-available with that of Irish-American author Frank McCourt, for whom near-starvation was the norm for the whole of his childhood and adolescence. He notes that those widely divergent experiences result in radically different approaches to the concept of food, and he uses the example to suggest that those of us who have never known the constant presence of hunger might have difficulty recreating the early realities of the eucharistic meal. Crossan feels strongly that the experience of want was the impetus for the beginning of the ritual meal and invites us to consider our nibble-and-sip ecclesial adaptations of it in light of those considerations.[20] As Christianity moved from rural, agrarian communities to the comparative affluence of the *polis*, the meal became more symbolic and less a necessity than a ritual of remembrance.

## Contemporary Perspectives

While religious systems come with full-fledged—and apparently immutable—theological or philosophical systems of thought, those systems are updated over time. Contemporary reflections on them, many of which are contentious and difficult for people to accept, help to challenge and eventually change and develop the system as a whole. The concept of animal sacrifice, for example, is amply presented in the Hebrew scriptures. In Leviticus 20:2, however, prohibitions of *child* sacrifice suggest that it, too, was a contemporary practice at the time. Although the ritual of human sacrifice may have been within the history of the religious tradition of the Israelite community, the prohibition of Leviticus chapter twenty reflects a contemporary condemnation of it. The story of Abraham's submission to Yahweh's demand that Isaac be sacrificed and the provision of a "substitutionary" ram at the last moment (Genesis 22) has often been argued to have been a story created to replace the already well-entrenched ritual of human sacrifice with its more "humane" counterpart.

Is it possible that we missed the progressive element in the sacrificial, substitutionary atonement theology of the story of the cross? Perhaps the theological message of the atonement was meant to have entirely eliminated the idea of a God who needed ritual sacrifice to be appeased. Merely refuting the appropriateness of sacrifice would have suggested that all that had been practised and offered in the past was unnecessary and perhaps even detrimental to the history of the Jews. It would have been inconsistent with scripture. Making an *ultimate* sacrifice allowed the community to save themselves from the humiliation of such issues. Jesus' death as portrayed by the evangelists would have provided the next theological step necessary to move a community beyond concepts that had worked for it in the past but that it had socially and culturally surpassed. The God who had needed sacrifice had eliminated the need for it entirely. What a different Christianity we might have had if such an understanding had been promulgated so that we felt called to free ourselves from religious ritual rather than binding ourselves to it! Of course, we'd still be grappling with the challenges of acknowledging that all theological suppositions are built upon a document that is not divine. Whatever theologians of the day were attempting to create or prove, it is only ever speculation.

## Discoveries in Other Pertinent Disciplines

Throughout time, disciplines that are evolving do so on their own trajectories. The disciples of one may or may not be aware of developments in another. It is then possible for two streams of thought to interlace in a cultural setting but not influence each other to any great extent. However, when one discipline makes its advances known beyond its own boundaries, that interlacing can cause incredible change. Rather than remaining distinct, they affect one another and each experiences change.

Because our major religions developed their core doctrines long before the establishment of some of our most elementary scientific understandings, however, it is difficult for us to imagine what advances were assimilated into their development. We look at how little astronomic, geographic, anthropologic, and scientific knowledge is affirmed in our religious institutions, scratch our heads, and wonder if those institutions have ever advanced at all. But before they took the static forms we're familiar with today, those same institutions undoubtedly incorporated the "knowledge" that existed at other times in history from a variety of disciplines.

For instance, some of the dietary prohibitions found in the Bible may have been the result of knowledge accumulated by the Israelites that was connected to wellness. If a food was likely to cause illness or was susceptible to contamination, over time it would come to be considered taboo. In the development of the Torah, prohibitions became embedded in the ritual life of what had been a nomadic people despite the fact that the original risks may long have been replaced with the primary need for cultural identity.

Taboo food beliefs continue to this day. In the early 1990s, researchers from the University of Campinas in Brazil examined the dietary restrictions of different kinds of fish by indigenous populations along the Amazon River. They found that many groups shared similar restrictions, particularly one which made carnivorous fish a prohibition for the sick.

Some fish are avoided only when persons are ill and others are recommended for these cases. The reasons for these avoidances were investigated and it was observed that carnivorous fish, more than any other fish, were avoided during illness. The toxicity of fishes might also explain some avoidances. Finally, medicinal uses of some species, such as rays and lizards, seem to explain some important dietary taboos: medicinal animals may be saved as a source of drugs.[21]

It is easy to see how health-related knowledge, with its life-and-death consequences, could take on religious significance, at any time in history. The medical understanding may change or develop, even while the religious practice stays the same.

## Testing the System

If a ritual is claimed to bring about certain results and those results do not consistently materialize, one would become suspicious of the veracity of the claim. For instance, if one's family had ritually sacrificed its first born child for several generations and still not seen an increase in fortune, it might move on to another form of sacrifice that didn't destroy so much potential or it may choose to reject the ritual in its entirety. Alternatively, like the Rapanui of Easter Island, the ritual may become more extreme and pervasive if the community's belief in the claim is stronger than the permission it feels to reject it. The choice will reflect the needs of the community; that is, if the community's most urgent need is stability, then it is likely the ritual will become more deeply entrenched. If the community's most urgent need is survival, it is likely such a ritual would be challenged and eventually rejected. As theologies and traditions develop within a system, they are constantly being tested in this manner.

One of the most powerful biblical messages is the inherent sinfulness of humanity, a state introduced through the story of the fall of Adam in Genesis and developed in Paul's epistles.[22] Integrating this dominant theme created a system that ensured the stability and ongoing preservation of a particular interpretation of the faith, a circuit of efficacy that landed responsibility on individuals rather than the church or the God described by that church. Prayer, sacraments, participation in ritual—any failure of these aspects of faith to produce the expected response—healing, peace, right relationship—needn't be pinned on the church or its deity. Rather, the individual employing the practice or participating in the ritual, as an inherently sinful being, could be identified as the reason the religious practice didn't work. The system stabilized itself.

## Insights from Outside

The area now known as the Middle East, womb for many religious traditions, was in pre-modern days a crossroads of culture. Its Mediterranean ports linked southwestern Asia, Africa, and the Greek and Roman worlds. Control over them was a constant struggle between the Greeks, Romans, and Phoenicians.[23] The interaction of those various cultures, prior to the encoding of doctrinal beliefs, could only have resulted in an interchange of ideas, rituals, and beliefs. There is a debate among scholars as to exactly how far that interchange went. Theologian Adolf von Harnack easily accepted that early Christianity and late Judaism had marks of this interaction within them. He saw the Nicene Creed as the admission of Hellenistic philosophy to Christianity, a process he argued had been necessary to break Christianity's ties with Judaism.[24] The conversation about the depth of those influences was re-ignited recently with the publication of Canadian journalist and Anglican priest Tom Harpur's *The Pagan Christ*. Harpur finds convincing evidence of the Egyptian God Horus nestled in among the religious icons and beliefs of classical Christianity, even going so far as to suggest that early Christians routed Egyptian libraries to purge them of any evidence of the hijacking.[25] Others, such as W. Ward Gasque, president of the Pacific Association for Theological Studies, deny such links.[26] Regardless of which side of this particular argument one takes, the influence of culture on the development of a religious system within it or in proximity to it seems likely.

Contemporary society and multicultural communities place us in intense juxtaposition with other cultures and faiths. Those we were once able to describe as having cloven feet and horns are now merely the next-door neighbours who kindly pick up the mail for us when we are on vacation. Proximity and the need for peaceful coexistence push us toward deeper understanding and challenge ill-informed stereotypes.

## Beyond Cohesion

As soon as a religious system recognizes itself as a cohesive system of beliefs, the tendency to protect it from additional refinements kicks in. When that actually takes place probably cannot be pinpointed, but the system's reaction to the introduction of new concepts is a pretty good indication of whether it remains a dynamic system or one which has become closed. Cardinal John Henry Newman, in 1845, wrote his *Essay on the Development of the Christian Doctrine* in which he argued that the doctrine of the Roman Catholic Church had not changed throughout its history; however, in the early decades of the Christian Church, much was in flux. As the church first moved from rural to urban settings, went from being recognized as a Jewish sect to an independent religion, increased in numbers, and moved into different geographical areas, it continued to assimilate the traditions of others into its own.

The most well-loved assimilation is the festival of Christmas. There being no recorded date of Jesus' birth in the Bible and no evidence elsewhere, the earliest record we have of it being set on December 25 is in the calendar of Philocalus, prepared in Rome for the year 325.[27] In the late fourth century, the Christian scribe Syrus explained the reason:

> It was a custom of the pagans to celebrate on the same 25 December the birthday of the Sun, at which they kindled lights in token of festivity. In these solemnities and revelries the Christians also took part. Accordingly when the doctors of the Church perceived that the Christians had a leaning to this festival, they took counsel and resolved that the true Nativity should be solemnized on that day.[28]

Obviously, up until the fourth century, the Christian tradition was still developing, still openly looking to more established traditions for its beliefs and practices.

But zeal for that kind of development didn't last. Those early councils set in place by Constantine began the codification of Christian doctrine—the first attempt to set it in stone, for all time. The result was that the introduction of new elements, often those from the indigenous culture or religion in which it was being established, quickly became condemned by the newly official church. The system protected its orthodoxy, adding theological explanations for any exposed inconsistencies as they became necessary. On December 8, 1854, Pope Pius IX brought into the canon the doctrine of Immaculate Conception in response to the clamouring of the people for a doctrine that released Mary from the stain of original sin. Prior to understanding the active role of the woman in conception, it didn't matter if Mary was stained or not. Once science disclosed her part in the mystery, if original sin could be transmitted through the mother as well as the father, then Jesus couldn't possibly have been sinless. The new belief cleared this up in a somewhat convoluted way by declaring Mary to also have been born of a virgin and therefore free of original sin. Pius IX's pronouncement included the dire warning to any who would suggest otherwise: "They are to know that they have wrecked the faith and separated themselves from the unity of the Church."[29] The church kept close rein over what could and could not be examined and how the results of those examinations were promulgated, if at all.

Reaction to an ecumenical conference held in Minneapolis at the end of 1993 polarized Christian response to syncretism and continues to reverberate throughout Protestant Christianity well over a decade later. The Re-Imagining conference brought feminist theologians and delegates from twenty-eight countries together to explore the concept of God and how it could be more accessible to women. Reports of feminist worship services, the invocation of Sophia (a personification of the biblical concept of wisdom), and edgy speeches that brought religious elements from other traditions into relationship with Christianity reverberated through the church. Denominations were pelted with angry reactions from members furious that church funds had been used to make the conference possible. A conservative magazine sent free of charge to United Methodists across the States included a tear-out postcard addressed to the church's head office with the inscription,

> We call upon the Women's Division to repudiate the radical teachings of the conference and make a public apology to the church for its participation in and financial support of such an event. This is a tragic betrayal of the trust of tens of thousands of faithful UMC women who now need from you a promise of no further involvement in similar feminist/womanist/lesbian gatherings.[30]

Denominations distanced themselves from the women in their employ who had been part of the conference's organization; at least one woman lost her job, another was charged with heresy.[31] Terry Schlossberg, then executive director of Presbyterian Pro-Life, believes that "this, and the 1994 General Assembly's promise that 'Theology matters,' seemed to restore the aggrieved congregations' trust in the leadership."[32] The Presbyterian Church (U.S.A.) launched the theme program "Theology Matters" in an attempt to appease its membership and staunch the loss of revenues it was experiencing.

## Questioning Authority

Over time, the many, many influences incorporated into Christianity came to appear to be a cohesive whole. The fact that it developed over time and from many disparate traditions and experiences is often lost or overlooked. We have had handed down to us a seemingly cohesive entity known as Christianity that in many ways grew out of the culture into which it was born but was also influenced by the many to which it has been exposed. There is no threat in recognizing this. Once we realize it, we can more easily dismantle it into its many parts, creating, after the manner of Crossan, little "heaps of possibilities," which we can then critique in order to identify what should continue to express our beliefs and what is no longer worthy of doing so.

It is extremely difficult to remove one's own prejudices, likes, and dislikes from such an examination. Speaking in 2004, Crossan made reference to the work of the Jesus Seminar, scholars who, upon hearing the explication of a particular passage of scripture, use a sliding scale to vote on how historically accurate they believe the passage to be. He noted that the scholars have to remember to take a pejorative position toward anything that, prior to their objective examination of the academic evidence, they think Jesus would have said or done. It is far too easy to project one's personal political, social, and cultural preferences onto Jesus. If you believe he was a feminist, you need to believe so because the examination of the evidence proves that he was, not because you believe he was a good man and as a good man he would have been feminist. If we allow our personal prejudices to colour history, history is of no use to us.

That process of deconstruction or dismantling in order to examine and understand something helps us to move beyond our own biases and recognize the presence of bias in the material we're examining. It challenges us to pose a number of questions to what we find in those heaps or, for that matter, in the heaps of any of the belief systems into which we come in contact at work, at church, in the media, and in the community.

Often, we won't find definitive answers, and our answers may differ from those of others; yet it is in the very questioning that power issues can be identified and defused. The exercise can lead to thoughts, ideas, theories, questions, speculation, and insights that can be both unsettling and liberating, and reactions—one's own and others—can be highly emotional. A supportive community can provide a safe place for sharing the experience. Here are some suggested questions to bring to the text—any text.

1. By whose authority is a particular statement declared to be true or untrue, necessary or unnecessary? Is the claim to authority supportable? Should other voices and perspectives be heard or acknowledged, either instead of or in addition to the established authority?

2. Whose interests are protected by what is being stated? Who benefits from it? Conversely, whose benefits are ignored or harmed? Who is excluded? What must one do to qualify for acceptance?

3. What language is archaic and outdated, and therefore easily misunderstood? Why has it continued in use?

4. Does the image, story, or claim set limits on what we can question, believe, or relate to? Does it expand or shrink our understandings of faith, the world, and our experience?

What would be the purpose of limiting our understanding? How would that have been helpful in the past? Is it still helpful?

5. What beliefs and behaviours are being commanded as universally obligatory and which are being condemned? What are the consequences for not believing or not behaving accordingly? What freedom and diversity does this inhibit? What harm might it cause?

6. Are there liberating truths within a story or image that are eclipsed by the interpretations brought to them in the text?

7. Does the concept or story incorporate and use images, symbols, and practices that mirror and support the world's systems of power and hierarchy out of which they grew? Are systems like these still in place? What are the costs of those systems, and who pays the price? What has been the influence of the world's dominant groups (male, European, affluent, etc.) upon the expression and acceptance of "divine truth?"

Whenever we approach a belief system, these questions can help us dismantle its assumptions and see it clearly for what it is. Rather than obliterating the established systems entirely, they will serve to help us see to which beliefs we *do* wish to attribute power. What exists within those systems that is worthy of being carried into the next generation and the next after that? The power to find those things, the power to choose them, the power to use them appropriately rests, as it always has, in our hands—only now, we know. It's time we accessed our freedom and took up our responsibility.

# RECONSTRUCTING CHRISTIANITY
## THE POSSIBILITIES

A Christianity that is worthy of continuing will be one that helps us to see beyond our own driving need for self-fulfillment, either spiritual or material. It will help us develop outside our own ego-centricity to a transcendent awareness of all life and the complexities of our just existence within it. This is the radically ethical living that I believe our values call us toward.

Spiritual tools distilled of their religious baggage are only that, tools. They are no longer considered to have purpose in and of themselves. We pick them up, put them down, and pick them up again only as we find they are helpful for our spiritual health and growth. And that spiritual health and growth must always be toward radically ethical living. The church can be the library for those spiritual tools. Christianity must be the impetus for their use.

Remember that list of life-enhancing values created in a small workshop? It listed things like beauty, forgiveness, delight, love, respect, wisdom, honour, creativity, tranquility, imagination, humour, awe, truth, purity, justice, courage, fun, compassion, challenge, knowledge, and trustworthiness. Remove any one of these from our communities or the world and we would radically alter our quality of life, the way we engage in relationship. The message Christianity can convey, one that needs no validation, is that these and all life-enhancing values are sacred. They make life worthwhile. They make us better when we employ them, when we seek to live up to them. And it is a message that we can share with those who do not call themselves Christian but name a different religious tradition or philosophical ideology. Indeed, it is a message all perspectives can employ when challenging the fundamentalist mindsets existing within them.

Yes, there will be conflicts when one of our values comes up against another. That is what ethical dilemmas look like—two values struggling to be chosen where only one can be upheld. But that is exactly the kind of thing our faith, our system of beliefs, should help us deal with, cope with, acknowledge, and heal beyond. It is what communities must learn to struggle with, too, if we are going to assert rights and assign responsibilities; neither can exist without the other, at least not with any sense of justice.

As we move into the possibilities that exist for a refreshed Christianity, there will be much to explore, many ideas to engage, and more possibility than we might ever have imagined.

## THE BIBLE: A HUMAN DOCUMENT

For the whole of Christian history, from the time that the scriptures came to be called so, we have been trying to figure out what they mean. After all, there are some weird things described in the book purported to be the foundation upon which our faith is built. So it's no wonder we have been working away, lo, these many years, trying to understand it.

I remember being in a Sunday school class in that limestone edifice known to me simply as "church" with the couple of dozen other children my age who had also learned to answer "Jesus" to every second question we were asked. In this particular class, the question we were asked was what the difference was between the

Christian faith and all the other faiths. Yes, "Jesus" was a most appropriate answer, but the teacher wanted more. The second answer eluded me. My child's brain couldn't intuit it with enough speed to get my hand in the air again with any confidence that I would be right. So I didn't answer. Neither did anyone else. We didn't know.

## Recorded History

The other answer, our teacher told us, was that the Bible, which was the book that recorded who we were, was a history book telling us things that really happened, in contrast to all the other holy books in the world, which were just instruction books or ideas that people had put together. (The Sunday school teacher had yet to explore with us the reality that people of the Jewish faith used the larger part of same book, so we had yet to assimilate the thought that much of it was their history, too.) It was an interesting thought, and I played with it for many years. It gave me a sense that my religion was more fact that just the airy-fairy stuff of faith.

Of course, that lesson took place some time in the 1960s. The idea of written history as factual was still predominant in most learning centres, or at least those to which most ordinary people have access. It was probably the case that in those institutions of higher learning, they were already talking about the *fact* that written history isn't fact at all. It is fact as presented from only one perspective. And one perspective among the millions and billions that might exist is a narrow one indeed.

I recall arguing with a colleague one day and, using words not original to me, saying, "Orthodoxy only means 'I got here first.'" His quick response: "Orthodoxy means it's right." Perhaps he was kidding, but given we were discussing current confirmation processes for youth in our denomination, I don't think so. Well, history, similarly, means, "I won, so I get to tell the story from my perspective." That is the history we were taught in school. And that is the history my Sunday school teacher was reading when he opened the Bible. If it was written as history, it was, like any other history, the story of the people who won, how they did it, and, with a skill perfected by the authors of the Hebrew stories of exile, how they made sense of it when they didn't.[1] The New Testament, our ecclesial history, canonical law, the whole shebang—all of it is nothing more than the history of the victors.

That being said, this "history" can't just be left there. It has to be opened up for further examination. All the people who didn't win should be given sticks and allowed to go and prod it, here, there, here, again, so that their blood can ooze out from between the textual lines and draw us a more factual picture of the history we claim is that of our faith. We'd have a very different history book in front of us if all those who are nameless had the opportunity to fill in the too-empty spaces where their names, their stories, their lives, their deaths, and their realities lie hidden from our sight.

Of course, that can't happen. Even if we had enough sticks to hand out, those who would do the prodding have long since died, and with them so has any kind of authentic memory. That's the tragedy of history. By the time we realize we need to hear what the other side has to say, we've killed them all off. So we can't ever understand the Bible as a true history book. My Sunday school teacher, unbeknownst to him, was wrong. The only answer to the question really was "Jesus."

One of the reasons it has been so important for the church to have us see the Bible as history is the validation of any miracle stories you find in it. If the book is history, then they happened. Far too many times to count, I have heard, "My God is big enough to do anything," spoken in response to any question raised about the veracity of miracles, the creation narrative, the virgin birth, anything a rational person might query. It is a silencing method and it works well. As soon as your God is so small that you can't imagine him being able to save a man in a whale for several days or cause a miraculous pregnancy in a pre-pubescent Hebrew girl or even wanting to, then you can only hang your head in shame at the puny God you've imagined and hide in the corner until it can grow big enough again to be worthy of your unquestioning faith. And if you don't, well, you're not one of us.

But rational questions *must* be brought to the stories we read in the Bible precisely because those stories don't make sense. From the very first page to the last one, we keep running across things that tax the credulity of most rational people. As long as we still have that niggling thought in the back of our heads that the Bible is history and therefore the people who wrote it believed it to be "true," we'll keep thinking that the people who wrote it believed what they were writing really happened. There are all kinds of interpretive perspectives on that question. But whether they did or didn't believe it to be what happened doesn't matter. *That's* the point.

## If It's the Authoritative Word of God for All Time, We're in Big Trouble

If the Bible is TAWOGFAT (the authoritative word of god for all time), then it is very important for me to figure out what it means, regardless of whether it was a historical rendition of the facts. If God is trying to get a message to me, to us through this book, then we had better sharpen up and pay attention. But if there is no such thing as a divine being trying to get through to me or a book that is that divine being's message, then it would be a major waste of my time to continue to pick one particular book and keep looking at it in order to squeeze out of it all the answers to all life's big questions. They just wouldn't all be there. My attempts to find the meaning in it would be mooted by the fact that whatever meaning may have been written into the original document was not being sent to the world for all time by God, even if the original authors wanted me to think that it was. Because we have looked for so long at the Bible as history, even a somewhat peculiar history, it is difficult for us to imagine it as anything other than an absolutely true picture of what has come to pass. And because we have believed it to be the foundation of our faith, it is even more difficult for us to imagine it any other way. But, as we've been shown over and over again, it isn't the authoritative word of God, and we need to keep reminding ourselves of that.

## Losing "The Meaning"

Recognizing the very human construction of the Bible means that we don't have to (a) find The Meaning in its stories or histories or (b) worry if we've got The Meaning right or (c) believe it all happened the way it's written. Those kinds of questions just don't matter.

Now, saying that we need to remind ourselves to stop looking for The Meaning in every story we read in the Bible does not mean that we necessarily throw the book out. Not at all. It means we place the book on our shelf with all the other interesting books that we look to for insight and enjoyment and challenge. The Bible has been the foundational document of Christianity since almost its very beginnings. Many believe that because of its connection to our past, because of the meaning we have sought in it, because of the beauty of its poetry, the sureness of its promises, that it should hold a privileged position even if we no longer believe or find comfort in those things. Many, too, fear that without it, we will have no moral compass, no guide to help us make choices when difficult situations arise. For much of its history, they claim, its stories and promises helped us make sense of our lives.

If we think carefully about it, we see that we have been bringing our own moral perspectives to the Bible and assessing it with our progressively broader and increasingly more informed knowledge of humanity, the world, and life for a very long time. Innumerable people have discerned right from wrong independent of its teachings. Had we never heard of the Good Samaritan, would we still not have discovered compassion? Where are those who condone the presentation of virgin daughters to be gang-raped as a sign of hospitality (Genesis 19:8)? We challenged ourselves away from such behaviour long ago, despite its presentation as a once biblically appropriate course of action. Those whose moral compass is grounded in the Bible often find it there only when it has helped to back up their prejudices. The book has been foundational in the formation of much of sacred and secular history, with helpful and unhelpful results, but it need not be foundational for our own beliefs, any more than any other source. We will continue, we must continue, to discern our way toward ethical living quite apart from the Bible as we have learned to do. The Bible can no longer assist us in that endeavour.

Choosing to see the Bible as another interesting book rather than a privileged book of divine wisdom means that there might be things in it that are interesting enough for us to think about for a long, long time. And it means that there might be things in it that we needn't spend another minute on. The question to bring to any of the stories of the Bible, once we no longer see it as TAWOGFAT, is: What do you make of it? not What is the meaning of the story? *You* bring the meaning to it. It's not there without you reading it and getting something out of it. You are the context in which it will be figured out and lived, if it's worth it. You might find that much of it is helpful to you as you move, headlong, into the next stage of your life. Or you might find that you shouldn't have wasted your time. Every story is different, and everyone's perspective is different.

For that matter, once the Bible is set aside as *the* spiritual resource, you can be fed by many sources. Use whatever it is you're reading—William Blake or Mary Oliver, Maeve Binchy or Thich Nhat Hanh, Dean Koontz or Philippa Gregory. Seek out the deep spiritual wisdom that your perspective might find there. I have a book about philosophy and comic-book superheroes. Since reading that, I've never been able to look at comic books as mere trash meant only for kids. Now my eyes have awe in them. Bet that's a stretch for you, isn't it? It was for me.

## Sonnet Snapshot

Imagine that I choose to read Shakespeare's sonnets one afternoon, and one of them blows me away. In it I find a synchronicity with my life that is stunning in its clarity. Indeed, I'm sure this happens fairly regularly or we wouldn't still be calling him the world's greatest bard. So say that I come across that synchronicity, and I carry that poem with me, whether on paper or just in my mind, for several weeks. Each time I regard it afresh, I am touched again by its power. Perhaps, as a result of what I have read, I determine that I have not been allowing myself to sink into the experience of love as it has been offered to me in what has the potential to become my primary love relationship but which I've been pushing aside for lack of some serious time to consider it. So, after reading the lines over and over again, I think maybe I'll let myself get a little closer to the possibilities. I dip my toes in for just a fore-taste of what might be—maybe dinner and a movie. I don't die. I don't stop breathing. I don't crash and burn. On the contrary, life seems brighter, more beautiful. So I read the poem again, and I go back to my potential lover and try exploring a bit further. No dive off the deep end, just another step into the swirling waters of relationship—more risk, more to lose, and much more exhilaration. It happens again. The world is completely different. I'm completely different. And it is utterly, unspeakably, perfectly wonderful.

So the sonnet has meaning for me. It has moved me past what might have been a huge obstacle and laid before me riches that I may never have explored had it not been for those lines squiggled out of the nib of Shakespeare's pen several hundred years ago. Does that mean that the sonnet was about getting me into a relationship that I might not have risked before reading it? Would it be right for me to say to the sad-looking woman on the subway next to me, as I tucked the piece of paper with the poem on it into her hand, that if she would only trust what it says, it could change her life? Could I slap my experience on top of anyone else's lifeline and say this is what you'll get if you read this? I don't think so. But that is so often how we use the stories of the Bible—as if they were some sort of a panacea, or at least a prescription: "Listen to what this says and, when you get the right meaning out of it, your life will all come together beautifully."

The struggle many liberally oriented Sunday school teachers have had trying to find The Meaning in many Bible stories is thus relieved. God destroying all but two of every kind of animal on the earth; loving Jacob but hating Esau; waiting hundreds of years to save his enslaved chosen people; commanding the destruction of women, children, horses, and priests of another religion; rescuing select people from death; requiring the death of his son in order that he could forgive the sins of the people he had created imperfectly; and so on. If these and other stories need be taught at all, if it is felt that they have something to offer, the question is not What is God telling us? but rather, What do you make of this?

Learning the subtleties of the difference between looking for The Meaning and looking for meaning is very important when we return to the text we have known for the whole of our lives as TAWOGFAT. The first is far, far, far too close to trying to maintain its TAWOGFAT status. Whether the original writers were recording history, story, myth, allegory, or some esoteric code, it remains that their words have come to be housed in a book called "Holy" and purported to be TAWOGFAT. No version I have seen is prefaced with: "This is a collection of ancient stories written by many authors who believed in a spiritual Being who created the world, made his will clear, and demands obedience to it. The publishers are not validating the authors' views but present the stories for your interest and edification." We think that because it's *the Bible* we need to look at it for its intended meaning for us. It might well have meaning in it because a particular verse resonates with us, say, the feeling of oppression or the importance of compassion. But let's challenge ourselves to think again if we open it looking for the meaning we think is in there, waiting for us to discover it. We must get away from that manner of approaching the Bible or we will be forever tripping over the bad stuff and never finding, in ourselves, the way the good stuff tugs and pulls at some little bit of our subconscious that needs to be thought about, mulled over, and brought out for inspection. The Bible should be looked at like Shakespeare's collected works. Some of his works, I can unreservedly relate to. Some of them I can make neither heads nor tails of. And I don't need to.

## GOD: A HUMAN CONCEPT

Once our idea of the Bible shifts away from its being TAWO-GFAT, everything in it is up for grabs. Everything. That means just what it says. Everything. It's not that there aren't good stories or dramas we can use metaphorically to challenge ourselves and set us back on the right path. It's that we can't say that anything those stories say or imply is factually true. It *may* be, but all we can really say about it is just that; it may be. There are no definitive answers.

It leaves us with a very big question then. Just who or what is God?

The Bible presents a whole bunch of different descriptions and understandings of God, although almost all are masculine images. That's no surprise since most of it was written before women were even counted in census numbers. In the creation story, we're presented with a somewhat bumbling God. The first thing we learn about him is that he tires easily. After uttering a sentence or two a day for six days, he needs to take a whole day off. He's not very insightful, creating a man in need of a companion and traipsing the entire animal population before the poor, lonely guy in the hopes that he'll find one attractive enough to mate with. After some time and, no doubt, a great deal of frustration on Adam's part, God gets the picture and creates a woman. (Of course, you'll note that creation took place from the least evolved thing to the most evolved thing and that women were last. Think about it.) We learn that God is passive-aggressive, placing a tree in the garden that has delicious fruit on it and telling them not to eat it, behaviour fitting a kindergarten child. We learn, too, that he is not all-knowing as we thought, losing track of Adam and Eve shortly after creating them and wandering the garden calling for them. And then, of course, we learn that he is a bully, forcing them to leave paradise because they fell for his little temptation scheme.

We travel through the early books of the Bible with a God who seems to try to work things out for us by swooping in to extract us from the very hot water into which he dunked us in the first place.[2]

We get the sense of God as this beneficent being who will always try to work things out until, as too often still happens, something goes seriously wrong and the idea of God has to be rethought. For the Israelites, it was the exile into Babylon, something that was definitely not supposed to happen to the people who were God's gift to the earth. Their captivity in Babylon also separated them from God, who at that time was living in Jerusalem, but a single good Ezekiel vision, and God was mobile, complete with wings and wheels, and able to join them there. In order to handle the reality that God had seemingly forsaken them for those seventy-odd years, shaming them with defeat in front of the whole world, their new idea of God included the concept of judgment: finding fault with their behaviour was not a difficulty and could, then, be logically proven to be the cause of their humiliation. That part of the idea of God rapidly took over and has remained, in essence, the basic understanding until now, excepting a little blip during which Jesus seemed to be suggesting that God, or the Kingdom of Heaven, was in how we treated one another. His idea was inconsistent, though, because, so the story goes, he also sent people who didn't believe him straight to hell. So who really knows?

## Thinking Freely

Why slog through all these inconsistent stories about God when I've just finished trying to convince you that the Bible isn't the authoritative word of God for all time, anyway? Because I want you to think for yourself when you approach it and not fall back on preconceived notions. There will be things within it that resonate with you. Keep them, ponder them, and set the rest aside. Create new concepts of God for yourself or reject them altogether.

The people who wrote the Bible believed they had permission. They made up all kinds of different ways to see God. In a single psalm you will often find two or maybe three seemingly contradictory ideas about God. My favourite is Psalm 139. It gives us an image of this loving God that is present to us no matter where we are, "If I were to dwell in the outermost parts of the sea, there you would be also," and then, before the reader gets too carried away by the images of being blissfully held in this eternal presence, the psalmist calls upon the warrior God to kill all the enemies known to his people. A loving God, an omnipresent God, a murdering God—all in one lyric poem. So, like the psalmist and other biblical writers of ancient days, print your own permission ticket and head outside the box.

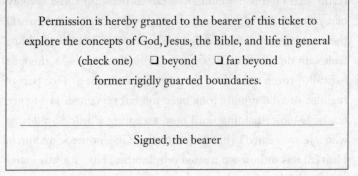

It is impossible for us to know anything about what it is we call God beyond what our personal experience might be, and we are only able to interpret that experience through experiences we have or ideas with which we are already familiar. In other words, say you've had an experience that you believed was God. Perhaps you heard words coming to you in a time of deep need and confusion. You attribute them to God. Many people would. But you must already have had an idea of God as a being that could speak to you in order to interpret what you heard in that manner. If you had previously only been exposed to the concept of God as light, for instance, it would never have occurred to you that it was God talking because light does not speak. You'd have decided that it was your Great Aunt Hattie speaking to you either from her ocean-faring around-the-world trip or from the other side of the great abyss or maybe just your conscience giving you a much needed drop-kick into a new perspective—and even then, of course, only if those ideas were previously placed in your brain in a manner with which your experience could resonate.

Michael Persinger, cognitive neuroscience researcher and professor at Laurentian University in Sudbury, Ontario, has experimentally recreated experiences of a "sensed presence" by using electromagnetic fields. By stimulating one or the other of the temporal lobes with artificial magnetic fields, a subject can be made to have either a fear-based or a bliss-based experience of a being that is close by them. Researchers working with Persinger and exploring the spiritual nature of his findings have suggested that prayer, a process of separating thoughts from feelings and so also the functioning of both sides of our brains, stimulates the brain in a similar way and makes it possible for individuals to create a sense of the presence many would then call "God." Those who become highly practised at the separation of brain function brought about through prayer might even have a constant sense of God's presence with them in their lives.

In order to explore the concept of God, we need to open ourselves to all kinds of possibilities, such as God being light or there being no God at all. We need to take note of the ways we have been conditioned to experience God and then, when we're having some sort of spiritual experience, be wary of the easy explanations. Step beyond the easy fit into the possibility of something other than what you might have previously thought.

## Not So Freely

In the past, any human experience that might have been claimed as spiritual was held up to the light of the church's doctrines on God and the Spirit and declared holy or otherwise. The church, as the keeper of "Who God Is," has used its authority to validate or deny any experience that we've thought might be holy. A weeping statue and a few miraculous healings? Stamped with the church's approval. Sexual orgasm, thought by many to be the ultimate in spiritual experience? Absolutely not.

It is time for the church to give up that truth-testing role. Those in leadership positions in the church are fully aware that whatever god is, it is not described by the church's doctrines. They are even aware that there may be no such thing as god. Since the leadership of the church is unlikely to discard the pile of doctrines they have created and protected throughout its history, perhaps it would be best if they were to shift the focus of their protection. Perhaps, instead of preventing access so that those doctrines could not be tampered with, church leaders should be preventing access so that we are forced to explore and name for ourselves that from which we might glean spiritual insight. Perhaps "the people" have been too timid. Perhaps it is time to explore beyond the safety and security of the answers wrapped in ecclesial favour.

Should the church have the wherewithal to do that, the first easy answer that you wouldn't be able to access any more is the idea that god is a being. Gone. Sit with that one for a minute. When you think about it, you may find that you haven't been thinking about god theistically—as a distinct, other being that is separate and definable—for a while. Flip back to Chapter Three and take a look at the definition of god that you probably agreed with (or at least didn't think was too crazy). You may think of god as a remote being some of the time, but you also may have often thought of god as a feeling that makes you want to be the best person you can be (and I don't mean getting your name in Fortune 500). You get that feeling when you plunk a quarter into a stranger's parking meter. You get that feeling when you talk to your kids about trying to make the world a better place, and they tell you some pretty great ideas they've come up with all on their own. You get that feeling when you stop and talk to that other person who has been sitting all alone the whole time you've been visiting with your mom in rehab. All he does is smile at you and nod, but that feeling is almost tangible. You get that feeling when you pick up the package you were expecting, and in it you find that perfect gift you ordered for your child, your lover, or your-self. Invite yourself to think of that feeling as god.

## A Worthy Heritage
So the idea of god not being a being isn't that crazy after all. Indeed, Lloyd Geering, author of *Christianity without God*, explores

the development of the concept of a theistic god, a god with "being"-ness, one able to act independently of us, and finds the roots of non-theism deep within the Christian tradition and the philosophical arguments it has historically rejected. In a mere 146 pages, Geering answers a whole host of arguments that might be made against a non-theistic understanding of god and challenges us to finally recognize that in its current doctrinal incarnation, the church can only be doomed.

Finding traces of non-theism already in existence in early Judaism, Geering steers his way through the development of the Christian scriptures, early doctrine, and subsequent theology and philosophy to arrive at his point—that non-theism not only grows out of the Christian tradition but is the only logical next step for the church to take.[3] Along the way, he points out several remarkable insights or assimilations that should have tolled theism's death knell long ago.

Hebraic understandings of God developed in the same tribal mythology as did those of other faiths. During the first Axial age, those understandings were being challenged and significantly changed. Within Judaism, polytheism gave way to monotheism, a belief in one God who, initially, ruled over the other gods. Eventually, the very existence of any gods other than the one God of Israel was completely denounced. Through the course of that shift, as the many different understandings of god melded into one, it became increasingly obvious that no one person or tribe could conclusively describe God. The understanding of God as being beyond description came to be the norm. Indeed, following that period, any attempts to describe God were considered blasphemous. It was as if in order to coalesce many gods into one, the description of the one had to incorporate all the characteristics of the many. Such a comprehensive God, of necessity, came to be beyond description.

As Christianity developed among those who claimed Jewish heritage, this comprehensive God was further refined by new arguments. The platonic concepts of a remote, impersonal god, *theos*, stretched the understanding of the Israelites, who understood a very personal God as having mucked about in history with them, exhibiting all too human characteristics. Complicating this relationship was the Stoic concept of *theos*, which was quite different. The Stoics understood *theos* as the principle of rationality and order upon which the whole of the universe was set. Early Christianity grew out of a delicate interweaving of these and many other different experiences and understandings.

In fact, Geering argues that the doctrine of the Holy Trinity was just such a feat. Unable to reconcile the complex perspectives of those for whom the Christian community had become deeply meaningful, it was not inappropriate to simply express all of them and perhaps all at once. Geering points to Paul's early benediction, "The grace of the Lord Jesus Christ and the love of God and the fellowship of the Holy Spirit be with you all." (2 Corinthians 13:14) as a straightforward inclusion of such a variety of experience and claims that each of the three separate natures appealed to a significant experience being grafted into a single, new concept; through the apostles was mediated a rich experience of the grace bestowed upon them by Jesus; from its Jewish roots came a deep experience of God's love; and within early Christian communities, experiences of fellowship were found to be transformative.[4] Geering argues that Paul never intended his words to be law. Like so many others at the time, Paul was merely writing it as he saw it, addressing situations in whatever way he felt most appropriate and accommodating his style to the needs of the moment. It was only in subsequent arguments about the exact nature of God, soon to be described as the Trinitarian "Godhead," that his words were argued to be Truth (with a capital "T").

If a single god could be argued to be of three persons and one substance (already confused by translation of oblique Greek terms into Latin), then there is nothing to stop it from becoming something else. We're reminded of John A.T. Robinson positing for us that if we can change our thinking of God as being "up there" to "out there," then we can start thinking of god in entirely different terms than "out there," too. Surely, Geering emulates Robinson's reasoning: if we can be as fast and free with the concept of god as one would have to be to create the doctrine of the Trinity, then we can do almost anything! Non-theism is one of those "almost anythings."

Among the tectonic thinkers, Geering notes, is William of Ockham, whose "razor" required that if an explanation for something could be made without bringing God into the question, then we'd best leave God out of it. Ockham, who explored the realities of his existence in the thirteenth century, couldn't possible have foreseen the effect of his words on the understanding of God, but they are startlingly clear to us. Simply put, as science has been able to explain more and more of what we experience in the world, God is needed less and less as an explanatory factor. Indeed, when we can understand the evolution of any life form as the simple trial and error progressions exposed in Richard Dawkins' *The Blind Watchmaker*, there is little reason for us to hold on to God as explanation.

In truth, Ockham had also introduced the notion that ideas were the creation of those who had them. They do not exist distinctly awaiting our discovery but, rather, come into being through our own creative efforts. Again, Ockham could not possibly have had the clarity of vision that would have allowed him to extrapolate the application of his thinking to the concept of god. He lived in a world very different from ours.[5] But Geering assigns him a place of esteem in the transition of Christianity from theism to non-theism.

## Free to Create

Once we recognize that it is absolutely acceptable, if not necessary, to explore beyond the idea of god as a being, we can come up with all sorts of ways of thinking about god (if we still want to, that is) that are unorthodox, that is, not protected by the church. We might, for instance, consider that god is what exists between two people, you and me, perhaps. Whenever we choose to honour what exists between us, we strengthen the god in our world; if we desecrate our relationship, we do the opposite. It's up to us.

Or we might think about god as everything that is good in the world. We often do. Life will be good or bad, and we might try to think of god as being only the good stuff and the bad as something else. The church used to tell us that the bad stuff was Satan or, more likely, human nature; I don't buy it and, I warrant, neither do you. Sure, we screw up, but the idea that we are evil by our very essence seems deeply wrong.[6] Restrict access to that kind of *mea culpa* thinking. Make it one of the things from which the church must protect us. It's too easy. There is just too much bad stuff that isn't anybody's fault—like tsunamis and category 4 and 5 hurricanes and earthquakes that wipe out whole populations.[7] It's not possible for us to take responsibility for all of that and, without access to that theistic all-powerful God (remember, the church in this imagined scenario is preventing us from falling back on the old answers and starting to force us to think differently), we have nothing to blame. So we are left with the responsibility of facing even the bad stuff with whatever strength and courage we can muster, as confounding as it is, and holding one another through the worst of it, counting on one another for finding and creating enough good stuff to get us through the night and into the next day. If that's the case, we're strengthening god, building god up in the world, one little act or smile at a time.

It will be very important for us not to create new dogma. Presbyterian Church (U.S.A.) minister and author Jim Dollar cautions us in his book *The Evolution of the Idea of God:* "We don't need another doctrine of God to add to the pile. We just need to torch the pile." He is right: we have way too much dogma as it is. "To replace an old doctrine with an updated doctrine merely perpetuates the practice of creating words without referents, and we debate the doctrines, and lose the center, and treat those who oppose us in ways that are not God-like regardless of how well we articulate our Godly views."[8] We must be very careful not to get it down just right, to leave room for creativity, for space to feel a different way of god, a new way to speak of our experiences.

I'm going to try to stop using the word *god* altogether. Robinson suggested that way back in 1963. That we didn't take him up on it has cost us decades of exploration time. But I'll try to drop the word *god* because I know you, and I know that every time I use that word, try as you might, you're going to go back to some sort of idea of god as a being or some otherworldly person. From now on, I'm going to use some other word—maybe *breath* or *love* or *pyntrilm*. I like *pyntrilm*. I made it up. The emphasis is on the first syllable, though it is charming on the second, too. But I think you'll probably think it's a proper name instead of, maybe, a verb and go right back to thinking about you-know-what/who as a being. So I don't think I'll use pyntrilm either. We'll see.

As we create new means for celebrating the vast number of ways we experience and are drawn into the sanctity of life, dropping that not-to-be-spoken-again word will seem to be a big thing. It really isn't. If you think it is difficult, just think how easy it has been to begin using inclusive language. Well, okay, maybe it will take time. But substituting words is something we do all the time. In the first sentence of this paragraph, for instance, I needed a different word for "ways" or I was going to have to use it twice. "Means" worked well, so I dropped it in. We actually substitute all the time and are almost unaware of it. Doing it with the word *god* will take some practice but is not impossible by any stretch of the imagination. One of the most difficult parts, and it may take a while to realize just how difficult, is imagining a way that is not active, that does not act upon you or me or anyone, that lacks the quality of agency. Don't worry about that too much to begin with. Just using new terms will sweep a lot of old stuff onto the dustpile and make room for the imagination to stretch and rethink and create. You'll get to the absence of being soon enough.

My son, in a creative writing class, was given a piece of paper with 101 different ways to say "said." Here are 101 ways to say "that word." Most are nouns. Some are adjectives. A few are verbs. Playing with the words helps us play with the concept and playing with the concept can help us experience it in incredible new ways:

> blessing, love, spirit, essence, being, light, heat, hope, sacred, holy, one, ground of all being, shining, flow, groundedness, lightness of being, emptiness, immensity, deep, joy, understanding, awe, life, deep unto deep, relate, creativity, healing, delight, whole, whole-i-ness, dream, strength, centre, root, intimate knowing, questing, power, wedge of possibility, stillness, grounding, whisper, heartbeat, thunder, longing, passion, compassion, spiritwork, womb of all life, truth, resonance, peace, edge of hope, laughter's echo, ultimacy, goodness, sense and non-sense, depth of being, ineffable, nothingness, that which is between, wealth of understanding, care, kindness, visionwork, depth of meaning, urge toward life, hallowing, shadow, window of opportunity, silent, pulse, purpose, forgiveness, mercy, wonder, absence of being, music, turbulence, order, justice, mirror, beginning, right relationship, it is when we _____, access, inexpressible, intangible, absence of sorrow, gift of life, promise of healing, world of blessing, realm of promise, surge of joy, all that's worthy, fulfill, presence, wellspring of life, thrill, song, voice, and heart.

As we seek to move beyond images that have constricted us and allow ourselves to embrace the being-ness of our own divinity, choosing to see and celebrate each creative, life-affirming experience as holy, we will slowly and steadily release the theistic grip in which we have held all that we have called good. We will free it to grow and develop among us. It will be in our laughter, in our loving, and in our caring for one another. It will be when we act justly and choose to fill another's need before our own. It will stir us toward sincerity, to the truth of who we are. It will well up from within us and overflow in kindness and delight. We will know it in our relationships, in our efforts, and in the depths of our souls. And we, too, will have been set free.

## JESUS: A HUMAN BEING

When we reconsider the concept of god and work our way toward exploring it differently than we have in the past, the whole idea of Jesus being the Son of God no longer makes much sense. Although we will have travelled a very different route, we find ourselves arriving at a place similar to that achieved by the Jesus Seminar, that group of scholars who gather to share research on the historical Jesus. Here we see the story of a man who lived his life in a relatively enclosed geographical area and who spent his short adult years travelling from town to town sharing his ideas about what is important in life. We might find that he seems to have lived in ways that exemplified our newfound understandings of god, honouring the sacredness of his relationships, challenging his peers to live radically spiritual lives; but even as we do, we will recognize our own interpretive biases being laid over the ancient picture the evangelists portrayed.

### If It Doesn't Fit, Make It Fit

We will also see the way the church stretched, pulled, and reconfigured the story of Jesus to give us that Son of God it said we had to have. With the help of scholars and authors who make academic research accessible, we will have set before us a very human Jesus, a man of emotions, wisdom, and desires. But we will not have the Son of God.

Having acknowledged that, we need to ask ourselves whether it is worth our time and effort to continue to focus so much of our attention on his life, sayings, and activities. Does it make a difference to how we read the Gospels if we are reading about what the Son of God said and did or if we are reading what a charismatic Middle Eastern teacher and healer said and did two thousand years ago? Of course it does.

The gospel writers' perspectives have been deftly exposed by scholars over the past century or so and most recently by those of the Jesus Seminar. As they have sifted through the evangelists' words and discovered the real blood-and-gristle Jesus who walked the Galilean shore and spoke to anyone who would listen, they have found themselves essentially aligned with the perspective Schweitzer had presented a hundred years ago. Accounting for the various audiences the texts were written for—Greek, Gentile, and Jew—and the purposeful direction of the writing, scholars, using very credible means, have found that, in the end, there is little left for us to get a good hold on. I doubt if they, like Schweitzer, had anticipated the result of their work—the picture of a man incapable of carrying either the weight of the world's sins or two thousand years of devotion upon his meagre shoulders and one who, truth be told, would have been shocked to see that he had.

It seems that Jesus, born into a world that presented him with a pre-set worldview within which he lived his short life, had much to say to the people with whom he lived and worked and travelled. That is, at least, how he is presented by the evangelists. But, stripped of the designation as God's only begotten, complete with its requisite claims to salvation, there is nothing that he said or did that we must take more seriously than anything said by anyone else. What he is purported to have said or done may, indeed, have been remarkable for his day and time and may, indeed, prove to be provocative material challenging us to think more justly and compassionately even today. We need listen and watch, however, only with the same attentiveness we would give to any person or piece of literature, film, or art, popular, classic, or otherwise. Our interest is not only for diversion but for inspiration, not only in passing time but in being affected, not only in positing who we are in the greater scheme of things but in clarifying who we are. The purpose of our attention to any of those people or things is the possibility of transformation, and, for this, there is no more import in the stories of Jesus than there is in any of the stories we see being lived out around us. We take from them the strength that may challenge us to live toward the good more fully and leave what is left over, what does not inspire or challenge us, defined as entertainment or diversion. When Jesus is not understood to be God, the stories of his life, the things that he said, and the way that he acted do not have the power of God attached to them. They become stories, and we are freed to read them as such.

## New View

Yet, we remain fascinated with the man, Jesus, and so it is important that we read the stories about him first hand, as though watching a movie, and decide for ourselves what we will call significant and what we find not to be so. I'm going to propose a different way to look at what Jesus is purported to have said, done, and thought. My method requires three things: a blue highlighter, a yellow highlighter, and a modern translation of the Gospels that you aren't afraid to mark up. (You need blue and yellow because you'll want to use both of them sometimes and come up with green. Or you can use pink and yellow if you have to.) Sometimes, it is helpful to also have a Gospels parallel book. It places, side by side, all the stories that are present in two or more Gospels. So, for instance, you can see what the birth narrative in Mark (there isn't one) looks like compared to the one in Matthew (the wise men), Luke (the shepherds), and John (there isn't one). That can save a lot of time and give you more than a few extra things to think about. However, if you don't have one at hand,[9] don't put off this exciting project while you wait to get one for Christmas. Just jump right in with the basics.

Once you have your things together, you are ready to do all the Jesus study you'll ever need. Remember, this is not TAWOGFAT. It is just a book. And you are not a scholar extrapolating The Meaning that God put in there for you to find. God did not write it. There is no The Meaning. There is only the possibility that something might resonate with you, challenge you, tug at something you need to think about a bit more, or disgust you and make you ask yourself why you're disgusted. That's all.

Decide which one of the highlighters is going to be for good stuff and which of the highlighters is going to be for bad stuff. You get to say which stuff is which. As you read, you'll want to work with whole stories or segments of stories within the different books, although you will also find that within a particular story, Jesus is purported to have acted in a particularly negative manner or saying something that really ticks you off. Feel free to mark these separately from the rest of the story. They are significant, and you'll want to be able to see when and with what kind of regularity that happens. Read until you come to an obvious end to the particular narrative, and then decide whether to highlight the whole thing or parts of it as good stuff or whether to highlight the whole thing or parts of it as bad stuff. By the time you've finished, you should have highlighted almost everything except, perhaps, the stage directions. They're pretty neutral.

It actually only takes about twenty-five minutes to read the Gospel of Mark, so you might want to begin with that one. It's the oldest Gospel, anyway, so it makes a good starting point.[10]

It can be very stimulating to have someone else or a group reading through the Gospels using the process at the same time you are. You will find that there are differences of opinions on a wide range of things, and the conversations that will come out of those different perspectives have the potential to be rich and interesting. Some of you will come with a feminist perspective. Particular things will affect you as they may not affect others. Some of you will come with a pacifist perspective. The same thing will happen with different results. Each perspective and each person reads any piece of literature differently.

Here are some questions to keep in mind as you read.

1. Is Jesus acting in a way you would be proud of were he your son/brother/friend, or not?
2. Does this story evoke a good feeling in you or a bad one?
3. What do you make of it?
4. How would you see the story if you were one of the characters in it?

This exercise is only to assist you in seeing Jesus as he has been represented by a variety of voices. My hope is that you will have used both highlighters by the time you are finished, not just one.

Some of the things you might notice about Jesus during your anarchic highlighter waltz through the Gospels will be new to you. They've always been there, of course; it is just that we haven't spent a whole lot of time looking for them. The liberal gloss through which the Gospels have been read has been thick. We've grown accustomed to the gentle Jesus of our childhoods. Or, if we believe ourselves to be radicals, every now and then, we've resonated deeply with the idea of tossing tables—even if we haven't had the courage to do it ourselves. But there is much to discover and think about, such as these provocative thoughts on the humanity and therefore fallibility of Jesus and our remoteness from most of the information about him. They were prepared for me for use with a study group at West Hill United Church, the congregation I serve. Not at all a comprehensive study of Jesus, the list was intended to draw attention to material right in the text or ideas drawn directly from it that challenge the idealized picture we've held for so long. Once you've caught the idea, it will influence your reading every time you open the book.

- Jesus wrote down nothing that we know of, and what was written about him was written years after he died; we cannot know with any degree of certainty whether we are hearing the words *of* a person named Jesus or the collected thoughts of the early church *about* a person named Jesus.
- No other historical record contains anything about Jesus' miraculous works or resurrection; we have only the words of those who believed he was the Messiah or the Son of God, a decidedly biased view.
- What *was* written is compromised by many instances of miraculous deeds, done for select people or situations.
- He declared no intention of starting a new religion or even another version of Judaism—he was just emphasizing certain parts of his Jewish faith as true spirituality.
- His teachings about love and forgiveness are found in the Hebrew scriptures and other religions long predating him.
- He taught a mixture of beliefs, some of which are helpful, some of which are markedly unhelpful, for example, divorce, hell, and eternal punishment.
- He is not recorded as having attempted to change any oppressive forces, but taught people rather to acquiesce ("turn the other cheek")—a stance that is fine to a point but not at all helpful in ending slavery, racism, patriarchal hierarchy, and so on.

- If our explorations find that he was a humble, sincere teacher, we can then assume that he would not want generations of people to be worshiping him, singing about him, and praising him. On the other hand, he might be very pleased that we agreed with some of his teaching.
- All human leaders are fallible, and themselves broken and imperfect. Jesus is not portrayed this way in the New Testament. He is an idealized figure, and all his ideas are presented by the evangelists as being right. Some of those ideas, however—banishment to hell, damning the fig tree, deriding his followers, and so on—we would now say are wrong. If we say we follow Jesus without clarification, we allow the assumption that we agree with all of his ideas, including the bad ones.
- Many claims recorded as having been made *by* Jesus are unsupportable and exclusive: "I am the way, and the truth, and the life; no one comes to the Father, but by me." (John 14:6) "I am the resurrection and the life." (John 11:25) "And whatever you ask in prayer, you will receive, if you have faith." (Matthew 21:22) According to 2 Peter, the elect will go to heaven and the unchosen will not. (2 Peter 1:10–11)
- Many claims made *about* Jesus in the New Testament present a highly exclusive way of salvation, for example, "The elect will go to heaven" (2 Peter 1:10–11), the unchosen will not. Jesus is the Lamb of God sacrificed for the sins of the world, and only they who believe this will go to heaven. All will bow their knee before Christ.
- Jesus' moral teaching is not outstanding. It would have blended in with that of countless other spiritual leaders and may have been superseded by many who actually did more to put their words into action.

It isn't all bad and it isn't all good. Not everything in a bad book is bad. Not everything in a good book is good. There are some interesting things that we can put in our satchel, pull out every now and then to look at, muse over, and reconsider. Those are the bits worth keeping. Those are the bits that make the story worth reading. And those are the bits that you will find yourself coming back to over and over again. Let the rest slip through your fingers and settle into the dust of two millennia of misrepresentation and misunderstanding.

## PRAYER: HEART TO HEART

One of the most lasting and significant aspects of almost every faith tradition is that of prayer. The world engages in prayer that is private, public, silent, spoken, calm, and energetic. It is used to celebrate and soothe, intercede and heal; to focus our energies and thoughts; and to open us to new understandings. In every case, it is an act of aligning oneself with that which is both immanent and transcendent, both at one's centre and beyond the furthest boundaries of the universe—the sacred, the holy, the divine.

Often, tangible symbols and objects assist us in our efforts to engage in prayer. Perhaps most familiar to those in the West is the Roman Catholic rosary. In the east, prayer flags have been used for centuries around homes, monasteries, and mountains, acting as offerings to those who have achieved enlightenment and as prayers that will bless all. Lights, floating on rafts made from slices of banana tree trunks and decorated with flowers and leaves, are set onto the waterways of Thailand as thanksgivings to the Mother of the Waters. Similarly, each morning in India, worshippers gather on the shores of the Ganges to cleanse themselves and set prayer lights upon the holy waters in thanksgiving.

## A Progressive Struggle

But for progressive Christians, many of whom struggle with the understandings of god that are normally conjured up by the concept of prayer, talking about the subject of prayer becomes difficult. Even more awkward for many is its practice, which becomes increasingly complicated by the theological struggles that a progressive perspective demands. Too often, as our images of what is holy shift and morph, prayer takes on a negative aura, becoming identified with things of faith that one is choosing to leave behind as no longer useful.

Yet those who regularly include prayer in their spiritual discipline seem to enjoy a sense of well-being, comfort, and strength regardless of the images of the sacred that they have developed. For the community with which I serve in ministry, prayer is one of the most important aspects of our spiritual life even though the images of god that are held by the members of that community are incredibly varied or the concept of god is entirely denied. Broadening an understanding of prayer can allow for its retention as a vibrant spiritual tool during what might be a difficult journey of faith. A little bit of history and some anthropology may help deepen our understanding and appreciation.

## How We've Imaged God

Traditional Christian prayer postulates an interventionist deity— one that is in control of the world, that is merciful and loving, but also judgmental and jealous. Such an understanding binds us to rituals and traditions that were created to appeal or appease, to ask for assistance or beg for mercy from that remote god. We say that the world, with its immovable natural laws, is often "cruel and heartless," recognizing as we say it that we desperately want a god that has a heart, that will watch over us, that will keep us safe. The theistic understanding presented in the Judeo-Christian scriptures proposes a god-being with the capacity to hear us, be moved, and respond; it is imbued with our human characteristics. And so, as Christians have lifted their prayers to give thanks or to petition for some kind of blessing, it has been to a god that would be moved in the same way we would be moved by such actions.

By way of example, imagine being asked to help someone out. They ask you politely, making you aware that assisting them offers you an opportunity to feel good about yourself. Such a request moves you to respond with whatever you can do that would be helpful. When you are thanked for your actions, you feel even better and are often, as a result, more gracious with your time and belongings. If, however, the original request comes with a bad attitude, with an "I deserve this so do it" sort of demand, your response is probably less than generous. You're less likely to be moved by the request—less likely to respond with a feeling of well-being.

We have projected these same human characteristics upon God throughout the centuries—please God and you will know blessing; offend God and you will not.

Similarly, we postulate, often based on scripture, that the human characteristics of prejudice and judgment also lie at the core of God's being. When suffering occurs, as it always does, we look first for a reason or a purpose. Perhaps we find a flaw in the individual's personal life, faith, or being, and we hang God's judgment on that. Or we find in their particular race, gender, nationality, or sexuality a cause for that judgment, and we find the heart of God conspicuously aligned with our own fears and explanations.

When we see how theistic concepts of God developed to help us cope with the random nature of pain, suffering, and blessing, we recognize that such an image is just that—a humanly created one. Our attempts to define something we cannot possibly understand or adequately describe has and will always be subject to the limitations of our human, fallible minds. God, spirit, the divine must be acknowledged as being beyond our explanations, or it becomes an idol, a useless tool in our struggle with reality.

It is important to note that by recognizing we have constructed an image of god that has existed for millennia, we do not trivialize that undertaking. It may be that we would never have survived as a species without such an understanding. We needed, during our struggles with an environment that was more often hostile than not, a vision of a future for our children and ourselves that we believed might be possible. Our understanding of an all-powerful, all-knowing, all-loving god gave us a belief in that future. It may have been the only thing that gave us the strength to survive. Our capacity to create an image of the divine that gave us that sense of security is awesomely wonderful. It speaks of the creative strength of the human species and calls us to draw upon that same spirit and sense of wonder to continue to imagine ourselves into a sustainable future. But just as our forebears did not stop developing their concepts to match their understandings of life and themselves in it, we have the freedom and responsibility to continue developing, to leave behind concepts based on certain images of god, and embrace ones that reflect our present understandings.

## Okay, But What New Images Are There?

As we engage in the practice of prayer, and the images we associate with it change, the experience of prayer changes, too. Several instances come to mind. For one woman, long before she had ever heard the term *progressive Christianity*, prayer took on the face of those she knew were holding her and caring for her through that medium. Waiting for news of her husband's condition following a life-threatening trauma, she had time to call only one person—a woman from a book study group at her church. She asked her to let others in the congregation know about the situation and ask them to pray for them. As she waited, eyes closed in her own personal prayer, she felt one, then another, then many of her church family become present to her. It was *as if* each person, as they heard of the circumstances, joined her and blessed her, and she knew that, regardless of the outcome, she would continue to know the blessing of the presence of those people.

In another situation, some years later, as prayer filled the mind of a man whose wife had experienced a similar life-threatening trauma and as he settled his mind upon God, to whom he was praying, no traditional image arose as the recipient of his prayer. Rather, one by one, the faces of members of his church family crystallized before him, and he had an epiphany, realizing as he prayed that he was, indeed, seeing the face of God but that God resided within his friends and family, not in an ancient and distant image.

And in another desperate circumstance, a different woman purposefully set out to address her newly formed, non-interventionist understanding of god. Willing herself to see god "horizontally," rather than "up there," she was yet unprepared for the resulting images. Members of her congregation, friends, and family "came" to her and galvanized her prayer. She speaks of the action of her prayer, adding the power of their prayers to the situation, despite their not knowing of the circumstances about which she prayed or that she was doing it. She drew upon their strength and received what was, for her, a tangible response.

Each of these individuals created images that deeply moved and supported them at critical times in their lives. Images are a significant part of our prayer life and can offer us as much strength as we have experienced with former interventionist understandings. But they aren't real, and we know they aren't real. We have created them in our minds. A participant in a workshop once offered me a P. D. James quotation in reference to this kind of prayer: "Consolation from an imaginary source is not imaginary consolation."[11] We strengthen ourselves through our own mental state. Images we conjure have an enormously beneficial effect, even if we know they are not "real."

Religious author Jack Good, at a conference in 2005, engaged delegates in a process of revisioning god. Taking a critical scholarly approach to the Bible, church history, and the development of the concepts of god that have tied us to a theistic image, Good helped participants come to a realization that we do not live in a world that is safely and securely within the arms of a "personal chaplain to the earth." Far too much reality belies that image, and any concept we hold of the divine must not contain that type of limitation. We must also lay down a false sense of rescue and take up responsibility for what we formerly put on God. We must live recognizing that there "is no safety net. It is we who must be the safety net for each other." [12]

This perspective offers us a radically new understanding of prayer—a liberating, challenging, empowering one. Rather than beseeching God's mercy, we find we are called to be god in the world to one another. Using the word *god* as a verb, we offer it to the world as we love and forgive and seek right relationship. We find in Jesus' ministry an incarnation of god simply because in much of his recorded work we see that drive to live out in his relationships all the goodness we associate with the divine: his challenges to the status quo, his recognition of brokenness, and his upholding of the oppressed. We see that same incarnation in any number of social-justice heroes and spiritual leaders, but we see it in one another, too. When we live out the values of love, mercy, compassion, and forgiveness, we, too, incarnate god. Or, in different terms, *when* we love, we experience and express our fullest humanity—our divinity.

So our prayer begins to resemble our commitment, our binding of ourselves to the work of living out those values. We listen for the cares and concerns of others and feel ourselves turning with compassion toward them to offer love and reaching out in whatever ways we are able. We search our own lives for the places where we are in need of challenge and change, and open ourselves to the perspective that living in community can offer. We are made aware of the many ways in which the world remains a hostile place and seek to offer ourselves, our time, our resources, our energy to soften the cost living charges to those in the world's most depleted and hurting places. And we find, in ways mysterious to us, that we experience healing, renewed strength, and courage when we have engaged in prayer, both privately and communally.

Scientific research seems to vary on the efficacy of prayer. Continued conflicting results make emphatic statements on its power potentially embarrassing and, therefore, impractical. Initial work, much attributed to Larry Dossey, suggested that prayer had a positive effect on people even when happening unbeknownst to them and from a distance. Tom Harpur's book *Prayer: The Hidden Fire* was highly influenced by those and similar studies. More recent work by Harvard Medical School suggests not, while the John Templeton Foundation and the Benson-Henry Institute for Mind Body Medicine continue working to find the links between the brain and spirituality that may, one day, conclusively determine the truth about prayer.

We are invited to move into new understandings of the realm of mystery we have long called God. It dwells in our relationships; in the urgent call from within to live responsibly and respectfully with the earth, ourselves, and one another; and in the inner strength we draw on even when the person or thing that once gave us strength is no longer with us. Seeing injustice, we move to challenge it; beauty, we move to celebrate it; pain, we move to heal it; love, we move to embrace it.

Although we may never fully know the reasons why prayer seems to be such a powerful spiritual tool even beyond the simple petitionary equation of its beginnings, our experience convinces us to hold up those values that we once saw as characteristics of a divine being and to live them out, to live god, through our spirits, throughout our own lives. To do so is to pray.

Often, it is easier for us to pray if we are able to imagine an external source of objective critique helping us assess our lives. That's often how we've used God in the past—as the divine being who expects certain things of us. Without that God, it's like leaving home for university before you're mature enough to take care of yourself. All the house rules no longer apply. That is not the case. We have to find ways to reinforce the challenging aspects of our prayer life and seek ways to commit to the values we have set for ourselves as worthy. It can be helpful to list these values, the highest ideals you might have previously thought God expected of you: compassion, kindness, respect, sincerity, humility, courage, humour, forgiveness. . . . Make up your own list. Then stick it up somewhere where it is convenient for you to consider it twice each day. In the morning, as you prepare to go about your day, read through the list and commit to trying to live up to these ideals *you have set for yourself.* At the end of the day, with the list in front of you, review your day and acknowledge those times when you accomplished your goals and those times when you fell short. This can be as brief or extended as your lifestyle allows it to be and can help you replace a former style of prayer with which you are no longer comfortable with a new and very powerful one.

Some time ago, I was approached by parents of the children in the congregation I serve. They were delighted with the progressive perspectives being offered in the morning's service but expressed concern that their children were not getting the same gifts in their own morning programs. Specifically, they expressed concern about our practice of having the children lead and recite the Lord's Prayer (known to us as the Disciples' Prayer) at the end of their time with the congregation each Sunday.

The parents' concern was very real. The image of God found in the Lord's Prayer was of a remote being upon whom we were entirely dependent: God gave us our food, forgave us our sins, and saved us from mortal ruin. Implicit in every line was our inability to do anything without God's gracious assistance. Our children were reciting a prayer about a God that almost none of their parents could relate to and most certainly did not want to hand down. What could we do?

Almost all change that happens in a congregation is a pastoral process. Spiritual growth is the goal, but it is often only possible in small, manageable bites. The congregation had seen significant change over the preceding few years. Removing the Lord's Prayer would be tantamount to blasphemy. I speculated that there would be many who would welcome the change and many who would not. In truth, it took almost a year for me to gather up the courage to introduce the topic to the congregation.

With the help of my songwriter husband, Scott Kearns, I began to address the issue. We wanted something that could live up to the familiar and comfortable feel of what the congregation had known for so long. At the same time, it needed to be non-theistic, a style that influenced all the other communal prayer in which we engaged. If it could embrace the values we had identified as worthy of our utter allegiance, those life-enhancing truths that call us to be more than we too often choose to be, that would be wonderful.

Beginning with the familiar feel of the prayer most often attributed to St. Francis of Assisi, but more likely from the turn of the last century, and removing any interventionist aspects of it, we got to work.[13] We introduced it to the congregation a line at a time so that we could play with the rhythm as we reworked it each week. On Easter Sunday, 2005, the congregation joined together to recite it in its final form. Every week since, one of the children has taken the microphone and, usually from memory, led the congregation with these words:

As I live every day,
I want to be a channel for peace.
May I bring love where there is hatred

and healing where there is hurt;

joy where there is sadness

and hope where there is fear.

I pray that I may always try

to understand and comfort other people

as well as seeking comfort and understanding

from them.

Wherever possible, may I choose to be

a light in the darkness,

a help in times of need,

and a caring, honest friend.

And may justice, kindness, and peace

flow from my heart forever,

Amen.[14]


## RITUALS: LIFE TO LIFE

No matter where we apprehend them, symbols are powerful. Whether changing language within the symbolic rituals we practise in the church makes any difference to how they are understood is questionable. At the first communion over which I presided at my suburban congregation in Toronto, I paraphrased the Words of Institution. I'd done it for years. We had never actually been told in seminary which words were the "magic" ones, very likely because our professors didn't want to suggest that there was any magic. So, from the very beginning, I didn't really know which ones were to be left in an unadulterated state.

My ignorance gave me a lot of latitude, and, fortunately for me, none of my parishioners seemed to suffer from the lack of "appropriate" phrasing. Over the course of a decade, the paraphrasing morphed into an entirely different interpretation of what we were doing when we gathered for communion. Gone was the *sursum corda* (The Lord be with you / And also with you) and the *kyrie* (Lord have mercy, Christ have mercy, Lord have mercy). Gone were the reference to body and blood and the long-winded preparatory thanksgiving to God for his unending mercy. Gone was the prayer for the dead, the intercessions, the ritual elevation of the bread and the cup. Gone were any vestiges of the sacrificial roots of the traditional Eucharistic feast. In their place was a description of the importance of our being in community with one another and a rededication to the challenges that such commitments present.

Strange then that a few short weeks after an article about my activities with the Canadian Centre for Progressive Christianity appeared in the *Toronto Star* in 2004, a parishioner should accuse me of not using Jesus' words when presiding over communion. Unless I had been reading someone else's prepared text (and perhaps not even then), I very possibly hadn't ever used the exact words in the entirety of my ministry there and certainly hadn't done so since this concerned individual had been active in the congregation. I hadn't used a written text for the prayer in several years, preferring to pray extemporaneously with the congregation and changing the supposed "magic words" each time, being careful not to simply substitute one "special" phrase with another of my own making. So powerful was the symbol, however, that the words had been completely lost on this congregant. They had simply not been heard, and it was only when an outsider pointed them out that my parishioner was able to hear them for herself.

## Handling the Sacraments

While it is prayer that is challenged when old concepts of an interventionist God are disputed and replaced, it is our symbolic acts that are the most unsettled when we let go of our doctrinal understandings of Jesus. The sacraments, those rites that have long been associated with Jesus' salvific power, can have little magic left when contemporary scholarship strips Jesus of his uniquely divine status and leaves him as only a Middle Eastern peasant with a few charismatic gifts and a great posthumous marketing team.

Most Protestant churches recognize at least two sacraments—baptism and communion (the Eucharist)—while the Roman Catholic Church recognizes five more—reconciliation, confirmation, marriage, the anointing of the sick, and the taking of holy orders as members of the male clergy.[15] Each is offered by the church, the repository of God's grace, to the people, the sinful, as a way of creating, affirming, and repairing their relationship with God (salvation). In Baptist congregations, baptism and communion are symbols that reflect the choice for salvation that an individual has already made. There they don't have the same "efficacy" that they do in most other mainline Protestant denominations or the Roman Catholic Church but only because the salvation, according to them, has already happened.

The power of the sacraments derives from the idea of humanity as being fallen or sinful and in need of redemption or grace. If we think about it for any length of time, the implausibility, if not the impossibility, of that idea becomes embarrassingly clear. God, in his high heaven, creates a world that is perfect but introduces into it human beings. Then he sets those human beings up to fail (the temptation and fall) and damns them to an eternal punishment (life on Earth for some, life in hell after death for others) that can only be mitigated by regular adoration of him and the slaughtering of countless birds and animals (to say nothing of the firstborn children who were very likely slaughtered earlier on) so that their blood could be offered as a sacrifice. Salvation is available only by faith or by works. When that doesn't seem to do the trick, God sends down his own child to be slaughtered on behalf of everyone; but, because that seems just too simple, God makes it possible for anyone to get the "Advance to Go" card only if he or she either utterly believes that (a) that's what God was really doing (salvation by faith) or (b) God gave the church the right to decide who gets salvation by carefully distributing the sacraments of grace, and she or he goes to receive those sacraments regularly (salvation by works). Pondering that précis discloses an incredibly capricious and masochistic God in whom I can't imagine anyone actually wanting to believe. And if our rational minds, as a result of our study and reflection, have rejected the concept that we are inherently sinful and then its corollary—that we need and can receive redemption from some outside source—the doctrine of original sin and its counterpart salvation, whether by faith or works, becomes nonsense.

## Your Personal Share of the World's Sins

There are few of us, however, who in our most private, reflective moments don't doubt our absolute goodness. Whether it is the result of years of chronic emotional abuse at the hands of the church or the pervasiveness of its most destructive doctrines throughout Western culture, most of us, by the time we've hit adulthood (and often long before) have deeply entrenched feelings of inadequacy and unworthiness. And in the course of a normal week, we find plenty of fodder upon which those feelings can feed. We stumble. We fail. We make mistakes. We hurt ourselves and others. We yell at our kids. We ogle the neighbour's wife (or husband). We wish our parents would die. We're jealous of our friend's happiness. We fill our bodies to the bursting point with plastic food, pharmaceuticals, legal and illegal (alcohol and crack) consciousness-altering drugs. We put other people down so that we can feel better about ourselves. We aren't pretty or good-looking enough, strong or healthy enough to prove to ourselves that we are blessed. Or, on the other side of the coin, we're not generous enough, loving enough; we don't give enough to charity; we're too absorbed in our middle-class privilege. Wherever our minds settle, we are not worthy.

Our culture picks up on our fears of inadequacy and builds us up with the mantra "You deserve. . . ." When we really think we are undeserving, it offers us a rich market of "affirmations" that will do it for us. The school of positive thinking (its most recent incarnation is the book *The Secret*) dangerously tells us to believe we are worth getting anything we want badly enough and if we believe totally, perfectly, unceasingly, we will get it. We only have to believe in ourselves and our inherent worth. If we don't get it, we manage to confirm our original belief that we really weren't worth it or we blame ourselves for not believing enough. The ego-building industry, built on the solid foundations of our own per-ceptions of unworthiness, has been safely in the black for years.

Set down into a culture of pervasive self-loathing, the belief that someone somewhere sees us as perfect and whole and for-given despite every screw-up we've ever accomplished is a very, very powerful thought. It is cleansing, healing, and restorative. It is transformative. Lives are made whole. They are saved. I've seen it. I've felt it.

Any evangelicals worth their salt, after reading those last few sentences, have promptly tipped their chairs back from the table and declared victory. The transformation of so many lives stands, in an evangelical mind, as sure proof of God's eternal goodness and love. Salvation, in such a mind, is a once and for all grace. You feel that forgiveness, you acknowledge it comes from God through Jesus, and you're saved. And once you get salvation, you keep it. Roman Catholics would join our evangelical friends in arguing that those who feel their burdens lifted after a soul-baring confes-sion and mass are undeniable proof of Jesus' redemptive work.

Wait just a minute. Rewind the tape. Now where did all the weight of that unworthiness come from to begin with? Let's see . . . . We're told a book called the Bible is the word of the most powerful God, and it tells us that we are sinful by nature and can't do anything worth doing without his help. Hmm. Let me check this out. Yep! It works. I'm feeling lousy about myself all over again!

Could it not be that what is lifted from our shoulders in those powerful moments is not our own unworthiness but the weight of the doctrines of the church? And could it not be that when we are told it is gone forever, we experience overwhelming joy? Or could it not be that if we are told it is gone only for a few days that we will feel compelled to return and receive again whatever it is that has taken that weight away? Whether temporarily lifted by the Catholic priest or permanently excised by the born-again experience of salvation, the release from such a burden is powerful beyond measure. The human spirit is immense. Its suppression is heinous. If it has really only ever been those doctrines that have weighed us down so pitiably, wouldn't it be a much better idea, a much more humane idea, a much more loving idea, to just offer up the truth about them to all and sundry and start nurturing a society of humans that acknowledge, not only their own, but their neighbour's dignity?

Yet the church seems bent on continuing to lay the phenomenal weight of doctrinal sin upon the shoulders of humanity rather than take it upon itself. Even in moderate liberal congregations where the idea of salvation is more corporate than personal, the sacraments are laden with the melodic language of another time and draw the unsuspecting participant, through the use of communal responses and actions, into complicity with the initial intent of the rites. The *kyrie*, often set to incredibly stirring and evocative music, underscores the dreadful, sinful state from which only Jesus' intercession can save us.

For many, new words offer a necessary departure from the history out of which the sacrament has grown and allow them to participate in something that would otherwise be only a negative experience for them. Guests at a Sunday service once confessed their desire to bolt when they found, much to their dismay, that communion was to be served. Neither of them had taken communion in years, being unable to stomach its routine theological propositions. But before they could make their way back out of their seats, the service began and courtesy held them fast.

Because these guests were excruciatingly aware of what was being said, they experienced the act of communion differently than others might have. They listened to the words rather than lost themselves in the actions. Once we open our ears to the traditional liturgical words, we find them utterly offensive—as we should. And because it was the words that had offended these guests elsewhere, finding a place where the words had integrity and were not connected with sin, sacrifice, and atonement, they could experience the gift of communion as a celebration of community, of our commitment to live in community.

Can the sacraments ever be anything other than what they were initially intended to be? When we change the words, strip the sacrificial overtones from the rituals and symbols, do we really rinse them clean of the power they have come to wield? Can we make them something beautiful or will the stain of original sin always be present in the reflection of the baptismal basin or smeared like blood across the table? I expect that, no matter what we say, communion will still have a strong emotional power for those for whom it brings solace. And for those for whom the words are only offensive, I hope that, along with the awakening that made them so, came the realization that there will be no need for the sacraments in the next incarnation of church. In the meantime, should they find themselves presented with communion in the midst of a worshipping community, I hope the words through which it is offered celebrate the beauty of their own whol-i-ness.

# RESPONSIBLE CHANGE

## FREEDOM WITH INTEGRITY

There is going to be trouble. No doubt about it. Start tinkering with worldviews, the symbols that bolster them, the language that classifies them, and the security systems that reinforce them, and it's bound to get ugly. We know that.

Our habitual behaviour in such situations is to duck. Or skirt the issue. Or point to someone else as the culprit. We don't like the mess, and we don't like being blamed for it.

But the mess is well underway; the only way out is through, and we're going to get blamed anyway. The best case scenario is to make our way to the other side without having sold ourselves out or too far short in the process. If we're going to manage that, we're going to need to be very aware of what it is we're doing and what it is we want.

## SLOWLY, SLOWLY . . .

A most endearing trait of small children is their ability to play make-believe, to enter into a story or a role and completely take it over as reality. Their world, originally only tangible and very concrete, begins to incorporate those things that are not visible and cannot be touched. As they hear adults and other children around them speak of these things, ideas join the world developing in their minds. At that young age, however, between about three and seven, they are as yet unable to distinguish between reality and imagination, and so they easily succumb to the cultural and religious behaviours and taboos that are suggested to them.

Some of the magical make-believe adults encourage children to develop are the ideas of the Tooth Fairy or Santa Claus. Television introduces them to purple dinosaurs and big blue dogs. Storks bring little brothers and sisters. Toys are marketed to reinforce the pretend world in which children play and develop. And while the wonderful world of Disney enchants them with fairies and talking animals, the religious concepts of the child's family are also being assimilated. These might include angels who care for them, the idea of a God who sees them and wants them to be good, or even Jesus at their bedside keeping watch over them at night. The child uses the various "realities" presented to her or him to begin the building of her or his worldview. Much of what is presented is sweet and lovely, but there is also much that can create in the child a deep fear of what cannot be seen, things over which she or he has no control.

I can remember my father using what I eventually learned to be a simple telephone trick in order to have it appear that the North Pole was returning his call so he could report on how bad my siblings and I had been. It is such a common threat that I'm sure he never once thought it was inappropriate; most people don't. But when I had children of my own, I tried hard to avoid making the link between their behaviour and Santa's benevolence (they picked it up anyway—thank you, socialization).

## Stages of Faith—Early Assumptions

These early assimilations of fantasy and religious belief constitute the first in developmental psychologist James Fowler's *Stages of*

*Faith.* As we turn our attention to what church can be, Fowler's stages are helpful. His straightforward categories clarify the changes we each encounter as we reflect upon and develop our faith. They also point toward hope, both for individuals struggling with faith issues and for the church as it seeks a credible and responsible future.

An integration of existing theories of cognitive and moral development, Fowler's stages initially progress in close association with chronological age. By the age of seven, most children start to differentiate between the real and imagined worlds, and they move from Fowler's Intuitive-Projective stage into a new phase. Here, beginning to understand that some things don't really exist, children are persuaded to belief by the authorities in their lives. A layer of requisite belief is added to the child's understanding. Indeed, in order to prove that one's belief satisfies parental concerns, the child learns to participate in the traditions of ritual and symbol being handed to them. Fowler calls this stage Mythic-Literal. As the child learns to distinguish between reality and imagination but faces a very real inability to affirm the reality of the beliefs held by his or her parents, he or she is forced to integrate myth literally and rely upon its truth despite experienced contradictions.

Throughout the school years, the child continues to check its place against those in authority, usually parents, but increasingly institutional leaders and peers. Each time she or he checks, the push to conform is reinforced. Thus does the child, by the time adulthood is reached, grow into Fowler's third stage, Synthetic-Conventional. Each belief has now been integrated into the reality of the young adult's life. She or he has learned how to express it, how to live it out, and how to affirm it when seen in others.

Here's where chronological and faith stage parallels end. Most people make it to the third stage and stay there. They have synthesized the belief system that surrounds them and established a comfort with it. Here is where conventional beliefs become the norm. Others who share your beliefs are known to you even if you don't know them. What you believe is straightforward, unchallenged, and simply there.[1] Marcus Borg calls this stage "pre-critical naïveté."[2] Questions are unnecessary and, in all likelihood, not even raised.

Many who live in this stage remain in it until they die. Their belief system, perfectly laid out to handle any of life's big questions, is sufficient for them no matter what happens. Very little can shake it, and, as we've seen before, as an established worldview, maintaining its homeostasis is important. Indeed, remaining committed to their beliefs despite what happens is applauded by the community as a sign of a strong and true faith.

When you walk into a church, the community that has gathered is all about reinforcing third-stage beliefs. We might even say that this is the chief purpose of Sunday morning services—to reinforce the belief systems that are assimilated at an early age by most Christians. Language, behaviours, readings, symbols, are all geared to this purpose. Very little is presented that would challenge it.

## Experiencing the Crash

But the beliefs peculiar to the Christian faith system and to many others, I would warrant, can sometimes be found to be contradictory and even downright insufficient. When we bury a child, see children abused by hands that should guide them, watch those we love struggle with depression or uncontrolled bipolar disorders or fade into the ravages of Alzheimer's before our eyes, when death comes only after prolonged periods of pain and suffering, the concept of a benevolent deity with a plan becomes a difficult one to hang on to. When we try to balance our delightful Sikh or Muslim neighbour with Christianity's exclusive claim to salvation, our desire to have the best for our own children with the reality that those on the other side of the world (or the other side of town, for that matter) starve for lack of basic necessities, it is difficult for us to keep in place the structures that have protected our self-indulgence.

Those who are challenged by such inconsistencies and inadequacies, something that can usually happen when accumulated life experience adds up to about thirty or forty years, find themselves in a position of danger. Often it includes a frightening free-fall right into the most difficult of Fowler's faith stages. This powerful stage, Marcus Borg's period of "critical thinking," challenges, reorients, and often destroys what has up until that point helped make sense of the world.

Much of this book, so far, has been focused on dropping you into the fast-flowing waters of dis-belief if you weren't already there. The undertow you will experience is what Fowler calls stage four: Individuative-Reflective. He means it. As one reflects on one's belief systems and the realities that life presents, the questions that begin to coalesce separate one from one's community by challenging what has been accepted as true. The consequent isolation can be a painful experience.

The challenges that "critical thinking" presents are similar across the board, but the experience of those challenges can be radically different. For those in the liberal Christian world, church has often only augmented the rest of their lives—it has been a part, not the whole. Church fellowship activities may have been a significant part of their social lives but not ones intricately connected to their religious beliefs. For them, the fall into stage four or "critical thinking" might be likened to that first big step taken by a novice parachutist—fear-tinged but exhilarating. Many reach out for new understandings, hungrily grasping everything they can find and milking it for every last bit of knowledge it can provide.

Those who have been enveloped within the safety of the evangelical world, however, are giving up a worldview that has ordered a much larger portion of their lives. Social activities, music, friends, and life-goals have often been nurtured by and synchronized with their beliefs. Questions present a very real threat to everything they have ever known and understood to be true. Within some religious groups, questions bring on efforts by others in the community to reinforce the established belief system. Friends and family members try to bring the individual back into the fold. Those who remain unmoved can be labelled apostates, permanently disqualified from the eternal life that came with their former belief. As belief crumbles, often family ties, friends, and profession also turn to dust. Loss is incredible. Isolation can be frighteningly huge.

Many who remain within stage four become bitter, angry, suspicious, and mistrusting. Up until whatever precipitated their questions, they had happily accepted what had been taught and upheld by the authoritative figures in their lives. It had formed the ground upon which they walked. It had been essential to their understanding of the ordered universe. The rejection of those beliefs wipes out their security. It is no surprise that anger is a very real part of the experience of this disintegration of belief. Adults are realizing that those they trusted lied to them.

It may be that many who were our teachers truly believed what they told us. They are forgiven. All pupils should reach for understanding that exceeds that of their teachers. Ignorance, however, is becoming less and less excusable as contemporary (and not so contemporary) scholarship is found to be utterly accessible in every sphere of life. Those who did not and do not believe in the many doctrinal concessions one has to make to be a leader within an ecclesial institution, in exactly the same manner as those parents who propagated a myth to their children, are spinning tales and reinforcing lies that the church has been telling for a very long time. When one learns that, when one comes to a place where one actually believes that, anger is only a hair's breadth behind. This should not come as a surprise.

A few of years ago, an Anglican bishop at a Diocesan Council meeting consisting of area bishops, church officials and lay members, reminded them that, when thinking of potential candidates for a then-vacant area bishopric, they should be looking for someone who held an orthodox perspective. He then looked around the table and, along with all the other bishops, chortled. A lay representative who was present was perplexed as to why they had laughed and mentioned his confusion in a conversation we had. I am fairly certain that I know why they laughed, and I don't find it funny. Perpetuating lies that safeguard one's position at the expense of others is not a funny matter.

One has only to consider the rift in the Anglican Communion between its Western bishops and its African bishops, and it becomes evident that the comedy may yet have a tragic ending. The bishops of the West, who have long been exploring the questions and their many and varied answers, find it hard to respond without sputtering when their African colleagues, to whom the West has much more recently spun the ageless story, angrily hold on to their beliefs.[3] The Lambeth Conference, at which bishops from the whole of the Anglican Communion gather every decade or so, has been, in the past, when bishops have hissed at those with whom they do not agree, what Bishop John Shelby Spong calls, "anything but an example of Christian community."[4] The conference called for 2008 will stretch the communion dramatically as it seeks to support diametrically oppositional beliefs.

Fowler suggests that many remain in the space of betrayal and anger, and, should we look around us, those people aren't hard to find. A 2006 newsletter of a community association of secular humanists included a piece by a young man searching for a humanist organization that wasn't entirely made up of old, angry men and women consuming all their time denigrating the church. He was looking for a community with which he could explore new ideas, argue and refine developing hypotheses, and think about the big questions life presents; but he was only able to find people who were still furious because they had found out the church had lied to them. His article urged them to get over it. I hope they will.

The recent spate of books by atheists, such as Richard Dawkins' *The God Delusion* and Christopher Hitchens' *God Is Not Great*, slap many Christians in the face with their vitriolic tone. While they offer much in the way of clarifying belief, because their pastoral skills are wanting, they will earn themselves few converts. A. C. Grayling, on the other hand, concludes *Against All Gods* with "An Essay on Kindness." It is in the vein of that essay that we are able to move beyond hurt and anger.

## Moving On

Symptoms of a move to the next stage begin with a coalescing of comfort with ambiguity. No longer having access to all the right answers and coming to recognize that one is not going to find them, individuals enter Fowler's Conjunctive stage. Things begin to come together again. The fragmentation, chaos, and much of the fear is overcome. Beyond anger, the individual is now able to return to the symbols and myths of his or her original belief system and find meaning and value in them—well, *some* of them. No longer held as factual, these bits and pieces of a former worldview are freed from the necessity of proof into a realm of mythic symbolism.

Fowler notes that, at this stage, the individual also begins to see beyond his or her own culture and people. Here, Fowler coincides with Lawrence Kohlberg's fifth stage of moral development wherein the individual broadens his horizon beyond his own tribe and, perhaps, even his own species.* Because so much of religious belief has been grounded in distinguishing oneself from others, as it falls away, so, too, do those distinctions. The concept of justice reaches far beyond just doing what's right by one's own people; it extends to everyone. The individual is in a stage of rapid consciousness-raising. The world looks very different than it did before; indeed, one's former perspective and those held by one's former peers are now seen as parochial, narrow, and even ridiculous. Were one still in stage four, one might even chortle.

The symbols and myths of one's former tradition become the tools by which the individual continues to explore his world. The mythic symbolism behind them can help to spiritually focus him on growth, a process that can be simplified because of the familiarity of the tools. Communion, for instance, can draw one into a deeper commitment to living in community. Candlelighting can be a call to contemplation of life's mysteries. Walking a labyrinth is resurrected as a tool for discernment, seeking out the wisdom of a variety of choices. Knowing that there is no efficacy in the item itself, one is opened to its effectiveness as a tool for spiritual growth and development in one's own life.

Marcus Borg calls this place "post-critical naïveté" and provides many options for the conversion of classical understandings to metaphorical understandings in his various books. Moving from the relative safety of "pre-critical naïveté" through the difficult and tumultuous period of "critical thinking," we are now, he argues, able to reinterpret our stories as myth and our actions as symbolic. Borg suggests we can then continue to use the same

---

*Kohlberg developed an expansive cognitive structural theory of morality that revitalized and altered the direction of the field. Kohlberg (1969, 1976) postulates a six-stage sequential typology of moral rules, beginning with punishment-base obedience, evolving through opportunistic self-interest, approval-seeking conformity, respect for authority, contractual legalistic observance, and culminating in principled morality based on standards of justice. "Social Cognitive Theory of Moral Thought and Action," *Handbook of Moral Behaviour and Development*, ed. William M. Kurtines and Jacob L. Gewirtz, vol. 1. (Hillsdale, NJ: Lawrence Erlbaum Associates, 1991), 47.

language, tools, and symbols because they are now imbued with new meaning gleaned during our traipse through the "critical thinking" stage.

## Looks Like, Smells Like, Wags Its Tale . . .

The church that does as Borg suggests is going to look, smell, sound, and wag its "tale" like a classic stage three Synthetic-Conventional or "pre-critically naïve" operation. But, as you now know, the mainline church and most of its leaders have had access to and assimilated contemporary scholarship some time ago. They've traversed that scary land of the big questions and come out the other side. Using Borg's logic, they have changed only what they mean, not what they say or do. Having done so, they believe they hold no culpability for the ongoing spiritual desiccation of their parishioners.

It has proven extremely convenient for church leaders, and for all who wish to retain the perception of security fostered in the comforts of stage three, that the accoutrements of the "post-critical naïveté" look just like what we've been using all along. Most people in the church don't know and can't tell the difference between the story of the virgin birth presented literally and the story of the virgin birth presented metaphorically. Ditto the salvation, resurrection, and all the other theojargon we've examined. It has been too easy to just switch the meaning and keep the wording.

Granted, those in the pews may, as a result of study groups, DVDs, and good reading, be entirely with Borg on this one, eager to experience the forms with which they are familiar in new ways. Worship leaders using archaic language who have before them a congregation eager to translate every word into a palatable, even mystical new understanding, will argue that they are being contemporary and relevant to their parishioners. That may be the case. And many a layperson will state clearly that she wants things to stay the same while assuming everyone knows she wouldn't ever actually take anything that is said literally.

## Take Me Literally

Literal is anathema to the liberal church. The thought that the scriptures could be interpreted literally has been widely ridiculed by any who have read anything on biblical authorship or context. But before we hasten to take it all metaphorically, which is what I hope we can all eventually do, literal is the state of mind I think we need to sit in for a good long time. The issue is not whether we can use the Bible metaphorically, whether we are able to change the meanings of our symbols, or whether the words of our songs can be understood as spiritual art and not theological truth. The issue is whether we let people know what we're doing. The church has been shirking its responsibility in that area. Remember the elephant.

Presenting to its members, many of whom still see through critically naïve stage-three eyes, what its leaders would identify as post-critical stage five material, spiritual messages based on metaphorical interpretation of scriptural stories reclaimed as myth is abdicating its responsibilities to the people. Not only does the church keep members from maturing spiritually, it reneges on its ministry to anyone who has explored faith critically and is unwilling or unable to translate everything they hear on a Sunday morning.

The future of the church is in no way certain. Borg knows that. Perhaps, convinced of its demise, he is recommending the most comfortable palliative process as any good doctor would do, seeking to mitigate the pain. A peaceful death is a more beautiful one. Struggling to breathe or make one's way free of the tubes is so ungainly. If the church is going to die, let it die nobly.

I believe, however, that there can be a very great role for the church to play in the world's ongoing evolution if it finds a way to (a) access the wells of spiritually nurturing material in the Bible and present it *as* myth or metaphor, identifying it as such *in the same breath*, and (b) develop material for spiritual nurture that does not need ecclesial, theological, Christological, biblical, or any other kind of "religious" language.

In order to minister to the growing number of people who are no longer content with classical Christian material—readings, sacraments, songs—presented in a manner that allows them to appear to be literally believed, the church will have to learn ways to deal with that material in a way that can offer metaphor but present it with integrity. While it sounds as though leaders will be making abrupt disclaimers here and there throughout the service, breaking any sense of continuity or flow, it doesn't need to happen that way.

Think, for example, of the story of Jesus coming to the disciples over the water. It would not take a doctoral degree in homiletics to preach a sermon about that passage, using it as a metaphor for rising above our fears and challenges. The preacher might develop the idea of the water as our subconscious, seeking to undermine our conscious efforts and controlling the choices we make. Only when we rise above that pull, knowing it for what it is, can we achieve our goals safely and surely.

Not bad. But think back to an exercise from Chapter Three. Someone (it was you in that early chapter) is attending the church who has never been there before. She's new to church, in fact. She's come because her relationship is teetering on the edge of disaster, and it is causing her incredible stress, stress which is undermining her confidence in the volunteer social-justice work she does when she is not caring for developmentally challenged teenagers during her day job. She's about at her limit, and she believes that she might get some strength from an hour or two of spiritually uplifting time "just for her."

The message would have a lot to say to her at that particular time in her life. However, if the reading of the gospel passage is followed with a declaration that it is the Word of God and that's going to cause her to pause, she won't be able to get past the references to the miracle of Jesus walking on the water. If he needed a miracle, wasn't she going to need one, too? But life has taught her that miracles don't happen to ordinary people. She slips out the side door, and the preacher doesn't get to meet her.

Make a few changes to the story, however, and see what happens. First of all, drop the constant reminder that this is God's word. We've already dealt with that, almost everyone in the liberal church knows it, and it is boringly repetitive. If you have to say something, write something new and vibrant. Here's one to try out: "We read this passage that in it, we might find wisdom for our journey." "Amen." There, now you don't have an excuse.

That problem dealt with, the preacher inserts the following few sentences into his or her message: "The author of this gospel sought to convince his (it was almost always a guy) readers that Jesus was God and added flourishes to the story handed down to him. In this case, what we've often called a miracle was introduced to remind people of the powers they believed at that time God to have. We no longer attribute such powers to God. We know about currents and air pressure and what creates storms. So we read this story not as a miracle story, but as a legend that can tell us more about ourselves."

It is simple. It doesn't overtake the message. It is over in less than a minute. But adding it makes an incredible difference to the experience that one can have in a Sunday morning service. Honesty and integrity come through first and foremost, and they are both necessary requisites for the church of the future.

Of course, if no one else in the church knows that the writers of the Gospels were using second- or third-hand stories, that the preacher believes neither in the miracles nor God's control over the weather, if they've never heard the word *legend* used in reference to the good book, look for some flack. It'll be on its way before the coffee hour is over.

## Simple Shifts

What does this mean for Sunday morning gatherings? To be sure, they won't be the same. The overall layout doesn't have to be all that foreign, but the content needs to change substantially. Each and every piece of the Christian tradition, when held up against the reality that the Bible is not the authoritative word of God for all time (TAWOGFAT), must be rigorously scrutinized for its message and purpose in church services. Here are a few examples.

At the end of prayer, we often say, "In Jesus' name, Amen." To conclude any petitionary prayer with that statement has a very specific meaning, perhaps long forgotten as its significance dwindled. It is included because we recognized that we were unworthy of standing before the face of God. Our prayers could not get to God if we sent them up there ourselves. The only way that our prayers could be heard is because Jesus had made us worthy through his atoning sacrifice. Because of that and that only, we could expect that our prayers would be heard and answered. To ensure that happened, we clearly stated that they were presented "In Jesus' name" as he instructed us to do (John 15:16).

After the presentation of the offering, many congregations sing some form of the Doxology: "Praise God, from whom all blessings flow; Praise him, all creatures here below; Praise Him above ye Heavenly Host; Praise Father, Son, and Holy Ghost."[5] (One woman in my congregation, even though she was open to the introduction of progressive elements into the worship space, so loved the old words of the Doxology that she continued to sing them regardless of what others were singing.) It is regularly argued that all that we have comes from God and that our offerings are a thanksgiving back to God. Such a belief makes for a strong stewardship program to raise funds in a congregation, but its implication is that we, who have so much, are somehow more blessed than those who have so little. God has, for some reason, maybe our race or our nationality, granted that we have a larger chunk of the pie. No, that can't be it, there are lots of people in your own country that are poor and, for that matter, a lot of them have the same colour of skin as you do. The Doxology, in this context, seems to offer up a thanksgiving for something we should not be able to so easily reconcile.

Some time ago we became sensitized to the inappropriateness of the concept of missions and have all but eliminated the idea of "Christianizing nations" from our understanding of our work around the globe. We speak of partner churches and mutuality in mission. But we still sing of bringing the light to the nations in our hymns, as though when we put something to music it doesn't mean the same thing any more.

Our baptism liturgies have always had that ring of washing away sin even though we have long since acknowledged, or was it just wishful thinking, that we are not born in sin and that, since that's true, we don't really need that hyped-up salvation we've been plugging all these years. In fact, the Bible says nothing about infant baptism and speaks only of the baptism of believers. So take another look at what we're making baptismal candidates and parents say, and ask whether it is still appropriate given what we believe about original sin and salvation.

When people come to church, they come to be fed, held, and supported spiritually so that the rest of their lives have some sort of meaning. That is what it is all about. And, while the words and the movements and the stated authority must all be examined, we have the skills and the resources to do that and to create new forms and meaningful ritual. All we really need is the courage to make the change.

## There's More

Fowler's stages don't stop, as do Borg's, at this post-critically naïve place. They call us further. They call the church to a greater mission. He plants a sixth stage, Universalizing Faith, that grows out of the previous spiritual development individuals have undergone. Here, true wonders exist. Individuals who achieve the sixth level of faith development are leaders in the quest for spiritual communion. Perhaps the characteristic that is most indicative of them is the absence of a desire for self-preservation. The awareness of the unity of all things destroys the self's need for survival. Caught without a requisite context by which it recognizes itself, it can expand beyond any borders previously identifying it. Language becomes clearer, metaphors are enriched when they are identified as such, and more people are able to connect with messages that challenge and support them in their struggles to live compassionately.

Fowler's ultimate stage in faith development is where I believe the church should be as an institution. It should be able to hold the role of leader, calling us to greater compassion and justice, challenging us to walk the way of love, and forging for us a path. Good spiritual leaders do that. They help individuals stretch themselves to embrace the challenges that less travelled paths offer. Many leaders in the church are prepared and eager to be responsible spiritual leaders in this manner, placing before the rest of us the possibilities to which we can each aspire. The church, in its denominational forms, must support its leaders' attempts, protect them from the criticism of their myopic and frightened peers and congregants, and provide them with the time and resources they will need to recreate what it means to be a church and develop new "*a*theologies" and commentaries on virtue instead of on ancient texts and fragments of texts.

This final, expansive stage in faith development shares with the former stage a deep sense of compassion. For the individual in it, the lack of self-preservation in the religious context means that there is no longer any need to use exclusively the tools, beliefs, and symbols of one's own tradition for spiritual deepening. Many tools may even become unnecessary. Here in the context of seeking out harmony with all things, the purest understanding of those values that enhance and sanctify life becomes the foremost spiritual practice. We call it love, radically inclusive love. It is here, in the caring, challenging, prophetic role with which it is so familiar, that the church can really shine.

## CREATING A SPIRITUAL TOOLBOX

As with all words, *toolbox* resides in the ear of the beholder. We all have different memories and experiences that will bring an image to mind when the word is heard. Perhaps you have an image of an uncovered wooden box, the handle greased and worn with age, rising above two large, solid compartments on either side. Or maybe you see a faded red metal box, the lock bent and never used, the paint chipped and dulled. Maybe it's a brilliant yellow plastic box with handy snap-lidded compartments built into the top. Or your toolbox might be an old treasured one handed down to you from a previous generation of fix-it-uppers or one as new as your own dreams of proficiency.

My father didn't have a toolbox. He had a whole garage. And a basement. And a cellar. Come to think of it, he had a neighbouring garage, too. And if my mother wasn't diligent enough, he covered any horizontal surface he could lay something down upon, often meaning that the dining room table, the tops of both the piano and the refrigerator, the arms of his favourite chair, and the floor were covered with the implements of the carpenter, machinist, mechanic, and handyman. When it came to tools, my father was a pluralist.

And so, in our home, there was a tool for everything. I mean *everything.* How many of you had your own key-cutting machine in the basement? Well, we did. No matter what it was you needed to do—rewire a lamp, turn a spindle, bend a wire hanger into the beginnings of a Halloween costume—my father had a tool that was made for just that purpose.

When I describe the church of the future as a spiritual toolbox, that's the kind of toolbox I mean. Not the traditional hammer, rasp, and a-couple-of-screwdrivers kind of a toolbox, but a messy, take-over-the-house one—one that, no matter what it is you need, you'll have a tool that can do the job. The only challenge, of course, will be the same one that perpetually faced my father—knowing where to find it.

The church holds tightly to a toolbox designed according to the principles of what is often called Baruch's Law: "When all you have is a hammer, everything starts to look like a nail." Bernard Baruch, an influential twentieth-century American financier, noted that if a business is proficient in only one method of dealing with issues that arise, all the issues that do arise eventually come to be seen as ones that are *supposed* to be dealt with using that particular method. Despite the promulgation of many varieties of spiritual expression, diverse personal and communal needs, myriad ways in which individuals and congregations interact with the communities around them, the church continues to see in every situation a single challenge and a single way to meet it: to discern God's will and to act in accordance with it.

Rick Warren, in his evangelically energetic book *The Purpose Driven Church*, breaks congregational life into five different areas—worship, fellowship, discipleship, evangelism, and service.[6] In each of these areas, the church has sought to know God's will. How should we worship? How should we be in our relationships? What is essential truth and how do we teach it? What is our calling in the world, and what is the most important thing we can do? All of these questions are answered through a process of discernment, a process of distilling out of all the complexities of life, the Bible, canonical law, and pastoral realities, and finding just what it is that God wants us to do. "What does the Lord require of us?" is the most prominent classic refrain in church meetings, worship services, mission activities, education programs, and marketing programs; and it is now made available to a new generation in the form of silicone bracelets stamped with WWJD—What Would Jesus Do? If you wonder about the answer to this question, the church opens its arms and offers you a time-tested way to find the answer. They are the experts in God's will. Just ask them.

Questions about the meaning of life in general and our lives in particular, however, are human questions. Those who seek the answers are those who embrace the complexities of life and, despite the challenges, set out upon a road winding through terrain that imbues all of life with meaning. It is a road that should be broad and wide with many different ways to tread its surface. Perhaps, to make the metaphor more appropriate, it might even be seen to be many different roads. But the church, because it knows only one way to see, interpret, and respond, repeats the question back to us in its theocentric language, and we find ourselves adopting its version of the existential quest. Once enfolded within the bosom of the church, our question is no longer about the meaning of life but what it is that *God* wants, what the *Lord* requires, what *God's* eternal plan is for the world, corporately or me personally. The church refocuses our quest so that its particular approach is the one that can provide the most suitable response. After all, if it's a question about what God wants, who better to advise than God's representatives here on Earth?

But the church's toolbox has been too small. The signs of its inadequacy are evident all around us and have been since we first welcomed someone from another tribe to join us around our fire. Diversity of belief, understanding, perspective, and of the practice of those things has existed since we evolved into social beings.

It may be that we have, since that first shared-fire experience, tried to deal with them using the same tools, the same questions, the same formulaic responses, but we have not been successful because it can only ever be an unsuccessful endeavour.

The church has long fancied itself one of the places, if not the only place, that one can find nurture and sustenance upon the spiritual journey. Struggling with existential questions is its forte. Although it has given the same response to that question for the past couple of thousand years, if it is able to accomplish a quick, albeit costly upgrade, it may yet still prove to be one of the best places to undertake just such a journey.

Being able to offer spiritual guidance in a postmodern world will be difficult though. The church's reliance on classical theological reasoning, which assumes both the presence of a divine being and the church's arrogant stance as its interpreter, leaves it little to work with when both of those foundational beliefs are undermined. Not only does it have to acknowledge, as it must in our pluralistic world, that it does not have a direct line to God, it has to cope with the ultimate result of postmodern critique—the dis-integration of the concept of god altogether.

The late socialist sociologist T. R. Young in an online publication, *The Drama of the Holy,*[7] provides clarity around what the church's role might be in the future, not by describing an institution that may rise from the ashes of the current ecclesia, but by presenting a concept of god that allows for and acknowledges its human conception and construction. Young sees all life imbued with what he calls the holy. Our responsibility is to lift up that holiness. To identify that as our work is to create god. Not "god" as anything real that exists separately and distinct from us, other than the real articulation of an ideal, but as a collection of those ideals that pull us up from our loathsome self-preservation tendencies toward the recognition that we can best preserve the future for those who will follow us by seeing and honouring the holy in our world, and in those with whom we share it, and seeking to preserve that holiness. That "god" is very real and is something in which we can believe, something we can love, something to die for; but it is not something that loves us, believes in us, or creates for us pastoral afterlives toward which we dutifully march. Unlike the former God, this one has no agency. Not only do we know that, we are able to acknowledge it.

For Young, as for many postmodern and progressive Christians, there remains much within existing religious systems that is worthy of being carried into whatever future might unfold before us. The concept of morality is perhaps the most important gift religious systems bequeath to this new, human undertaking. The morality of religious systems has challenged us to live for that which transcends ourselves—usually a deity but often, too, those things that would concern that deity, such as the poor, the weak, and the downtrodden. Young acknowledges, however, that morality in a postmodern world no longer exists as an objective reality. Any one particular moral perspective, in a world where nothing can be regarded as the absolute truth, might be either upheld as right or cast down as illegitimate. In a world in which we must consult myriad perspectives to ascertain the truth, it is impossible to name one moral position as absolute.

Young manoeuvred his way through this relativist argument by placing values on the moral proposals before us and calling us to choose those we would identify with the values that are the most life-enhancing not only for ourselves but for the earth and for all life upon it. We must recognize all life and the earth as holy and seek to preserve both as best we can. If we do not do this work, we consign ourselves to a nightmare of personal, social, and planetary destruction, a world in which power and privilege have no moral consequence despite the dire results they manifest in all that cannot survive against them. This, then, is the work that is demanded of the church in the postmodern world—to identify that which is holy, to uphold those values that would preserve it, and to challenge us to live according to them in a way that ensures holiness remains in our lives and in our world.

This new church work will be engaged by those who are spiritually aware of its import, who are quite willing to honour what is identified as a humanly constructed god. The church's new mission then will be to develop spiritual awareness in individuals and communities around the world. Its new evangelism will be to introduce and support the living out of these humanly identified principles to those in relationship with it, that is, everyone. Spreading the news of their import for us, our children, and the planet will be a key task. Charged with living out this radically ethical mandate, the church will have to be deeply responsive to the needs of each constituency in which it offers its message, seeking first to find the holy within the context rather than applying a definition of holy derived elsewhere.

I don't recommend actually using the term *god*, at least not in the short term. Perhaps my made-up word, *pyntrilm*, won't work either. But without a constant reiteration of a postmodern meaning for "god," it will continue to be laden with anthropomorphic features and the powerful agency of an otherworldly being. And since the percentage of people who believe in that anthropomorphic all-powerful being far exceeds the number who actually go to church, even were we to change the message given from every pulpit in every land this coming Sunday, it will take an awfully long time to get the word out that we've remade god and, this time, it's for the better.

With a new mission and consequent evangelistic message, the church will, of course, need some retooling. It is interesting to note, however, that its old hammer, discerning the will of God, is still useful in the new paradigm. The only difference is that, this time, we're not pretending to be able to understand the will of a cosmic being that doesn't exist. In the postmodern church, we're looking for what our small-g god—the humanly constructed set of life-enhancing values we strive to uphold—challenges us to do. What will bring about the most life-enhancement for all? What leaves the earth best able to heal from our misuse of its resources? What is the choice that manifests the best not only for our time but for generations to come? Discerning the answers to these questions will be enormously important for us. Providing us a place in which we can develop the strength to challenge ourselves to make the right choices, the courage to confront one another when we do not, and the grace to move into new healing relationships is an essential role for the church. These are things the church knows well how to do. With language that reflects this new understanding, a variety of "tools" with which to do the work, and a newfound humility, the church can offer a great deal that can help us cope with the postmodern crumbling of so much that has been familiar and comforting.

# CRUCIAL CHANGE

## FULFILLING A RESPONSIBILITY

If I had a nickel for every time I wanted someone else to take responsibility for whatever mess I found myself in, well, you know the punchline. It simply doesn't happen. A sentimental Hollywood technique, having someone else pick up your mistakes and take credit for them rarely happens in real life.

So while it may be easy and even exciting to link our arms together, shackle ourselves to the front gates of the church, and chant challenges at the ecclesial structures and those who maintain them, if we really want to make any change happen in the church, we are going to have to do it ourselves. It is time to roll up our sleeves, get ourselves involved, and make change happen. We may be all we've got.

## PERFECTLY PLACED TO MAKE A DIFFERENCE

### The Big "Why Bother?"

Naturally, there is a big "Why bother?" attached to the suggestion that the church might be salvaged. While many who believe the church's survival is connected to the ongoing will of God and any suggestion that it not continue is blasphemy, there are many others who wonder if it is even worth the effort. Over the course of the last century social institutions have picked up and now provide many of the supports the church once offered. Even its once sacred role as the agent of hatching, matching, and dispatching (baptism, marriage, and burial) has seen a slow and regular attrition rate as the social stigma attached to the first two diminishes and the number of those who choose secular or no services for the latter grows. If social concerns and personal life transitions are adequately covered by secular organizations, then what's the use of church?

I do find it hard to imagine that preserving an institution for preservation's sake itself is anything more than an enormous waste of time and energy. But I do think that the church is well placed to bring about some significant change in the world. And change in the world is desperately needed. A quick example might illustrate the powerful effect the church can have on critical issues facing the planet today.

The year 2003 was the United Nations' International Year of Freshwater, named in an attempt to "to galvanize action on the critical water problems the world faces."[1] In 2005, churches across North America picked up on the emergent concern and cooperated to bring the issue of freshwater resources to their communities of faith. The United Church of Christ, the Presbyterian Church (U.S.A.), the Mennonite Central Committee (all in the United States), Kairos (an ecumenical partnership serving mainline denominations in Canada), and many others focused their mission activities and denominational programming on this important issue. *That* is when concern hit the streets of North America, not before. Whenever I ask a group familiar with the water issue if they had heard of it prior to the programming their church offered, very few respond affirmatively. Most had their consciousness raised through their congregational connections. The impact of that awareness has led, I believe, to pressure being exerted on local governments, restaurants, and multinational corporations to ban the use of bottled drinking water and to act responsibly in drought-stricken areas of the world.

That's the kind of thing that church can do. No other organization has that networking ability. No other organization has that kind of access to adults, many of whom are quite prepared to change their lifestyle if it is going to positively impact the world.

While the list of things perceived to be threatening the future of the church might seem long and even trivial, the list of things threatening the future of the planet is much longer and exponentially more serious. That threat to the planet can be distilled to a single item—humanity. Biologist E. O. Wilson clarifies our impact on the earth in a dramatic way. He tells us that if ants became extinct tomorrow, the earth would begin to die; but if humans became extinct tomorrow, the earth might just begin to heal itself.* That makes it rather difficult to get a handle on how we might be able to create a sustainable future for the planet without shuttling ourselves, and all the damage inherent in our way of life, off to another solar system. And, even if we do get it all right and figure out how to save the planet, the question of whether we will be able to save ourselves from one another will then become the burning issue. We need to address both problems—what we're doing to the earth, and what we're doing to one another—and we need to do it now.

What we're doing to the earth is well documented and rapidly gaining the attention of more and more concerned world citizens. Global warming, even when viewed conservatively, offers

*E. O. Wilson, recipient of one of the 2007 TED awards, continues to point toward the earth's dependence upon *biodiversity*, a term he coined. In his acceptance speech, he stated, "If we were to wipe out insects alone . . . on this planet, which we are trying hard to do, the rest of life, and humanity with it, would mostly disappear from the land and within a few months." Wilson is quoted by David Suzuki, *From Naked Ape to Superspecies: Humanity and the Global Eco-Crisis* (Vancouver, BC: Greystone Books, 2004), 47–8. As North America contemplates the impact of current massive hive losses in bee colonies, Wilson's words ring frighteningly true.

such catastrophic pictures of what the too-near future holds for us to even consider ignoring it.[2] Corporations faced with angry consumers who refuse to allow toxic waste to defile their own backyards have found a willing market for their poison—the developing world.[3] Fragile ecosystems struggle to maintain their homeostasis in the face of pollution, development, and changing weather patterns, each of which is directly related to human activity.[4] What's left of the earth's resources we consume at a rate that would require many more Earths than we will ever have time to discover at the rate we're going.[5] That hasn't stopped the West from assuming its priorities should be those of the world and moving to secure its interests using military and economic methods.[6]

As for what we're doing to one another—HIV/AIDS rises easily to the top of the list through several avenues. A global humanitarian crisis being experienced in dramatic proportions in the developing world, primarily Africa, our response to it discloses wide discrepancies in the accessibility of treatment.[7] Pharmaceutical companies use intellectual property rights laws to profit from the disaster by demanding premium prices for antiretroviral drugs.[8] The dismantling of public health systems as part of the Structural Adjustment Programs required under the terms of loans managed by international monetary organizations, such as the World Bank and the International Monetary Fund, leave the most vulnerable without adequate care.[9] The distribution of wealth has reached unprecedented levels of disparity with 2.5 billion people living on less than $2 per day while less than a thousand people hold assets in excess of $3.5 trillion. Neoliberal globalization contends that economies grow as barriers to trade are reduced or eliminated. However, it is well documented that such growth does not benefit everybody.[10] The combined assets of the world's top three billionaires exceed the gross national product of the world's least developed countries, home to 600 million people.[11]

## We've Evolved Ourselves to Vulnerability

Over the past two hundred years, we have done incredible damage to the earth and its resources. That can't be easily disputed, though there are those who believe the earth is up to the beating. But there is another aspect of the harm we have done that, to my knowledge, has not been systematically explored. That is the question of whether our progress has made it impossible for us to physically evolve. Even if we managed to get ourselves out of the jams we are in environmentally, what we have been doing medically might be playing against us in terms of evolution.

Species evolve as their needs change. Their legs grow longer, their eyes grow better, their hearing develops, and all of it according to the needs they encounter and the genetic advantage that one "mutation" has over another one. At the same time as we have been developing new ways to challenge the earth's equilibrium, we have also been tampering with the unfolding of our own evolutionary path. Each time we use antibiotics, transplant procedures, dental reconstruction, and any one of the hundreds of thousands of medical interventions that exist, we get in the way of natural evolution. The result is that while we have evolved technologically, we have stymied our ability to evolve physically in ways that will allow us to accommodate gradual changes experienced in the environment.

Perhaps the easiest way to point toward our potentially catastrophic veer away from natural selection is to look at the fact that I have two children. Prior to the medical wonder of antibiotics, my feeble, asthmatic lungs and constant childhood bronchitis would have ensured I never made it to reproductive age. Now, another generation will transmit genetic codes that might otherwise have been eliminated for very good natural reasons.[12] Remove access to ever-improving medical technology, and we find ourselves far more vulnerable to disease than our forebears may have been.

It becomes very important in that scenario then for us to be able to find ways to accommodate those gradual changes in our environment without relying on our physical ability to do so. One of the ways we can absorb these new challenges will be by improving our technological ability to deal with them, continuing to develop more and more products and procedures that will assist us (think of sunscreen, for example). The enormous challenge of that solution, however, will be its distribution. As humanity becomes physically less able to adapt to its environment, the way that technological advances are made accessible will be a highly charged ethical debate.

Evolution will no longer be a natural process. For humanity, at least, it will be a technological one. That means it will involve choice. The one process that will allow us to both improve our ability to technologically evolve and to make the correct ethical choices as we do so is that of consciousness-raising. No one seeks to bring about change, to evolve either technologically or ethically, without first being aware of the need for it. When we were evolving in the same manner as life all around us, we didn't have to think about it. Now we do.

As people become aware of their interconnectedness and the inherent value of things outside of themselves, a value that is not contingent upon the "use" to which the "thing" might be put, human or otherwise, respect and responsibility naturally grow. When experiencing the break-neck speed with which world issues sometimes demand such consciousness-raising, I have often longed for periods of time during which the radio would be mute, the television blank, the newspaper yellowed on the doorstep, and my mind safely sheltered within its already rationalized comfort zones. But we cannot afford ourselves the luxury of insulation from these urgent issues or the inattentiveness of busy, distracted lives. It is time to face them straight on, with all the angst and fear that doing so will raise.

When we juxtapose saving the world with saving the church,

however, the latter seems pretty trite. The time and energy put into religious obligation, as distinct from spiritual practice, and the maintenance of religious institutional structures, were it redirected to other humanitarian purposes, would go far toward making substantial inroads into the work of substantive change toward a sustainable future. In my own rather small community of faith, with about 150 worshippers on a Sunday, the number of hours that go into church and church-related activities in a year comes to around twenty thousand, only some of which are given directly to humanitarian efforts. Multiply that by the number of church communities gathering on any given Sunday, and imagine the number of hours put into church by the whole of them. Then start thinking about all the other religious institutions in the world and the amount of time spent on religious activities is mind-boggling.

The work of transforming a religious institution, congregation by congregation, from a religious activity-focused community to a sacred-values or humanitarian or eco-centric spiritual community is unfathomable. But no change happens in the world without the action of an individual or a group of individuals in response to how their consciousness has been raised. And if we could do it, the base we'd have for transformational work would be amazing.

## More Outlets Than Your Favourite Fast Food

If the church has the heart for consciousness-raising work, it certainly has the facilities. A quick Internet search identifies 63 churches within a ten-minute drive of my suburban home and 514 within a ten-minute drive of where I used to live in downtown Toronto. In contrast, there are only half those numbers of public and private schools within the same distances.

Across North America, there is no single organization that can boast the number of sites from which the church does business. Dunkin' Donuts and Tim Hortons, should they wish to reach the full extent of their market, would be envious of the number of outlets the church has managed to establish in every kind of neighbourhood. Without taking the time to research it, I believe it would be safe to say that there is not a community in Canada or the United States of America that does not have a church of some kind in it. The church has ground level access to millions of people. And millions of aware, reflective, conscious people is exactly what this world needs. We just have to figure out how to get the message out to them.

## Essential Conversations

Educator Meg Wheatley explores the transformational nature of conversation in her book *Turning to One Other*, pressing the point that we need to practise these behaviours; we've forgotten how to do conversation well and will have to work to relearn its patterns. The essential principles she notes are that we (1) acknowledge one another as equals; (2) try to stay curious about one another; (3) recognize that it is only with one another's help that we can become better listeners; (4) slow down in order that we have time to think and reflect on what we are thinking; (5) remember that conversation is a natural way for us to communicate; and (6) expect messiness—conversations are difficult and don't always lead to a tidy resolution of difference.[13] The church, placed as it is by its social history and its access to the topic of our spiritual lives, that area of our lives in which values and meaning are pursued, is exactly the place where we could learn such principles as these, practise them, and hold the conversations that are most desperately needed.

## Tools of the Trade

Religious and philosophical traditions have been dealing with the issues of life and death in difficult conversations for the whole of human history. Religion's self-granted mandate has given it purview of exactly these things—pain and suffering, justice and compassion, morality and ethics, values and meaning—those components of our lives relegated to the "spiritual." Leading minds and orators have addressed life's issues in challenging and provocative ways. Weekly, Christian leaders call their people to lives that reflect the values they present. The work of consciousness-raising falls naturally within an area with which the church is most familiar. The arena of sacred values, those principles you can't imagine life without, seems to fall within the part of life to which the church has ready access. Challenging individuals to engage in the discussion of spiritual values is work with which it is indeed familiar and ready to engage. Supporting them as they struggle to live out those values could be the church's new, but very worthy, calling.

## RECONSTRUCTED CHURCH

### "I'm Spiritual, not Religious."

A few decades ago that sentence wouldn't have meant much to anyone. Spirituality and religion were inextricably entwined. Now, as a divide grows between the two, it has become a frequent response to the question about whether someone is a Christian, a Jew, a Muslim, or any one of the dozens of faith traditions to which one might ascribe. People don't like to align themselves with organized religion of any sort. "Religion," seen to be institutional, doctrinal, authoritarian, anti-intellectual, and guilty of crimes and atrocities in the name of faith, has been tainted. "Spirituality," its ethereal, individualistic, anything-goes counterpart, has not. The result is that people who may believe in God or even practise some sort of discipline formerly associated with a religion will use the word *spiritual* before they will ever admit to being *religious*.

Producer Frank Faulk, in a 2005 Canadian Broadcasting Corporation (CBC) Radio documentary, *God and Other Dirty Words*, explored the negative reactions he and others have received when they've disclosed a belief in God or admitted to interests synonymous with Christianity. In a homogenous community, everyone understands what a word means. Spoken in a multifaith, multicultural milieu, a term that once made perfect sense loses its clarity. The multitude of interpretations people bring to words such as *God* stain them, Faulk says, leaving marks that, if one is not careful, pollute whatever may have been meant by the person using the term: "All I can do in using words like 'God' is to be aware of the countless human stains that cover it." A spiritual Brita might do the trick, he teases. It might be the only thing that could cleanse it and other words from such stains, giving them back the clarity they once enjoyed.[14]

Faulk's experience is backed up by recent market research done for The United Church of Canada. Participants in the surveys identified church words that were negative for them: *hell, sacrifice, confession, sin, commitment, offerings, holy, Jesus*. Positive words included *caring, sharing, friendship, giving, support*, and *teaching children good values*.[15] The former are all, with the tenuous exception of *holy*, related to theological dogma. The latter are all values-based. It is an interesting split.

## Is Church Too Churchy?

But what about the word *church* itself? What can we ever do to redeem that one? If we *are* able to create something that will help us build the sustainable future we want, *should* we call it church? There are many good reasons to ponder that question.

Suffering from the caricature it has allowed itself to become, all churches are stained in the same way as Faulk's "God," regardless of the denomination. The same research noted above showed that many think the church is staid, intimidating, and judgmental.[16] It's all about sin and making you feel bad. The clergy, when they haven't their own abusive and predatory behaviour to blame for their bad press, are cast in popular media as kindly middle-aged or older men who show up to do weddings on the daytime soaps, dispense insipid advice in feature films, or struggle with their irrelevance, as does Pastor Lovejoy on *The Simpsons*. Non-church people who find themselves in a church service, forced to attend a baptism or wedding, too often have most of the church's stereotypes reinforced for them—you can't talk in church, swear in church, or wear your everyday clothes to church; the sermon, hymns, and service are all foreign, weird, and incomprehensible in the ritualized language; the stand-up, sit-down routine is embarrassingly unfamiliar; and, of course, all they want is your money. Like I said—it's a caricature.

Breaking those stereotypes is a challenge for the church, particularly for those congregations and leaders who are comfortable operating in the closed system the church has become and who don't see the need to change the stereotypes. But there are those who have taken a good long look at contemporary culture and are working to make the church, at least its physical attributes, attractive to those who might be interested in exploring "life's big questions"—the seekers.

## Contemporary Church

The work being done to accommodate this discriminating crowd is substantial. Primarily operational in the evangelical church, the elemental feature to its success seems to be a strong, charismatic leader. Bill Hybels of Willow Creek Community Church and Rick Warren of Saddleback Community Church are two such leaders. Each has described his vision, its implementation, and the successful ministries he has built in a bestselling book: Warren in *The Purpose Driven Church* and Hybels in *Rediscovering Church*. The passion they have for leading people to Christ is a powerful impetus for the work they do. Because of their visions, the passion with which they engage them, and the twenty-first-century trends to which they have responded, they and others who have learned from them have been able to build very purposeful ministries.

Technology is one of the most powerful ways for church leaders to connect with a new generation. Those who are adept at it use its versatility to connect through a variety of media both inside and outside of the congregation. Ministers write blogs (online web logs—commentaries and reflections from the perspective of the blog-writer), and churches try (sometimes with very limited success) to create and maintain upbeat websites. Sanctuaries are being revamped to include the latest in technology—state-of-the-art sound and video systems, more microphone outlets than the local stage theatre, multiple, often retractable, screens, and the requisite theatre seating that will make it all the more appealing. Many churches have supplemented or replaced the classical sounds of the pipe organ with the adaptability of electronic midi-systems and contemporary music that often mirrors or exceeds the best of what you'd hear on any adult contemporary radio station. (Some evangelical bookstores even cross-reference their Christian music with popular music. If your kid likes Streetlight Manifesto, Gorillaz, or The Shins, but you want them listening to Christian music, you can go in, check out the store chart, and find out what bands make that particular kind of sound.)

"Worship hosts" in such churches are highly trained in the most welcoming techniques—casual, friendly, and well informed. If it is your first visit, a host will make you feel like an honoured guest. He'll invite you to join him for coffee afterwards and remember your name when he shows up at your side at the end of the service. He'll offer you an easy-to-follow map of the facility and, rather than point you in the direction of the nursery should you inquire (your children will always be welcome to stay with you, of course), will walk there with you so that he can introduce you to the trained, professional nursery staff, who will point out the many safety features of the modern play/sleep area. One of those features will very likely be a security process that ensures your child only leaves the room with someone authorized to pick him or her up. You might even be offered a vibrating pager to take with you so that you will feel completely comfortable during the service knowing that if your child needs you, you will be discreetly alerted and can be there in moments.

The facility itself will be bright, clean, and easily accessed. Studies have shown that adequate parking and attractive washroom facilities are two of the most important things for which church "shoppers" look. Larger congregations may provide valet parking. Smaller ones that don't need such a feature often reserve the spots closest to the building for visitors. Long-term members consider parking at a distance from the church a significant part of their ministry to newcomers. Northridge Church in Plymouth, Michigan, shuttles its regular attendees from a parking lot two miles away. Newcomers get the parking at the church facility.[17]

In emerging churches, information is provided throughout the service to help visitors understand what is expected of them. The worship leaders, and there may be several, will tell you what's coming next, or it will be projected on a large screen or printed. Options for participation will be offered but not forced. Printed materials will be professionally designed and prepared, easy to follow, and offer a variety of things to visually stimulate you. When it comes time for the offering to be taken up, you will be advised that it is the congregation that supports its ministries and that you, as a guest, are not expected to put anything in the offering plate. If you want to anyway, but you have forgotten to bring any cash with you, there may even be debit or credit card processing available. A *Dallas Morning News* poll recently found that 55 per cent of two hundred local churches accept credit and /or debit cards.[18]

Church organizational structures, too, can be changed to reflect a more dynamic, mission-driven organization. Approval processes, once dogged by multiple layers of committees, are streamlined. Every activity is considered an integral part of the church's ministry, right down to changing light bulbs. Committees are called ministries, and volunteer opportunities are matched with spiritual gifts in order that volunteers can maximize their ministry potential and grow spiritually at the same time. Board members do more than rubber-stamp committee decisions. They are spiritual leaders.

It all seems very good. The church needs to be appealing and engaging. The more we are able to accomplish that, the more likely that people will be attracted to us and listen long enough for us to get our message across. Leaders who are able to offer us direction in these areas, and there are many who are enormously gifted leaders, have much to teach us, and we would be wise to accept their lessons. We can do these things.

## The Seduction of Postmodern Packaging

Liberal Christians can't claim the same passion for Christ's saving grace as their impetus for church-building—not in the literal way that drives their passionate evangelical counterparts—and they aren't exactly wallowing in charismatic leaders either. Those who are passionate about church, who have found ways to incorporate tools that growing evangelical congregations have introduced, because of increased numbers, are able to claim success. They are often what some call "soft evangelicals," using resources and styles developed for more conservative settings. Members of these churches who are supportive of the growth and excitement are still prone to acknowledging their indifference to, if not their discomfort with, the increasingly conservative theology that comes with it.

The liberal church, a church that is possibly the most apt to survive the shift to a new non-supernatural understanding of religion, faith, and Christianity, is falling for the packaging. They see the bright lights, they hear the great music, and they want the excitement. They are ready to buy the delivery system even though they haven't bothered to think carefully about whether they really want what's being delivered.

Mainline denominations have been obsessing over their packaging for decades. As numbers have fallen, they've watched the evangelicals—so much more adept at reading pop culture—to try to figure out how to do church in a way that will draw people. The evangelicals, of course, mastered the art of the powerful soundbite, evocative music, and visually engaging technology long ago. Frantically trying to catch up, mainliners are installing projection screens, using video clips, and offering cappuccino before the service. They are embracing the musical style of the evangelicals, offering choruses and songs about a personal relationship with Jesus, and introducing worship bands, song teams, and a polished informality.

Without recognizing the value of their own product—that is, the progressive theology they've developed over the years—liberals are on the brink of sacrificing their greatest gift for the glitz and glamour of the evangelical church. They're learning the lingo, beginning to feel comfortable waving their hands in the air, and hoping their efforts will save the liberal church from fading away to nothing.

While I don't think many congregations that make a move to a more evangelical style of worship (and theology) really spend a whole lot of time defending the existential reasons for their doing so—it's more about numbers than meaning—I do wonder if their decision to do so isn't strengthened or validated by the belief that it is a very postmodern, and therefore "progressive," thing to do. It is "with-it," "hip," and "where it's at." Maybe that alone accounts for its popularity.

Leonard Sweet, the avant-garde, charismatic (in the generic sense of the term) prophet of the "with-it" side of the evangelical church, identifies the church's response to postmodern culture as its single most important concern. He likens the effect of post-modernism on the world, culture, and the church to a tsunami and argues that we try to hold onto the status quo at our peril. To do so will leave the church blasted and broken, a heap of rubble amid all the rest of the shattered icons of the past, unrecognizable detritus blanching on the ruined beaches of what might have been.

The seismic events that have happened in the aftermath of the postmodern earthquake have generated tidal waves that have created a whole new world out there. We are now in transition, and thrown from terra firma (if ever there were such a thing) into the tossing seas of terra aqua, we end up on *terra incognita* (Sweet's terms). A sea change of transitions and transformations is requiring a whole new set of ways of making our way in the world.[19]

Sweet argues that if the church's choice, in the face of this reality, is to keep doing things the way it has always done them, it will be destroyed. What we have to do, he says, is learn to swim, ride the wave, get the language of postmodernity down, and become comfortable enough with it that we will be able to speak our truths to a new generation. The gospel, according to Sweet, still needs to be told.

The gospel about which Sweet is so passionate, however, is a gospel that was inspired and interpreted; written down; circumscribed; moulded into creeds, rituals, and rites; and manipulated and mauled by so many imperfect human minds with just as many vague and too-human purposes long before even the Chinese invention of the matchstick.* Since that time, we've managed to

---

*Sources disagree on when and where the matchstick was invented. Reported to be first referred to in a book written in the late tenth century by Tao Ku entitled *Records of the Unworldly and the Strange*, little sticks of pinewood impregnated with sulphur were ostensibly used by impoverished court ladies during a siege in 577 CE. The Western invention of matches didn't happen for another thousand years. Who knows when it

improve on controlled combustion with incredible results, but Sweet would have us hold on to the good news of Christianity as it exists in the church-controlled manifestation that has been handed down, generation to generation, since the fourth century. The only thing he thinks we need to change is the way in which we propel it into popular culture. According to Sweet, if we get the language just right, if we use the sleekest terms, mix the metaphors into the perfect "Extra-hot Grande Global" Starbuckian delight and save ourselves from the "lukewarm Americano," in which the gospel continues to cool, it will sell as well as it ever did.[20]

Postmodernism is used to excuse a lot. In 2001, I served on the planning committee for the worship component of a denomination-wide conference. When objections were raised to the language and theology of songs chosen for use in the conference's worship services, postmodernism was hauled into the discussion to justify the choice. Since postmodern critique challenges and undermines all absolute claims, the argument went, then we are free to pick and choose what we use—language no longer confines us because it has no absolute meaning. In other words, exclusive language isn't really exclusive and salvific theology isn't really salvific—it's all in the ears of the beholders and, if they think it means something negative, that's their issue, not ours. Postmodern critique recognizes the multiplicity of meanings present in any word (remember Faulk's "stains"). Because we have no control over what anyone is going to hear and take our words to mean, in the postmodern world, anything goes.

It is true that in such a world there are no absolutes and that we are all free to interpret what we are exposed to, deciding for ourselves what is worth keeping and what is no longer relevant to us, whether we want to wear our T-shirts inside out or not. Evangelical Christianity, however, can only ever pretend to be postmodern.

really happened? The point is, once we figured it out, we kept improving on it. Once we nailed down the gospel, it stayed nailed down.

The claims it makes are absolute claims and are believed to be so. Presented as postmodern, evangelical Christianity co-opts a progressive, inclusive language that is then used to present a regressive, exclusive argument. It is a sleight of hand. If the audience doesn't pay very close attention, it will lose sight of what is really happening. In 2001, at this particular denominational conference, this sort of evangelical misuse of postmodern relativism was still an understudy in the liberal church, learning the tricks of the trade and only being given the spotlight in a few isolated congregations. It has since moved centre stage.

The most recently published denominational hymn book in North America is The United Church of Canada's 2007 *More Voices*, a sequel to its popular *Voices United*, published in 1994. The editorial team presents it in response to "a wonderful explosion of new songs of the faith" combined with the expansion of understanding within Christian congregations of "the kinds of instruments and the types of songs that can help to shape and deepen our worship and faithful living." In addition, the team notes that "We are . . . becoming increasingly attuned to the music of our sisters and brothers throughout the global village."[21]

If I thought the church was long past the gender-inclusive language debate that was at its height in the years of my theological training, *More Voices* proved me wrong. More than 10 per cent of the songs in it are copyrighted with exclusive male imagery language. Usually the male-dominated language takes the form of the word *Lord* for which the editors gently suggest the substitution of a non-gender-specific alternative, usually "God." The "feminine wound,"[22] poignantly described by so many able women writers, continues to be incised in the souls of girls and women who are required to rise in Christian denominations around the world and sing words that reinforce a "God-given" male privilege. My compassion—for the young who do not yet feel the pain of that wound and for the old who know it intimately—wells up as

I read the words to these songs and lament the insensitivity that allowed the editors to include them. In the area of inclusive language, as with the whole feminist experiment, the achievements we thought we had secured are at constant risk and, without diligent attention, will be steadily eroded.

But it's not just the gender exclusivity that has crept into the refrains and songs of the newest hymn compilation in mainline Christianity. Under the guise of "world" music, of Latin liturgical elements, of scripture verses set to music, continues a theological perspective that can no longer be justified in postmodern Christianity. It was one thing to be shocked when we opened up our *old* hymn collections and carefully explored their words, recognizing within them the deeply divisive theology we so blithely sang and which so many naively internalized. It is quite another thing, and that much more challenging for us, to read the words of songs set to music in the past decade that implore a heavenly God (Lord, actually) to pour power out on us,[23] or sing the catchy predestination* song about Jesus choosing those who will believe in him.[24] Does the liberal church still believe in a heaven that spills power out upon the faithful to be used as they see fit or that Jesus opens or stops up our ears at whim so that some may and others may not hear his message, as some lyrics would suggest? For a long time, the answer to that question has been no, yet we are happily bringing it back through what is offered as the best, most up-to-date music.

To include such theological propositions in the liturgical resources of a mainline denomination that teaches contemporary scholarship and postmodern critical interpretation at its seminaries can be explained only by the misapplication of postmodern thought. If none of it matters and nothing means anything, then

---

*Predestination refers to a Calvinist doctrine in which those who will be received into heaven have been preselected by God. There is nothing anyone can do to get themselves on or off the list; our fates are predestined.

it is fine to sing whatever we want. Well, it's not fine. Not by a long shot. If it can't be said in the pulpit, it shouldn't be sung in the pew.

When I speak publicly, I am sometimes approached by individuals who are eager to let me know that they have a very progressive understanding of the Bible and Christianity. They know that the Gospels were written years after Jesus died. They are able to contextualize the horrific stories of the God of the Israelites and dismiss them. They know that Christianity is not the be-all and end-all when it comes to religious paths, and they respect the rights of others to believe in different things. Because they are so progressive, they can easily sit through Bible readings, intercessory prayers, the singing of outrageously worded hymns, and eat and drink the body and blood of a first-century Middle Eastern Jew. Their rational mind understands all of it and can flip the channel to "metaphor" or "context" and be done with it. Nothing fazes them. In fact, because they are so comfortable with their intellectual interpretations, they sometimes challenge my suggestion that we need to become literalists about our language, using metaphor and symbol only when it would never be mistaken as truth. They argue that they should be able to use the old, comfortable, familiar words, the old theology, the old rituals because, "No one believes they are true, anyway!"

## Integrity

In a postmodern world, however, we still need to act with integrity.

Evangelical congregations, whether they employ postmodern techniques or not, have integrity down pat. Their interest is your soul, and they're going to work to save it, no matter what it takes. They believe the Bible is the word of God, whether infallible or not, and seek to live that word out in their lives and make it the centre of yours. Those that lead have the conviction of their personal beliefs empowering their public leadership. It's like harnessing the energy of pure lightning, and it makes a powerful impact on any who experience it.

Senior pastor Bill Hybels lives, eats, and breathes his beliefs. When he speaks, integrity galvanizes his words. Annual video recordings of the full-immersion baptisms he and his team perform in the creek outside the church are so profoundly moving that those watching can almost produce enough tears to do their own full-immersion service by the end of the clip. He tells the story of being at the dedication of a new church building where one of the members took him aside and pulled back a corner of the newly laid carpet. There, engraved in the recently poured concrete, were the names of family members and loved ones who had not yet given their lives to Christ. Every month, the core believers in that church meet to stand over those names and pray for their salvation. The names lie there, carved in stone and as solid as the Ten Commandments, calling those believers to a commitment they have made.[25] Leaders such as Bill Hybels believe solidly, fervently, and passionately.

I don't believe most of what they say. But then, as a guest at one of their worship services, it is almost as though I don't have to. I can feel their passion, their conviction, and their belief. In the face of it, who cares if I believe? I feel like I'm being sheltered in the arms of my hero, convinced that I will always be safe because, even if I'm afraid, he isn't. Integrity is a powerful thing.

The liturgies of the church once held that integrity, shaping, through a ritualized process, the individual's response to faith. It was deep in the movement of the liturgical process that individuals developed the strength, courage, and grace to face the challenges of everyday life, particularly living up to what was identified as God's will. The liturgical flow, in its many varied styles, often provoked an experience of holiness that transformed lives.

Traditional liturgy offers an accessible drama by which the individual is led through (a) an awareness of the transcendent, (b) one's place in relation to it, (c) a convincing and persuasive argument in favour of the community's ideals, to (d) a powerful rededication of himself or herself to living in alignment with those ideals. Good liturgical process, whether traditional, contemporary, postmodern or something else, draws the individual out of their isolation and brokenness into the communal undertaking of a transcendent mission, a commitment to the recreation of the world in the image set before it as ideal.

But it has to have integrity. It has to come from a gut-level belief that what is happening is stunningly important, true, real, and transformative. It has to be offered with a clarity of belief that rips through any doubt that might enter into the heart of any one of the participants.

Exposed to contemporary and postmodern scholarship, belief in the message of the Bible, the Christian faith, and of an interventionist God has eroded the integrity with which liberal clergy have been able to lead their congregations. They fall back on the "art" of worship, attempting to capture something they can no longer offer. Caught in the cracked effigy of the sacraments, they attempt to imbue objects, movements, and responses with the power once held by the mystery of grace. When we no longer believe that sprinkling water on a baby's forehead is necessary to its salvation, we seek to shift the import of the moment from the sacramental nature of the ritual, its nostalgic elements, to the idea of belonging. When we no longer believe that our sins are absolved through the ripping apart of a loaf of bread, we, again, look to the ritual, the community gathering with us, the desire to find the "simpler times of the past" in what we are doing, and we put great effort into keeping it "holy." That is great and meaningful work if we use language that recognizes the shift in our belief and doesn't suggest or pretend something is happening that is not. Those who do seek to offer hope through these rites, using words and symbols they cannot believe, do so without the impassioned, visceral belief of the evangelical pastor calling us to stand upon the names of the loved ones we wish to save; they are shrivelled by what they do. Devoid of sincerity and meaning, their rituals become dry and stale. The bread of life turns to dust that is no longer needed nor wanted. And so the liberal church continues to disappear.

Lloyd Geering has noted, in keeping with New Testament scholar Kirsopp Lake's 1925 prediction, the church is shrinking from the left. Lake argued that three divisions cut swaths across all denomination lines—the Fundamentalists, the Experimentalists (the Radicals), and the Institutionalists (the Liberals). His chilling prediction seems to be coming true: "The Fundamentalists will eventually triumph. They will drive the Experimentalists (Radicals) out of the Church and then reabsorb the Institutionalists (Liberals) who, under pressure, will become more orthodox . . . The church will shrink from left to right."[26]

As progressives have become more and more frustrated hearing things they do not believe from congregational leaders—who are willing to chat about their own progressive non- or a-theistic beliefs over coffee on Saturday but not from the pulpit on Sunday—that loss has reached hemorrhagic proportions. Progressives are fed up with translating, taming miracles as metaphors, and replacing "Lord" with something other than "God" because "God" doesn't work for them either.

But those who recognize the dangers inherent in leaving the church to moderates who allow the old language to remain in use (supporting the illusions of those fundamentalists who would argue its veracity) are loath to depart. They want to change the church, not abandon it. For the idea of a future built on unchallenged ancient worldviews can be a very frightening prospect. Sam Harris, speaking in 2007, expresses it with a frightening clarity:

Our ability to cause ourselves harm is spreading with twenty-first century efficiency and yet, we are still, to a remarkable degree, drawing our vision of how to live in this world from ancient literature. This marriage of modern technology, destructive technology, and Iron Age philosophy is a bad one for reasons that . . . nobody should have to specify much less argue for.[27]

## The Liberal Inheritance

The church we need to create will move forward without the negative trappings it has dragged with it from our distant, fearful past. The liberal church, unlike the evangelical church, has in hand the single most important tool needed to do just that. It has been the womb of critical contemporary scholarship for decades. Without being open to that scholarship, without carefully excising the supernatural from its beliefs, without staking more import in this world than the next, no church will ever help humanity ably deal with the issues facing it now. The liberal church is poised to do all these things. It has only to acknowledge its responsibility and take the next few steps. But it needs to carefully manage its inheritance. This it has not done well.

As the liberal church discerns its way forward, the cost involved with keeping contemporary scholarship confined to the odd spirituality or study group and away from its primary worship services will become apparent. That cost goes back to the similarity between the third and fifth stages of faith—respectively the one in which we literally believe the Bible and the church's doctrine, and the one in which we understand those things metaphorically. Members who have been presented the latter without being challenged to think of it that way, who, in other words have had their childlike faith preserved, will find it much easier to talk themselves into "format" changes than "substance" changes. They will move into contemporary forms of worship and church mission, believing them to be a progressive response to the world's needs. The liberal church risks losing its critical edge, the progressive scholarship it has been home to, because it didn't take care to tell enough people it had it. We risk the fulfillment of Lake's prophecy—leaving the church to the fundamentalists and losing a church that had much to offer the world.

Keeping itself true to its birthright, its commitment to critical thinking, the liberal church can have an effective and powerful ministry. It can still make use of what it has learned from the evangelical church about style and contemporary market devices. It can still wrap itself up in packaging that attracts different user and age groups. It can still structure itself using the most up-to-date management theories available. The message it has to offer is worthy of those very important improvements to its delivery. It can then be offered in language that is chosen intentionally, not with so-called postmodern carelessness or insincerity, and that will, itself, always be open to critique. Such a church might offer a very real hands-on, world-changing hope. An open, welcoming, honest, self-critiquing, dogma-free, values-based, spiritually engaging community—that's what church can be.

If the liberal church does not accept its inheritance in this direction, much will be lost. If it finds itself trapped by its inability to speak clearly and truthfully about the Bible, about Jesus, about the cross, it will slowly disconnect itself from what might have been its strongest asset. Churches that currently support the dwindling numbers of people who passionately care about the kind of work that challenges corporate power and who choose to forgo personal comforts that come at the expense of current and future generations—human, plant, animal, the earth—those churches will die for lack of a new generation. With them will die a vision, one that has always been ours, of a new world in which we live together in justice, peace, and love.

## In Lieu of "Church"

If the liberal church chooses to move in a progressive direction rather than a regressive one, it may be that, like the word *God*, the word *church* will be found to be beyond redemption and have to go. After all, the people the church needs to be interested in attracting are those who call themselves spiritual but not religious, and "church" is about the last place those people think they'll ever find anything spiritually significant. Call it something else and you might find yourself a market.

In September 2006, political economists Jonathan Ezer and Colin Agur started Salon Voltaire, a trendy lecture series that opened in Toronto with sold-out events at an upscale museum restaurant. Word of the series spread informally and by the end of its first year, Salon Voltaire was still filling its venue with inquiring minds at each of its evening sessions. Topics ranged from international trade to the environment to things of the spirit in a format that offered two thirty-minute lectures by guest speakers on divergent topics, each followed up with a half-hour question-and-answer period. Conversation was lively, respectful, and engaging. The audience spanned an age group absent from most pews on any given Sunday morning—the twenty- to forty-five-year-olds that congregations long to attract.[28]

Salon Voltaire is perhaps an early form of what church might morph into over its next generation. There is currently a dearth of places where people can engage in serious conversation about serious matters without the obligatory religion-bashing that characterizes many a humanist gathering. Programs such as Salon Voltaire, with the proper marketing and staging, are almost assured success.

But Salon Voltaire is only one of the many ways people are gathering together to talk about important things. Al Gore, by jam-packing every venue at which he shows up, proves that people are eager to engage around core issues. Other events draw people to ticketed programs or casual evenings; "Every month people who work in the environmental field meet up for a beer at informal sessions known as Green Drinks."[29] The Green Drink movement brings together people interested in environmental issues in, at last count, twenty-eight countries around the world. Another Toronto series filled one of that city's largest sanctuaries for each of the six evening programs it offered: The 2004–2005 Seekers' Dialogue, a series of lectures that offered itself as an alternative to traditional Christian worship, featured speakers such as theologian Thomas Moore, author Marianne Williamson, statesman and HIV/AIDS activist Stephen Lewis, and Lieutenant-General Roméo Dallaire, outspoken veteran of the Rwandan holocaust. As well, people show up in droves for documentaries, such as *An Inconvenient Truth*, *Why We Fight*, *Sicko*, *March of the Penguins*, and *Jesus Camp*, or movies, such as *Blood Diamond*, *Children of Men*, *Syriana*, that expose them to critical issues facing the world today or the world we may live in tomorrow. More and more, people don't just want to be entertained. They want to be engaged.

The church could be part of this movement. As I said early on, we certainly have the outlets. Not only that. We have another unrealized potential that most of the above don't even consider of interest.

## When They Say It's About the Community, They've Got It Right!

Most faith traditions, not just Christian ones, are in fact experts at creating community. That's what the roots of religion were all about—reinforcing your affiliation with your tribe, strengthening community. Of course, some of them do it better than others, particularly those who are incorporating some of the evangelical church's welcoming ideas. But almost all of them, whether large or small, work hard to create and maintain relationships.

Mainline denominations have often been criticized from both evangelical and sacramental perspectives for being nothing more than "clubs," places where people go to meet like-minded people, perhaps commit to some shared values, and enjoy one another's company. Perhaps that isn't a criticism after all. Perhaps community is exactly and only what we need to be.

When you go to the movies, you go with someone whose company you enjoy. When you go to hear someone speak about a topic in which you are interested, you go with someone who shares your interest. When you read a book that introduces you to an issue you believe is of great importance or that tells a good story, you pass it on to someone you think would enjoy it or benefit from it. We experience our world more richly when we experience it in relationship.

If, as the credits roll, the speaker finishes her speech, or the book is closed, we reinforce the experience we have had by sharing it with others, we broaden our experience to include ones we would not have had ourselves, we open ourselves to relationship, and we strengthen our resolve to address a particular issue or incorporate a certain behaviour into our lives. In community, we are able to reflect and process our experiences more broadly than we might on our own. Through the reflection of others and our internal processing of shared ideas and concepts, we grow and develop. The company we keep has a great deal to do with how we do that and who we become through that process.

Establishing *communal* values allows those who choose to participate in the community to assist one another in the task of establishing those values *personally*. But remember, there are lots of different values and they aren't always good. Groups elevate all kinds of values, many of which we would consider unhealthy. Those that have an unabated allegiance to the value of profit may not pay attention to the way in which that profit is accrued. Fun and good times are the chief values of many cruise ship operators. The effect of their activities on the communities they visit is of little value or import to them. In an extreme example, one group

I encountered, whose chief value was the right of all seniors to live independently—regardless of a client's diminished competence—was oblivious to the havoc created when it removed any "potentially life-threatening objects," such as stoves, kettles, scissors, electrical cords, and glassware, from the apartments of those it sought to empower. The seniors living alone were sitting in the dark, if they hadn't remembered to put on the overhead light before the sun set, were left with microwaves they did not know how to operate, and with food turning to poison in the refrigerator. This group worked diligently toward its well-intentioned value—the right of all seniors to live independently—and in the process risked sacrificing the safety and dignity of its clients.

Church, or whatever it comes to be called, could be a place where we reflect and process our life experiences with others in ways that encourage us to become compassionate, just, and loving human beings. The values Christianity has often aspired to and that liberal Christianity has focused on honour life and argue for its inherent dignity and worth. Those values have compelled Christians to achieve incredible good works over the course of history. Maturing in our understanding and application of those values is essential to our being able to live in right relationship. Teaching us how to do that is the work the church could identify as its purpose. It has no need of dogma or doctrine, canonical imprimatur, and scriptural affirmation. It is simply the best of what is left when liberal Christians clear their desks of what they no longer believe of the Christian message.

With community based on life-enhancing values now becoming the "product" that liberal Christians have to offer a challenged world, it is important that we explore how best to develop strong, welcoming communities that can share a newfound passion. Again, the evangelicals are often way ahead of the liberals, and we have much we can learn from them. Aware, now, that the packaging is not the same as the message, we can glean community-building concepts from the best of them and use them to deliver our own values-based message.

Many evangelical churches have learned to structure themselves around relationship-focused communities rather than around a collective Sunday morning experience. Groups are sometimes based on interest, neighbourhood, or lifestyle. Relationships strengthened within smaller communities reinforce each member's commitment to the wider community. Values are uplifted during gatherings of the whole community and reinforced in the relationship-focused groups. Individuals are challenged to live up to the values shared, supported in their work to do so, and comforted when they have not been able to.

We all know that values often conflict. Trying to live up to them, regardless of how clear they seem to be, is a challenge in our complex world. While we might like to take care of the world's starving children, giving all our money away to them may recklessly imperil our own. Choosing a school that can provide the needed supports for a child with learning challenges may require that we drive more than our ecological sensitivities would allow or compromise the family time to which we have committed. And those are the easy issues. Others weave us into complexities we barely begin to understand. We need support, the wisdom that can come from those who care for us. The church can be a community that builds and nurtures those relationships. Those who struggle with how difficult it is to live a conscientious life—whether they should even try to make a difference when their efforts seem so dramatically insufficient and when indifference seems so much more highly prized in our culture, whether having another child is even an ethical question, or whether burying oneself in work or relationship or some exercise isn't easier than engaging in the challenging issues that face the world—struggle with these things because they are hard-pressed to find many within their social and work-related groups who are willing to converse on these sorts of topics. The church can be, create, and support this kind of community.

In the past, we have sometimes fallen short of making the right choices. Armed with a desire to "do good our way," we have often failed to reflect on the effect of our imposed values before sweeping in and damaging cultures, lives, and ecosystems. The task of discerning what we should do in any given situation will not become easier. We will have to be attentive to our choices, to subject ourselves to ongoing critique, and, using Wheatley's conversation guidelines, to approach each other with humility. But we mustn't err on the side of omission either. We must become experts at ethical discernment. It will not be easy.

## Beyond the Beliefs that Divide

We who move beyond the traditional boundaries of Christianity are often thought of as not believing in anything. But beyond the beliefs that have divided us for millennia are beliefs that challenge us to hallow all that life is. It is our responsibility to seek these beliefs out, share them with one another, embrace them, and try to live by them. The following words were written in an attempt to defend the work that was unfolding in the congregation I serve at a time when that work was being challenged by others in the church. I offer them now as an invitation to conversation, an invitation to open yourself to what they might offer, and, in turn, for you to offer as you invite others into this most important work.

We believe in the sanctity of life that is often experienced in ways that cannot be measured and that far outstrip what we can see and taste and touch. We believe that there is much in this world that challenges the sanctity of life and that it must be defied. We believe defiance to be very hard work and that it takes all the shoulders in a community to bear the burden of the responsibility. We believe our experience of the deep sacredness of life is dynamic and cannot be named.

We believe that the Bible is a human construction, and it is, therefore, full of both human promise and human error. We believe that no humanly constructed book can be the authoritative word of God and that we, who recognize this, are responsible to challenge such claims and behaviour that suggests such claims, particularly where we find it in our own tradition. We believe that some of the stories of the activity of the divine in the world that are collected in the Bible are rich with metaphor and meaning and can enrich our understanding of ourselves, each other, and creation. And we believe that much of what is described in the Bible as the activity of God is destructive of relationship and equality, that it is tribal and divisive, that, despite the best attempts that the authors were making to describe their experience of the divine, they have created a legacy of judgment, horror, and despair, and we no longer choose to burden ourselves with that legacy. We believe it is wrong to call such words holy or sacred.

We believe that some of the words attributed to a man called Jesus, myth or reality, are words that can challenge us to seek alternate ways to live together and break down humanly constructed barriers. And we believe that some of the words attributed to that man are words that can divide and destroy relationship, not just by the way they are used but by how they are recorded. We believe that they describe a concept of hell that was very real to that man but is no longer relevant to us. And we believe that, too often, his words have been used to imprison people in that hell, a place only the Bible and other religious texts continue to describe and make real in this world. We believe that we have the right and responsibility to free ourselves of those concepts that are no longer meaningful and relevant for us because we do not believe that he was speaking as the only begotten Son of God but as one who sought, as we do, to understand the sacred reality that he embraced and we call life.

We believe that all that is constructed upon the church's claim that the Bible is the authoritative word of God must be questioned because of the error of that claim. We believe that the church's creeds, doctrine, liturgy, ecclesiology, sacraments, hymns, and theology are based upon it. We believe they should be assessed for their ability to support our attempts to live in right relationship with ourselves, each other, and the earth, honouring the sanctity of life as we each experience it. We believe that, though there are costs associated with such work and that much we have loved will be lost, we must accept those costs, grieve openly, and, with love and caring support for one another, leave behind that which would encumber our work. We believe we are gifted to create new understandings and that they can be rich and meaningful. And we believe that these new understandings, too, must be questioned as time and experience lay hold of them.

We believe that there are many who have spoken of or through their sacred realities in ways that open us to our tasks of building right relationship and loving from the core of our being. We believe it is right and proper to nurture ourselves with their words, our own words, and the ways that we and others see and know and celebrate the divine in our own lives.

We believe that we are light to the world, one another, and ourselves and that the world and all its inhabitants can be light to us. We believe that our values will guide our choices and that our choices are the incarnation of our beliefs. We believe that because this is so, it is more important for us to struggle to develop solid values for ourselves and society in order that we can strengthen the reality of love in the world than it is for us to be conversant in ancient theological terms.

We believe that our experience of the sanctity of life is best expressed as and in love.

To these words I would add a few more. We believe that there are no supernatural beings, forces, or energies necessary for or even mindful of our survival. What we have dreamt in the past have been dreams. They have enriched us and challenged us to seek out what we needed to survive. What we need now cannot be found in those dreams. We need to dream again, recognizing that our visions, ideas, choices, and challenges, all come from within us, not from somewhere else. We are our creators, and we have the challenge before us to create a future for this planet in which love, made incarnate through justice and compassion, is the supreme value. What we create must come from a deep and rich desire to connect ourselves, one to the other; to be responsible for one another in ways we have been called to by so many brilliant speakers, leaders, poets, and prophets so many times before. Believing as I do that all religious, philosophical, and ideological understandings must be challenged by their adherents so that we might all move into a place where foundational beliefs are shared and held in common, reviewed and revised as necessary, challenged and changed when appropriate, I extend the confrontation that is this book. May it irritate us all into the growth we so disturbingly need.

When we arrive at that place of shared values and beliefs, it will be arrestingly obvious. Rather than mocking or even tolerating the faiths and ideological positions of others, we will be delighted by the kaleidoscopic beauty of the ways in which different lives, experiences, understandings, and traditions have sought to express what for them is of the utmost worth, holy, and sacred. We will find them, not only in those things we so easily call sacred, but in all that enriches and makes palatable the ordinariness of our days. Because, after all, that is where, for each of us, the beauty we must see and know and celebrate resides.

May we each believe in and hallow the inherent beauty of the other, the earth, and ourselves, and as we find ways to honour our connections, may the love we learn to share enrich us all.

# APPENDIX
## A TOOLBOX

The purpose of this appendix is to provide ideas, options, and resources for those who wish to engage in religious practice within gatherings that are progressive to the furthest extent of our knowledge at this time. Many liberal denominations consider themselves progressive. Many social justice congregations consider themselves progressive. Many who gather together and utilize alternative ways to explore their spirituality consider themselves progressive. It is true that each, in its own way, is. The resources and ideas offered here, however, are for those of you who have progressed to the place that the supernatural no longer fits with your understanding of spirituality. You live in the most progressive Christian paradigm available *at this time*, and you want your religious practice to reflect this. It is to be expected, even hoped perhaps, that in due course these ideas, too, will need to be set aside as new understandings evolve.


## PRIVATE FAITH, PUBLIC FAITH

The resources and ideas offered all relate to the communal rather than private aspects of a progressive Christian faith. A person's private faith is unique to that individual. The images, readings, activities, and disciplines that enable one to experience and express one's spirituality may be very different from the things that enable others to experience and express theirs. Privately, we are each responsible for finding and engaging in practices, participating in rituals, and accessing resources that "work" for us. Our only responsibility in the exploration of our private faith lives is to our own spiritual growth. As soon as we join with someone else, however, we must be reciprocally cognizant of those things that work for the other and the reality that what works for us might not stimulate them spiritually in the least. The language we use must allow both of us to access what it is that we need.

How do we do that when we may have widely disparate ways of understanding the sacred?

## INCLUSIVE LANGUAGE

If we are going to be inclusive, we must use inclusive language. Gender-inclusive, of course, but a new kind of spiritually inclusive language is also required. Spiritually inclusive language can touch people whose worldviews are decidedly anthropomorphically theistic (Father God), non-anthropomorphically theistic (Father/Mother God and all its permutations), just plain theistic (God, Holy One, First Breath of Life, and so on), non-theistic (Tillich's Ground of All Being), or even secular (love, peace, beauty—all without agency—"phenomenological facticities"[1]). It seems almost impossible to be inclusive until we get beneath the *naming* of whatever it is we are talking about to exactly *what it is* we are talking about.

When we worked our way through the gender-inclusive language debate, we had to identify the *characteristics* of the Father God we wanted to speak to and about, and then find other ways to express those characteristics without using an exclusive term. Since the late 1980s, in workshops across Western Christendom, we've shared our understandings of the compassionate, loving, challenging, nurturing, justice-seeking, and peacemaking images that arise when we spoke of God as father. We've also shared images of a judgmental, authoritarian, rigid, unforgiving, controlling, abusive, and vengeful God that were just as powerfully evoked. All are laid out in black and white between the endpapers of your Bible.

During the shift to gender-inclusive language, we had the opportunity to fine-tune our understandings of God. Letting go of an image that evoked characteristics we did not believe described the God we chose to worship (interesting how we get to craft the God we want, isn't it?), we were free to find images that supported those characteristics we wished to reinforce. So, although *bully* is a non-gender specific word, it isn't likely to be heard in most churches at the beginning of a prayer. The non-gender specific word *peacemaker* may very well be. We did much more than make a shift toward gender neutrality.* We cleansed the theistic concept of God of much of its negative, power-based connotation.

If we move through the same exercise now, we quickly find our way to spiritually inclusive language. We crawl underneath the titles and names used for god, find the essence of what we believe is worthy of being named in sacred space, and bring it forward.


## WORSHIP

Speaking of "sacred space," what we will call "the communal gathering that draws us together to recognize life's rites of passage and

---

*Even before coming out as a non-theist, I was not a proponent of feminine names for God. Mother is just as exclusive a term as Father, and people I have known and loved have been just as deeply wounded by mothers as have others by fathers. Non-gender specific terms are essential in all areas of the church.

reflect upon and deepen our understanding of the things we value and wish to enlarge in our lives while recognizing the challenges facing us as we do, the triumphs and failures we experience along the way, and which yet manages to uplift us enough to re-engage and recommit to living according to those communal values while filled with a sense of our own promise and interdependence" has not yet emerged. Obviously, a long descriptive title is not going to work. A single word doesn't cut it either, so it will take some time to come up with something that fits, feels right, and means what we want it to mean.[2]

Religious humanist William Murry, in his very helpful book *Reason and Reverence*, notes that "religious humanism finds great value in human beings coming together in religious community to deepen their understanding, support and strengthen their values, celebrate life's passages, and work together for a better world."[3] It's much less wordy than the line I strung together above. Throughout his book, Murry lifts up religious acts as those things we use and do to interpret our lives, to seek and ascertain meaning. Picking up on his recognition of the value of the word *religious*, I will use the rather bland and uninspiring title *religious gathering* to denote what liberals have always called worship in the past.* The term distinguishes the gathering from other times that we come together, such as study, discussion, social justice work, and so on, and picks up on the intentional inclusion of ritual, symbol, and myth as forms used to help us experience and translate the meaning in our lives. The sections following will indicate ways in which tools we are adept at using in traditional settings can be transformed for use in progressive settings and how new tools can be incorporated and created.

---

*Worship, for evangelicals, is the act of adoring God. While some mainline worship services may include times evangelicals would describe as worship, calling the whole thing worship would not make any sense to them.

# RESOURCES FOR RELIGIOUS GATHERINGS

If you are able to create a religious gathering from scratch, you will have a freedom that many do not. The forms, rituals, and symbols you create and choose, and how you decide to use them, will be entirely up to you and the group with which you are gathering. Although individuals may bring particular tastes and preferences with them, there will be no longstanding tradition with which you will be breaking, and the group will be able to make decisions in a more democratic process, examining the significance and symbolic nature of the elements with which you choose to work and creating a religious gathering that is uniquely and meaningfully their own.

Much of what follows will be geared toward those who are working in existing Christian congregations and groups. Much of the change in my own congregation has been able to happen because the basic forms have remained the same. We didn't ditch the organ and bring in a drum kit. We didn't pull out the pews and start worshipping in a circle. We didn't make major changes in the worship format. We still use a fairly traditional liturgy.

Each congregation will have its own structure and elements with which it will be grappling. While the resources offered here are elements of a middle-of-the-road liberal liturgy, you will want to pass over that which is not applicable, adapt that which may be, and create, create, create. While you're at it, don't forget the excellent material on packaging (style, format, technology) available from the evangelical church—just be very careful when it comes to using their actual resources as the theology will be far from what you may be seeking to provide.

## If You Can, Write
For too long, too many of us who have "put together" the Sunday service have relied on resources written by someone we consider

to be an expert or more creative or more spiritual than us. We have ignored or distrusted our own creative abilities to the point of dormancy. We think we can't write anything beautiful or meaningful. It may be that you are truly useless at such a task. Do rely on others if that is the case, and use the examples here to help you adapt public-domain resources for non-theistic use. If you are creative, and this is no time for modesty, write. A frequent accusation aimed at the progressive movement is that without the biblical story, as the metaphoric and symbolic matrix through which we seek to explain and understand our lives, all is dust—dry, intellectual, and lacking in spiritual beauty. Everything that you can do to prove that belief incorrect will be helpful. If you can't, you can't. But if you can, you must.

## Unison Prayers

If unison prayers are used, they must be for a greater purpose than congregational participation. Prepared prayers are not a form of congregational participation. They may have, at one time, been a step along the way, but they fall short of that lofty goal. While some suggest unison prayer creates a sense of community, a couple hundred people trying to say the same thing at the same time feels like dreadfully contrived community, particularly if the reading is punctuated with exclamation marks to which no one pays any heed. (Some alternatives will be presented in a subsequent section.)

## Symbols

In non-theistic religious gatherings, many of the symbols we have used in traditional settings are no longer relevant. But we need symbol and metaphor to explore ideas and concepts that are intangible and indefinable—life and forgiveness and courage. In the pursuit of spiritual growth, symbols help us engage these concepts and understand what they mean for us individually and as communities.

A recent worship service, at which women and one married man were ordained as Roman Catholic priests by the Roman Catholic Womanpriests movement, included a number of powerful symbols. It was very much the production of a sacramental tradition, and many of the symbols reinforced the beliefs such a tradition holds. But, again, with a bit of creativity and revisioning, symbols can come to mean very different things than they once did. The essential task of the individual introducing the symbol is to make its meaning clear, particularly if the symbol has been used and understood in a different way in the past.

At the opening of this ordination service, a liturgical dancer entered the space waving a heavy white silk flag on a long wooden stick. Her movements forced the flag to carve the air, beating it into thunder and disturbing the rainbow-coloured streamers that hung from the ceiling as she moved down the aisle of the sanctuary. A harpist offered background music and overlaid the dance with an interpretive reading. A story of life, the energy of spirit, the unity of our breath unfolded through music, dance, and word. A symbol that could have been used to express the presence and work of God's spirit in the world, through the actions and words of those using it, was teased into something larger, more open, more accessible, all the while being directed by the actions and words of those creating it.

Later in the service, a bright red prostration cloth was laid at the front of the church. Those who had been ordained lay face down upon the cloth and remained there during the singing of a litany of thanksgiving. The cloth traditionally symbolizes the priest's and deacon's dependence upon the Holy Spirit for their lives and their ministry. But at this service, the cloth was laid by Irshad Manji, author of *The Trouble with Islam Today*, and me—a radical feminist Muslim and a radically progressive Protestant. Our participation in this part of this very Catholic service brought new meaning to the symbol and stretched it beyond the theistic connotations it traditionally held. Included in this new symbolism was the acknowledgement of the challenging and difficult work undertaken by women in every religious tradition to bring about change, open the establishment to the perspectives that women offer, break barriers, dis-integrate, and disturb privilege. We were recognizing that those ordained were not only dependent upon the spirit in which they believe but also upon the risks that had been and were being taken by those within their own tradition and the traditions of others to bring about equality and a recognition of giftedness.

For many people, particular symbols in religious ceremony are required for them to feel spiritually connected. Without symbols, they cannot open themselves to deeper experience. These individuals have what might be called an extrinsic religiosity—they access their spirituality through extrinsic religious symbols. Others who have a more intrinsic religiosity won't need symbols. Although symbols can be interesting, engaging, and helpful, they are not essential for an intrinsic spiritual experience. Eliminating a symbol from the religious community will not significantly affect them. When we eliminate a symbol (or a word) used as *the* access point for an individual, however, his or her religious or spiritual experience will be significantly stressed, and his or her ability to be nurtured spiritually in the community may be severely compromised.

In order to assist those who have an extrinsic religiosity make the shift from a traditional spirituality to a progressive one, it may be helpful to allow as many symbols to remain as is theologically acceptable. Candles handed to baptized babies can easily be referred to as the gift of light that a life committed to love can be. Any previous connection with the Holy Spirit or Jesus as the Light of the World is intentionally replaced verbally and, with each subsequent reiteration of new meaning, mitigated. Similar shifts and new explanations can be made for other signs and symbols as well.

If, however, the symbolic meaning is anathema to the new understandings the community holds, its removal may be absolutely necessary, despite the emotional and spiritual significance it holds for many individuals. If this is the case, the elimination of the symbol from the religious community must be done with care and, if appropriate, ritual.

Obviously, the cross is the most powerful symbol with which the Christian Church will have to contend. It has been a symbol of hope, healing, peace, horror, and abuse for almost two thousand years, and it will not go quietly into the dark night. When we were having difficulty selecting an appropriate spot to mount a projection system in the sanctuary at West Hill United Church, one of the members of the board suggested that it would be much easier if we just removed the thirty-foot high steel cross that looms above us at the front of the sanctuary. I must admit that I was not at that time, nor am I yet, ready to take responsibility for lighting the acetylene torch that would bring it down. I'm not quite that stupid. Since that time, Christians in the community who know of our ministry have asked that we remove the cross on the outside of our property (another thirty-foot steel giant) out of respect for those who are "real" Christians. Perhaps until progressive Christianity is seen to be a legitimate maturation of the Christian faith the cross's presence can act as a sort of affirmation for those who wish to explore beyond the traditions of Christianity but continue to consider themselves Christians. It is my hope that, in time, as the horrific story the cross represents loses its place at the centre of Christianity, the cross will become obsolete, a silent reminder of the past.

## Liturgical Garb

You know why this has to stop. Make sure it does. Excuses about distracting street clothes are just that—excuses. Even though it might cause more "church fights" than anything else, the reasons to stop are so rock solid it doesn't matter.

## Sacramental Traditions

Sacramental traditions that have approved liturgies and overseeing bishops to deal with will have far more challenges than the rest of us. Requesting permission to experiment with the liturgy can provide some room, but most offerings will have to be approved by the presiding bishop. This requirement will seriously curtail much of what you will be able to do within the confines of traditionally held services. It may be that gathering outside of regular services in a place other than the church is an option that conserves for you the energy you need to engage the power systems in place within the congregation.

If you are ordained within such a system, you will know that leading services outside of the building does not remove you from the jurisdiction of the denomination. You may still be called to account. Only you can assess the dangers present in what you choose to do and how you will deal with them. Above all, you will need to develop a strong support system outside of the church that might, eventually, help you to change what happens inside the church.

## The Service . . .

The opening moments of any religious gathering aim to make the participants attentive to what is happening. It is accomplished in many different ways and with many different results, most of which are aimed to draw the participant's attention to the deity. It may seem then that, without the focus a deity provides, non-theistic religious gatherings will have no direction, no particular place toward which people's attention can be drawn. It will be the responsibility of those who lead the gathering to ensure that people don't feel lost or that their purpose for being there is too vague. Reiterating the purpose of the gathering, perhaps with the use of symbol or metaphor, can help people feel grounded.

## Centring Time

The ideas of "creating sacred space," the Wiccan concept of "casting the circle," and allowing a time for people to "centre" themselves are all useful when preparing a group for spiritual interaction. The congregation I serve uses a Centring Time, during which they are invited to set aside the busyness of everyday life to become attentive to what they hope to find, feel, receive, and offer in the time that we are gathered. Candles are lit and set on a table, a ritual that replaced the processing of the Bible. A time of silence, followed by a short reflective song, is included. Although the invitation to the Centring Time is always done extemporaneously so that it feels more intimate and personal, something that works in my own community but may not in yours, the following are examples of what might be said:

> Each of us comes to this place from a life filled with engagements, occasions, commitments, challenges, and opportunities. Yet we take time to gather in this place, in the midst of our busyness, because we experience a deep sense of our need for community and for time to be attentive to our own and one another's hearts, dreams, goals. In this time, we bring those things to mind, to heart, place them here in the midst of our gathering, and call ourselves to be attentive to them—to love, compassion, wholeness, justice, beauty. May we centre our thoughts on the place these things have in our lives and throughout our gathering, may we be strengthened in our commitment to living them out, not only in the times that we gather, but through the whole of the living of our lives.

> I come to this place as one with hope—hope because I have seen our hands and hearts working together to change the world, to help it realize the beauty it deserves to be. I come to this place,

too, as one without hope, made brittle by promises I have broken and self-serving choices I have made. Each of you entering here comes with conflicts such as these deep in your hearts. In these few moments of silence, may we be attentive to what it is we need from this time together—strength, forgiveness, encouragement. And may we, too, find what it is we have to offer those who gather with us—strength, forgiveness, encouragement. In our need and in our giving, may we know love.

## Prayers of Confession

Often one of the initial prayers in a religious gathering is the prayer of confession followed by an assurance of pardon. Drop both. Think about them and then drop them. Enough said.

## Prayer at the Beginning

When we pray in a non-theistic setting there is no "who" to whom we are praying. Thought by some to be a major stumbling block to prayer, a simple shift will get you comfortable in no time. The following is a theistic prayer I wrote for use in a worship service focused on our music ministry several few years ago:

> Open our hearts to the whisper of Your presence, Holy One.
> Surround us with chords of music
> that fill us with deep reverence
> for the wonders we see and know in creation.
> Steady our pulse
> with the rhythms of life
> that come constant to us
> through the blessing of music.
> Let us overflow with the gift of past and present
> and feel You in each note, each chord, each harmony of life.
> Amen.

As you can see, it is directed to a deity called "Holy One." We're asking Holy One to do something for us. But obviously we are capable of doing these things for ourselves without Holy One's aid, becoming attentive to what it is we wish to see, know, and feel completely under our own steam. Once we realize that *we* are responsible for what we've been imploring God to do, it is easy for us to replace the concept of "do this for me" or "make me do this" by using the world "may." Our prayer then challenges us. The responsibility to act, change, accommodate, or resist is ours. The simple shift to "may" accepts that responsibility.

Adapted for use in a non-theistic setting, my prayer would then look like this:

> As we are surrounded with chords of music
> may our hearts be open to the whisper of holiness.
> May we feel a deep reverence
> for the wonders we see and know in creation.
> May our pulse be steadied
> with the rhythms of life
> that come constant to us
> through the blessing of music.
> May we overflow with the gift of past and present
> and feel beauty in each note, each chord, each harmony of life.
> Amen.

Exercise 2: A prayer from the Thanksgiving service of the same year:

Theistic:

> Holy One,
> at the very core of our being
> You have placed the need to relate to one another.

Our souls long for communion,
for fellowship, and we gather in this place to seek it out.
For the opportunity to share in this fellowship,
to know the sense of home this place is for us,
we give thanks.
Open us to the possibilities this fellowship offers us—
to see each other as unique and yet one,
to celebrate our differences
and to hallow what we find
when we look into each other's eyes.
Open to the possibilities to which our souls call us,
we overflow with thanksgiving.
As light into light, we pray
Amen.

## Non-theistic:

At the very core of our being
rests a deep and urgent need to relate to one another.
Our souls long for communion,
for fellowship, and we gather in this place to seek it out.
For the opportunity to share in this fellowship,
to know the sense of home this place is for us,
we give thanks.
May we be open to the possibilities this fellowship offers us—
to see each other as unique and yet one,
to celebrate our differences
and to hallow what we find
when we look into each other's eyes.
Open to the possibilities to which our souls call us,
we overflow with thanksgiving.
As light into light, we pray
Amen.

This prayer expresses gratitude that is directed at no particular being, person, or thing. It is just simply and intentionally expressed. To live as people with a deep sense of reverence for life fills us with gratitude. Living without a recipient for that gratitude may seem strange at first, but pouring it out, undirected and unnamed, can be a very rich spiritual exercise.

## At the End of Prayer

Several years ago, my discomfort with the phrase that most frequently punctuates Christian prayer—"In Jesus' name, we pray"—demanded attention. The roots of the phrase lie deep in the concept of intercession, worth, and intervention.

As noted in Chapter 6, Jesus' biblical direction to "ask in my name" was believed to have the effect of moving your prayer to the head of the line so God would consider it. Praying "in Jesus' name" brought all his merit to bear in the appeal. Without it you were, simply put, unworthy of being heard, laughed out of the line; God was not bound to listen to your request. Obviously, even in a traditional theistic setting, this theology is troubling.

Preserving a sense of closure for prayer that extended beyond a perfunctory "Amen" required a new way to end prayer that didn't suggest either an interventionist deity or our own unworthiness. "As those born into light yet ever seeking it" is the phrasing I now most usually employ. The words reflect my belief in the inherent worth and beauty of all human beings. We are born into that reality as our inheritance—nothing can take it away from us. And though we may have within us what some would call the divine spark, we spend our lives trying to achieve it, to become fulfilled. Although we are spiritual beings, we never complete the quest for spiritual meaning in life. We are born into what I refer to as "light," the capacity for spiritual awareness, but we spend our lives trying to achieve it—"born into light, yet ever seeking it."

In addition to whatever we might come to know as the divine spark within us, it is nowhere near the totality of the wonder we seek to know and understand in the universe. There is much that remains and will remain beyond our understanding and beyond the capacity of our minds to encompass. In traditional terms, one might say that God is immanent, within us, and transcendent, beyond us. We have an individual "incarnation" of divinity which we contribute to the whole, but that whole is much larger than we can even comprehend. So to pray as "light into light" is to recognize that we offer what we as individuals have to offer, that which transcends us—be it the community, the spirit, or the challenge to work for good that calls us beyond our own self-serving wants and desires—and what we as individuals seek to receive from that same ineffable transcendence—"as light into light, we pray."

## Music

Remember, if you can't say it in the pulpit, you shouldn't sing it in the pew. Although it is still difficult to find adequate music resources, theology you do not believe is no more acceptable merely because it is set to music. Begin by choosing hymns that need only one or two verses taken out of them; then get creative.

Copyright is key. You will need to figure out if copyright applies to the words, music, or both, and what you may need permission to change. Check with your lawyer. Are you "copying" the whole work, or a substantial part of it, or are you "performing" it? Generally, with most contemporary Christian music, the words and music are copyrighted in one piece: this may mean that if the language doesn't work in your setting, you simply can't change it without permission. If the music and words are copyrighted separately, you may be able to write completely new words for the music. In some cases, you can receive permission to alter words from the copyright holder. If there is no copyright, you can change the original words, such as replacing *Lord* with *love*, or similar substitutions.

The following is a completely new hymn, "Sing Praise to All," written to the tune "Lobe den Herren," commonly used for the hymn "Praise to the Lord":

Sing praise to all that has offered us life and sustains us—
All that has opened our hearts to the love borne within us:
Family and friends,
Beauty we see without end—
Gifts that our lives lay before us.

Sing praise to all that has opened our minds to new vistas—
All that has called us to seek out new truths through the ages:
Vision and word,
Music that sought to be heard
These are the gifts that will mould us.

Sing praise to minds that will fashion our bold new tomorrows—
Yesterday's wisdom released from its dogma and credos.
Evermore free
To live out what we believe
Walking the path that Life hallows.[4]

The following song, "Then Sings My Soul," is an adaptation of an old hymn, "How Great Thou Art," written by Carl G. Bobergin, and now in public domain:

When I this day, in deep and awesome wonder,
Consider all the myst'ries of this earth;
I see the stars, I hear the rolling thunder,
The universe unfolding since its birth.

*Refrain:*
Then sings my soul in wonder full and free,

Amazed at all I hear and see
Then sings my soul in wonder full and free
A sacred gift is life to me.

When through the woods and forest glades I wander,
And hear the birds sing sweetly in the trees.
When I look down, from lofty mountain grandeur
And hear the brook, and feel the gentle breeze.

*Refrain*

When Life is done, and all the love I've given,
with love received, what joy shall fill my heart!
Then I shall bow, in humble adoration,
to Life's great myst'ries, each a work of art.

*Refrain*[5]

## Readings

I have covered concerns regarding the use of the Bible and lectionary elsewhere and will seek here to provide some tools for assessing alternate readings you may wish to use in religious gatherings. It is important to note that without the common story the Bible has previously provided, the struggle to identify with a tradition will be challenging. I highly recommend a gently progressive change with gradual steps.

The sources for readings are innumerable. Appropriate readings can be found in spiritual writings, philosophy, the sacred texts of other traditions, literature, drama, music, contemporary novels, poetry, inspirational books, children's literature, and greeting cards, to name only a few. And, as with the Bible, inappropriate readings can also be found. At any one time, the same reading may be one or the other—it depends on the community you serve and the purpose you are trying to achieve.

Generally, you will need to keep in mind some simple criteria for selecting readings. These questions are offered to help you assess readings you are considering.

1. *Does it make a claim that cannot be substantiated?* Readings may appear to be spiritual because they include some of the traditional spiritual characters or language with which you are familiar. They may offer comforting images and ideas, but if they make supernatural claims identifying causes and promising interventions that are beyond the "realm" of objective evidence, they should not be used unless explicitly identified as metaphor or symbol. For instance, the presence of guardian angels, the guidance of personal daemons, the attributing of circumstances to Fate—all these present "spiritual" ideas that cannot be substantiated. Including a reading from Philip Pullman's His Dark Materials trilogy that involves daemons, however, might be a perfect way to begin a conversation about being attentive to our deepest truths, sometimes referred to as our inner voice. As long as the existence of daemons is not presented as or intimated to be truth (because you simply cannot know), it could be an appropriate reading. Frame any questionable reading with a qualifying introduction.

2. *Does it lift up universal values (I know, technically, there are none) or universalize local or tribal values (I know, technically, we can only really do this. See the discussion on relativism and absolutism in Chapter One)?* Readings that universalize local applications of values are no longer acceptable in a postmodern world in which differing local perspectives must be acknowledged. Even a seemingly banal statement such as "We are all God's children" is universalizing a single perspec-

tive that may be rejected by anyone who does not accept that statement of relationship. As well, cultural priorities, gender issues, and perspectives on sexuality are always contextual and must be recognized as such.

3. *Does it lift up the life-enhancing values the community has identified as sacred?* Just because a reading comes from an authoritative voice doesn't mean it is worth reading in worship. Some of the works of Thomas Jefferson, beautiful in form and style, would be highly worthy of reading in a religious gathering. Others, such as those regarding the differences of race (none of which are now considered factual beyond the obvious characteristics of hair and skin colour), would be absolutely inappropriate. Almost every voice that has broken down a social barrier of its time has been tolerant of another, broken later by someone else. Readings must be held up against those ideals to which we aspire and agree. If they do not meet them, they are not worthy of being brought into our religious gatherings.

4. *Is it engaging?* There is no excuse for reading a boring or overly challenging text to people just because they are sitting in front of you waiting to hear something. Difficult texts, regardless of their merit, create distance between the speaker and their audience. Save them for study groups or online conversations when people have an opportunity to spend time with them and digest them. A brilliant mind will explore a simple but inspiring reading to the extent that it is able, although that might very well be far beyond what an average mind might be able to do. Your responsibility is to engage both. Don't leave the average person behind in order to win the respect of the extraordinary few. And don't bore the extraordinary few to death with trite and trivial passages.

## Baptism

Baptism, as a sacrament (an efficacious act intended to engage God's participation in an event), requires particular words and actions in order to validate the effect. As something sacramental, however, that acknowledges and celebrates the pre-existence of the sacred within the child, such prescribed words and actions are no longer necessary. It may be, as with so many other terms, that the word baptism will need to be replaced in order to clarify the shift in purpose. Calling it a Celebration of Baptism instead of the Sacrament of Baptism is a good first step.

Helping people to understand what baptism means within your particular community is very important. A printed resource is helpful, especially if guests who may not have the same understandings as the congregation are present. The following is an example.

### An Understanding of Baptism

So many aspects of life are beyond our comprehension. While through the centuries science has revealed and explained much, there still remains a realm beyond the concrete, beyond the tangible. We refer to this as the realm of the spirit: a realm of mystery and of miracle. It is here we sense the concepts of meaning, values, and purpose. It is here we discover the inherent worth of life, the dignity and equality of all human beings. It is here we are moved by the beauty in the created world; here we are inspired to contribute to that beauty.

And it is here, in this realm of mystery, of spirit, that we sense a call to wholeness: to integrity in our relationships with ourselves, with others, and with the world around us. We call this wholeness, this "greater than, and beyond us, yet within us"—the Divine. And we sense this call to wholeness coming to us as individuals, but also as a community, for we believe that the way to this wholeness to which we feel called is the way of love—of justice and compassion.

We believe that life is a journey of the spirit, walked in faith. By faith, we are ever learning, ever growing; ever experiencing the Divine within us; and ever reaching toward the Divine beyond us.

(Long ago, it is told, a man named Jesus broke into a highly regulated and oppressed community with a vision of wholeness, of harmony and peace, equality and justice that turned his bleak and tiny world into a place of hope and new life. He saw and knew and spoke of that we call the Divine as though he, himself—indeed, as though all who listened to him—were indwelled by that Divine. For many in that time and place, it was a new thought. We struggle to understand the power that caused his life, his words, to cast reverberations through two thousand years to us. Even now, we sense the challenges that flow from the stories of his life, from the way he is said to have understood God.)

So much in life calls us away from community, from wholeness. We are torn in many directions. We see through different eyes. We learn fear and live, too often, by its demands. Yet each day, there comes at least a moment, too often fleeting, wherein the choice is ours to seek out what might bring back to us that sense of wholeness, of unity, of peace. We sense it as a working of the spirit. For some, the task of choosing an awareness of the spirit is easy. For others, the struggle to reach into that place from which deep calls to deep is ever that—a struggle. But still, the need to find a place of hope within us calls us to the task.

Having explored these concepts with the baptismal families at a prior event, the parents can then be engaged in the service in the following manner.

You come to this place bringing your children. You speak for them. Their care and nurture is entrusted to you. You bring them here to commit both them and yourselves to a life of faith, a journey with ever new experiences and challenges.

Do you see the act of baptism as a symbol of our celebration of the life of your child, filled as he or she already is with the spirit of the Divine? If so, please say, "I do."

Do you believe that as we share the stories of life, yours, ours, those of your children, and those of people of wisdom and faith who have gone before us, as we share those stories, we come to know the Divine more fully? If so, please say "I do."

Do you commit yourself and your children to a journey of the spirit with this community of faith, seeking to find and nurture the wholeness within yourself, your children and the world? If so, please say, "I do."

Congregational commitment is, of course, important. Often, creeds are used to reinforce the beliefs being embraced through the act of baptism, but if they are not commonly held to be true by the candidates, the officiant, or the congregation, don't use them. In many mainline denominations, creeds are included as practice not as polity; you don't need to use them. Where they are required, again, you must consider the implications of acting in a manner that places you in opposition to the authority of the denomination.

> One: We gather at this font
> to celebrate the Spirit of Life
> that connects us all
> and through which we come
> to love ourselves, one another
> and the whole of creation.

> All: This fount and the water in it,
> are our symbols of community
> and our common need
> for the refreshing waters of the Spirit.

One: Through water we are born,
   of water we are made,
   by water we are sustained.
   (To the congregation)
   Each of you, whole and loved, yet knows the need
   for support and care upon the spiritual journey.
   As this family gathers to commit to the journey,
   let us pledge our care to them.

All: We stand as witnesses to the commitment
   this family makes to the journey of faith
   and pledge ourselves,
   through the symbol of this water,
   to their love, support, and care
   as they discover the ways
   that the Spirit unfolds for them.

Baptismal formulae, the words we use when we baptize an individual, are consistent within denominations seeking common acceptance within the World Council of Churches (WCC). The gender-inclusive language debate introduced some options, although those options were not recognized officially by any WCC denominations. If you choose not to use the WCC accepted formula, "I baptize you in the name of the Father, the Son, and the Holy Spirit," parents must be made aware that the baptism does not conform to WCC standards. Certificates presented to the family should reflect this.

It may be helpful when making a shift within a congregation to use a somewhat Trinitarian form such as:

I baptize you in the name of Love,
   its beginning and its end,

its purpose and its power,

its commitment and its challenge.

If being Trinitarian isn't as important to you, you might branch out into something a bit more dramatic such as:

I baptize you in the name of
Life who created you,
Wisdom who knew you first,
Hope by whom you shall be sustained,
Delight in whom I pray you to live,
And I baptize you in the name of Love.
May you live every day in its embrace.

And, because these things can come to hold a power of their own, if you are able, develop several versions to use randomly so that none assume an authority and become understood as "the magic words." Over time, as congregants explore further, the personification of "life," the capitalization of "spirit," and the definition of "the Divine" will all become important aspects of an ongoing, dynamic conversation.

## Adult Affirmations of Faith

Occasionally, adults wish to make an affirmation of their faith. Perhaps it is a regulation required for full membership in a denomination; perhaps they have begun a new stage of their spiritual journey; perhaps they have moved to a new spiritual community. Whatever the reason, it is an excellent opportunity for the community to embrace them and to recommit to the communal nature of the spiritual journey. The following questions and affirmations might prove helpful and can easily be combined with a baptismal service:

One: Do you wish to unite with us on this journey of faith, to discover and rediscover the meaning of the holiness within you, between us, and surrounding us?

Candidate: I do.

One: Will you let Love be your guide, opening yourself to the spirit of truth, even, and especially, when you may be led to something you had never planned to know?

Candidate: I will.

One: Are you willing to share with us in joy and reach out with us in love?

Candidate: I am.

One: (To the congregation)
We gather in community
to offer our gifts to one another
as we share the spiritual journey.
It is in community
we learn who we truly are;
in community,
we come to honour the *other*ness
of those who travel with us;
in community,
we become bound to one another
by a connection deeper than words.

All: In this community,
we share our common desire

to know love,

to seek truth,

and to speak the truth in love.

One: Each of you, whole and loved, yet knows the need

for support and care upon the spiritual journey.

As these individuals gather to pledge themselves

to the journey,

through a profession of faith,

let us pledge our care to them.

All: We stand as witnesses to the commitment

these people make to the journey of faith

and pledge ourselves,

through the symbol of the laying on of hands

to their love, support, and care

as they discover the spiritual strength that is theirs.

One: We have committed to these individuals that we will

offer them love, support, and care as they journey

with us. That means we will be, for them, as they

need us, their strength. For any journey, strength is

a prerequisite and a spiritual journey is no exception.

I invite you to join us here at the front and symboli-

cally, through the laying on of hands, impart to them

our own strength to support them as they travel the

often difficult, winding paths of life.

Those who wish to will gather with those already at the front, including those baptized, and join in a laying on of hands. The leader can offer a brief blessing as we move through the group of gathered individuals.

## Communion

Within the congregation for which this liturgy was written, baptism is understood to be the declaration of a commitment to the spiritual journey or quest by an adult or on behalf of a child by her or his parent(s) or guardian(s). It is a commitment to live with an awareness of one's spiritual nature, value, worth, and connectedness to the rest of humanity and creation. Such an understanding of baptism leads easily to the celebration of communion as a symbol of recommitment to and nourishment for that journey.

We come to know one another around tables. We share our lives around tables. Relationships grow in intimacy around tables. We look one another in the eye around tables. That we gather around a table to share our struggles, take strength, and go out again to the world, is fitting and good. This is what we see ourselves to be doing as we gather for communion.

Because we are reclaiming a very powerful symbol, however, it is essential that we reiterate what we are doing *every* time we participate. If we assume that everyone understands our new interpretation of communion, the power of the previous meaning could easily overwhelm it for any who are new to the community or aren't confident of the new symbolism. For that reason, the liturgist welcomes the community to the table or to the time of communion with the following or similar words:

> One: It is around the common tables in our lives that we
> come to understand nourishment, love, challenge,
> and caring. We gather around them in our child-
> hood to share our day's adventures. As adults, it is
> there that we reconnect with friends and family,
> grounding ourselves in what is real. In our senior
> years we share the wisdom we are with those who sit
> at the table with us. We are cared for there. We face

challenge there. We look into one another's eyes and face truth there. Tables are a powerful part of our lives. Tables are an ordinary part of our lives.

So it is that we gather here today—to be about what is, for us, at once both common and exquisitely beautiful. In this community, we pledge to be strength and en-*coeur*-agement for each other on the spiritual journey, to wrap our hearts around one another as we travel together. And it is here, at this table, that we symbolize the power of that pledge. The road is long and, too often, we are weary. When we gather here, as we look into the eyes of those we know or do not know, we see the light of love and feel our hope lifted.

(So it may have been, that night so long ago, when Jesus lay with his disciples, sharing a meal, burdened by the realities of life. In that place, perhaps they offered one another care, lifted burdens from each other, and planted possibility in their overbrimming hearts. So may it be for us.)

The elements of the table are prepared. It is no more "progressive" to take communion by intinction than by taking it in the pew. Either method has its positives and negatives. If you're changing the words of the liturgy though, I'd suggest you stick with whichever form you regularly use. Make it look as "normal" as possible. The following prayer is roughly the equivalent of a traditional "Great Thanksgiving" without theistic elements. The liturgist may or may not wish to include the opening responses.

One: May it we well with you.

All: And also with you.

One: Life is a gift and we its celebration.

All: May we rejoice in the beauty that we are.

One: Let us pray together. (*pause*)
    The morning has awakened the earth
    and we arrive to celebrate.
    Day unfolds its possibilities before us,
    and we stand ready to embrace the options life offers.
    May we ever do so with courage and grace.
    The beginnings of time are so long past
    that we can neither see nor understand them.
    Each of us gathered here,
    the consequence of billions upon billions of chance
        connections,
    miniscule moments of opportunity taken,
    was in that beginning so long ago.
    Our breath began that day.
    The elements within our cells came into being then.
    The energy encircling such cosmic craft
    moves through our hearts even now.
    And we are wondrously and beautifully made.
    Through the millennia,
    before our eyes were blessed to opening,
    the earth folded, creased, burst wide, cracked.
    Mountains rose, continents drifted,
    land separated itself from land.
    Water flowed and froze, smoothed surfaces, carved
        canyons,
    then rose and misted, fell again upon irregular
        terrain,
    and life moved ever onward.
    And we, once wakened to the world around us,

set our hearts upon that subtle ever-forward pull of
   creation.
For we see the ills that we have wrought upon the
   earth.
We know the pains we have caused ourselves and
   others.
The burdens we now shoulder are great.
We pray that life might carry us forward from this
   place,
free us from the yoke of our unfeeling.
We pray there might be within our breasts
the wisdom necessary
to bring about an age of goodness,
an age of truth, an age of love beyond measure.
May life move surely onward.
We pray, too, that we, who gather at this table,
might see and know the humanity of those who
   gather with us.
May we feel their individuality, sense their fears,
believe the strength of their confidence.
May we be nourished by who they are.
We pray that we might, in turn,
be instruments of grace for them.
May we find within our own hearts
the hope that will light another's way,
the strength that will not fold beneath another's weight,
and the courage to face another's fears.
May they be nourished by who we are.
We have on this table,
the common things of life—
bread to break with each other
and wine to quench our thirst.

May they be for us as they have been for many,

strength and faith,

(*the bread is broken*)

nourishment and hope,

(*the pitcher is lifted but not elevated*)

blessing and forgiveness.

(*the cup is filled*)

And may we who come to this table,

know the presence of that which is beyond all our

 understanding

and which yet resides within our own hearts.

Amen.

(*Instructions may be given at this time.*)

The table is ready.

Come, gather 'round.

(*Music can be played in the background or songs sung as
the congregation gathers, prepares, or comes forward for
communion.*)

## Prayers of Petition, Intercession, and Thanksgiving

Prayer, as noted previously, is a significant spiritual discipline within many spiritual traditions. We count on "something" happening even if we can't explain what that something is. Any concrete evidence established by further study will likely disclose that there is no supernatural occurrence that assists or impedes the efficacy of prayer. Given the enormous strides taken in our scientific knowledge over the past century (strides that have unbalanced much of what we thought was "true") and the acceleration of scientific discovery we are now experiencing, it is possible that we will have definitive results in a very short time. Those of us for whom prayer is an important spiritual practice, unless we are prepared for its complete demystification, are going to be severely unsettled.

So let us assume that there is nothing supernatural occurring and prepare ourselves for the harshest reality. We find that the effect of prayer, as with all spiritual pursuit, is within us, in our perceptions, actions, and understandings. All spiritual experience is mediated through our physical, mental, and emotional processes, even those argued by the most convincing voices to be *super*natural. There is nothing beyond our natural capabilities that processes or seeks to understand the effects. It is, therefore, quite reasonable and appropriate for us to simply set supernatural powers aside and focus on the natural responses we are capable of when we address the topic of prayer.

We are, however, often most susceptible to falling back on former supernatural images when it comes to prayer. Murry reminds us of Freud's suggestion that traditional religion evolved out of the adult projecting onto the supernatural the infant's dependence upon the parent.[6] For many, prayer has been their lifeline, their connection to that point of security, wherever they may have anchored it. Tampering with that very deeply held need for security is a challenging and unwelcome task. It must be approached with enormous sensitivity, respect, and care.

As soon as a person moves into whatever prayer posture he or she normally assumes, a whole set of impressions, assumptions, and expectations tumble into place along with accumulated memory, either supporting or denying the efficacy of what she is about to do. There is little point in trying to reconcile the great diversity of experience that will be present at any single religious gathering. Each person will have a different story, a different experience of the "power" of prayer, and trying to urge all to agree on what that is would be a waste of time and an opportunity for conflict to brew.*

*Don't ever hesitate to ignite the conversation about prayer at times other than during the religious gathering time. For too long we have shied away from discussing complex ideas for which the answers are difficult. Acknowledging the different experiences people hold is one thing. Denying them by telling them it only works in one particular way, which always happens to be yours, is quite another.

As we move into new ways of doing things, the magician's skill of focusing the audience's attention in one direction in order to do something different in the other is one that might be kept in mind. What we focus people's attention on is their agreement that they have experienced the effects of prayer. What we divert their attention from is what made that experience happen, from what they cannot agree upon—their understanding of prayer—to what they can—that something happened.

Actively drawing attention to what is shared and away from what is not will help create a sense of community and comfort. Remember, even those who are radically progressive in their intellectual appreciation of Christianity often experience its supernatural comforts very deeply. Non-interventionist prayer removes that comfort and can challenge even the most forward thinking in the group.

Until the new form of prayer is widely accepted by the community—that is, until there is little threat to the security of those who have been going through a shift in what they expect of a religious gathering, and until those who wander in can be advised ahead of time (through websites, advertising, for example) of what actually goes on—it may be helpful to introduce the prayer time using words that affirm the common experience and divert attention from the differences. The following introductions are offered as options:

1. As we come together as a community of faith in the activity known to us as prayer, we feel our roots reaching deep into the history of our tradition. So, too, do we feel them spread broadly across the many religious traditions that also employ prayer as a spiritual discipline. While we do not claim to have a definitive answer to the question of how prayer works, we each have felt its power or seen it working in the lives of those for whom we have prayed, and so we join those who

walk the road of faith and enter into prayer with them and with each other now.

2. It is as those who seek connection, reconciliation, and forgiveness that we open ourselves in prayer. Touched by its power, we release the need to know how it works, what it does, where it goes. For us, prayer operates in the moment our hearts are joined as one, our needs are expressed, our celebrations shared. It is in the energy of those moments we find ourselves most open to the work of sacred transformation. May we step toward that transformation now as we share the joys and concerns of this community.

3. In relationship, we come to know ourselves, share who we are, and be confronted by what we see of ourselves in our sisters' and brothers' eyes. Prayer, here, is the hallmark of our relationship. Within it, we are held to our pledge to one another: to live together in truth and in love. Within us, it works to challenge, heal, and transform. May we hold one another as we gather now in prayer, once again, feeling and knowing the depths at which we are one. As each has need, may it be spoken, heard, and held within the shelter of this community.

Over time, the responsibility for offering prayer has shifted from me, as ordained worship leader, to the congregation. As Hal Taussig notes early in his book *A New Spiritual Home*,[7] many congregations have recognized the power imbalance implicit in the offering of prayer by a single, usually ordained, person. Rather than relying on an ordained worship leader, they have begun offering "Joys and Concerns" times, during which individuals rise and share their prayer concerns with the gathered community.

## Unison Prayer Responses

For those transforming congregations whose religious gathering is built around traditional liturgy, formal responses are regular and comfortable. Finding a way to maintain the rhythm of the response while eliminating theistic overtones can, once again, draw people's attention toward what it is they have in common— the flow of the liturgy—and away from what they don't—belief or lack of belief in an interventionist deity.

The congregation I serve had moved into a highly ritualized liturgy during the term of my predecessor. One of the additions to the service was a set of versicles following their prayers of thanksgiving and prayers of intercession. For thanksgiving prayers, the following was said:

> Leader: For this, O Gracious One,
> All: We give you thanks.

For prayers of intercession, the response was classic:

> Leader: O, God, in your mercy,
> All: Hear our prayer.

Since, in many cases, it is the emotional connection, not the intellectual understanding, that is most likely to be disturbed, it can be that the "feel" of the response is more important than the actual words. It may be helpful when attempting to create a new set of responses then to keep the rhythm and length of the statements similar to those being replaced. The "feel" of what the individual is doing remains the same, and the emotional connection remains intact. As with any congregational involvement, always put responses in writing, either on paper or projected, so that guests and newcomers do not feel excluded. And remember, if you are using resources from elsewhere, give proper credit. Some suggestions:

Generic
> Leader: In joy and in sorrow
>> All: We do not walk alone.[8]

Paired (Joys/Concerns),
Set I
> Leader: In the light and beauty of day
>> All: We give thanks in awe and wonder.

> Leader: In the dark and stillness of night
>> All: We dream of healing and hope.

Set II
> Leader: As one heart is lifted
>> All: May we share its celebration.

> Leader: As one heart is burdened
>> All: May we share the pain it knows.

Set III
> Leader: In this abundant blessing
>> All: We share the joy.

> Leader: In this, our time of need,
>> All: May love abound.

## Finally

When we come to the conclusion of the religious gathering, the traditional benediction is often pronounced on the gathered community, sending them out under the protection of God. The world is not a safe place. We know that. Intoning a benediction does not make it any safer. *We* must do what we can to make it as safe as we can and rely upon community to support us when we cannot. The words used to conclude a religious gathering need to be words that inspire, that attend to the commitment individuals have made to be attentive to the sacred ideals upon which they have agreed and to be available and present to one another as they do so in the coming days. If it is at all possible, do it without reading. Look them in the eyes, honour who they are and who you are as one of them. Tell them simply what it is you believe the world requires of them and what it is you believe them capable of doing. Or tell them how what has happened in that time together has changed you and how you hope it has changed them. Don't lift your arms over your head. Don't make the sign of the cross over them. Don't change to your preaching voice. Don't point your first two fingers to heaven after the applied manner of Jesus. Don't pretend you're doing something you're not. Just speak to them.

> The world you go into is a world filled with challenges, with crises, with pain, with disappointment. You go as people who know these things intimately because you have felt them, experienced them, and railed against them. Go now as those who would see not only what the world is but what we can make it be, and may your hands, your heart, your voice be turned toward making it so. Go in peace.

Or,

> In this gathering, we have spoken of love, sung songs of freedom, held one another's pain, and smiled at each other's blessings. As we leave this place, go knowing you are part of a whole that is beyond our understanding and yet enriched by your own particular beauty.

Shine as who you are. May all you meet be blessed by your beauty, and may you be blessed by the beauty of all you meet.

Simple. Meaningful. To the point. And nothing said that isn't true.

## AN ONGOING EXPERIMENT

Whether non-theistic religious gatherings can thrive and survive is anyone's guess. We are in the midst of a great experiment. I fervently believe that we need to see that experiment through to the end, giving our all to the creation of communities of "faith" that celebrate the communal nature of life and challenge us to engage in right relationship with self, others, and the planet. There is much that depends on the survival of love. If we transform church into a vessel in which love can be held, shared, and offered to the world, then we will have been successful. And if we find along the way, that church is not necessary to the work of making love known and teaching one another ways in which it can be lived out radically, ethically, beautifully, then we will be able to let church go and face a world without it with confidence and grace.

The Light of Love
*by Scott Kearns*

By the light of the sun and the glow of the moon
we can see the natural world all around us.
But the world of the spirit is a world of mystery,
and natural light won't help us to see.

In the light of love our lives have meaning.
In the light of love our purpose shines.

Whenever there is justice to be dared,
compassion to be shared—
this is our calling
in the light of love.

So lift it up, hold it high—write it clear across the sky;
burn it deep within your soul—live it well and live it whole.
And nothing more is needed, but nothing less will do,
for nothing else can take the place of love.

In the light of love our lives have dignity.
In the light of love our purpose shines.
To celebrate the beauty everywhere
with deep respect and care—
this is our calling
in the light of love.

Not our forms, not our creeds, neither plans nor empty deeds;
no, nothing else can take the place of love.
Not our status, not our health, not inheritance or wealth,
no, nothing else can take the place of love.

So lift it up, hold it high—write it clear across the sky;
burn it deep within your soul—live it well and live it whole.
And nothing more is needed, but nothing less will do,
for nothing else can take the place of love.
Nothing more, nothing less, nothing else could ever take the place
of love.
. . . so write it clear across the sky. . . . [9]

# ACKNOWLEDGEMENTS

"I no doubt deserve my enemies, but I don't believe I deserve my friends."
—Walt Whitman

Several years ago, the congregation I serve had fleece vests imprinted with the image of a tapestry that graces the space where we gather each Sunday morning. Under the embroidered image of the colourful, double-swirled design is stitched—in a funky, purple, off-kilter script—the phrase "Life is a journey."

Those four simple words, sewn long before anyone would have predicted the path we have since walked, are used by many on the margins of traditional religious institutional faith as a casual creed to explain the ups and downs, challenges and blessings, clarity and confusion that are all part of the complex reality we call life. On a journey, stuff happens. Some of it is great. Some of it is less than great. Some of it is downright awful. But all of it, when shared with people you love and respect, is worth every single step.

The journey of this book has been no different. Parts of it were shared with me by those who had long pursued the path, treading smooth a way I could then follow; other portions of the trail brought new faces alongside, and strengthened the purpose we shared; and from time to time, paths diverged and called to those whose interests lay elsewhere.

Over the years, I have been joined by a host of exquisitely beautiful and passionate people. They have challenged me, supported me, affirmed me, needled me, cajoled me, helped me, impassioned me, inspired me, infuriated me, encouraged me, enlightened me, assured me, moved me, soothed me, provoked me, cared for me, and pointed me in new directions when I could not find my way. Through it all, I have been humbled by their love. On particularly difficult days, when a positive way forward seemed devastatingly unlikely, bright flecks of hope would find their way to me, each sent by a heart who knew me well—a poem about crocuses, a torn paper heart left for me to find, "something like a breeze" to conjure comfort, an email with the simple subject line "Whither thou goest," a plush butterfly with a note explaining that ugliness is sometimes just beauty struggling to get out, powerful notes and cards and voicemail messages, and innumerable expressions of support. Each individual, each thoughtful gesture, each moment of encouragement has contributed to the creation of what lies in your hands. I regret only that the vast number of kind gestures makes it impossible for me to name them all.

The actual writing of the book came about through the particular gifts of a number of people. John Shelby Spong will happily tell you he merely opened the door for me. The truth is quite something else. His confidence, encouragement, enthusiasm, and faith did much more for me and for this book than he will ever know. I am deeply honoured to have been blessed by his wisdom, courage, and vision. Christine, as well, shone her grace and love upon me and my work, brightening the way and making things happen, as she always does. Thank you to you both.

Completely oblivious to the toll footnoting and research would exact, I recklessly engaged the assistance of Matthew Herrington who, fortunately, was as ignorant of the requirements as I was, and so, keenly jumped right in. His enthusiasm was marvellous, and I thank him for the work he did. David Barker, who undertook the research task at a much later date, with twice as many pages of manuscript to engage, brought to it an extraordinary grasp of the subject matter and was ever diligent in exploring sources and material to bring depth to my perspective. As life has unfolded, Matthew has become my son-in-law, and David a close and trusted friend. I love you both.

It has been amazing to work with the people at HarperCollins Canada. Their encouragement and patience has been unending. David Kent's confidence in his remarkable team allowed him to take this leap of faith. Iris Tupholme placed me in the capable hands of Nicole Langlois, who remembered to care not only about the manuscript but also about the writer as she guided me through my first editorial process. She gently pushed for more detail, lobbed off all that extra stuff you didn't need to read, challenged me to focus, focus, focus when I found it much easier to just shoot from the hip, and exposed to me her personal reactions to the content in ways that, I hope, have helped me empathize with a religious perspective that is not my own. It has been a delight to come to know her. I have so enjoyed working with Jim Gifford, who offered a calming strength through the final months of the process. His humour has often brightened the dark days and sparkled the bright ones. These are but a few of the many to whom I hold a debt of gratitude.

Dana Wilson-Li, chair of the board of West Hill United Church and a constant source of clarity, solid judgment, and wisdom, has been hugely important to the process the congregation has undertaken. In what she so aptly identified as a perfect storm, she has been the consummate leader and an excellent friend. Ken Ramsay, charged with the responsibility of keeping me and the congregation in a healthy relationship, knew full well what that would take and yet accepted. He has splendidly balanced the burden throughout the writing of this book. Peggy Hall graciously covered many of the gaps that my writing created in the fulfillment of my pastoral responsibilities and did so with discretion and care. Her presence and support have been enormously helpful and are greatly appreciated. Keith Hagerman and David Hallman each read the manuscript and offered reactions that were honest, insightful, and most helpful. Those who know Debbie Ellis will know that there is no person on the planet who could possibly show more enthusiasm for a piece of work. A constant source of encouragement, passion, and exclamation, she has shed delight on every moment we've shared, even and especially while offering her discerning critique.

Thank you to my parents; there are few who get to explore ideas such as these with their parents and know they will be met with non-stop support and praise. Thank you to my children, Hazel and Izaak; you are constant sources of inspiration. As you take up the tools with which you each choose to challenge and change the world, know that words could only ever fail to express my love and pride in you.

It is also impossible for me to express in words what it has meant to walk this road with Scott Kearns, my partner, husband, lover, and friend, who lives, more intentionally than anyone I know, by Cicero's challenging creed: "Seek the truth, come whence it may, cost what it will." He has sheltered and exposed me, challenged and protected me, affirmed and confronted me, held me fast and set me free. I walk upon the firmament of his love. He has been my intake of breath, my every liminal moment, and has proven beyond a doubt that the possibilities are endless.

# NOTES

## Chapter 1

1  Richard Holloway, "The Church Organist and the Jazz Pianist," in *The Future of the Christian Tradition*, ed. Robert Miller (Polebridge: Santa Rosa, 2007), 95.

2  Ibid., 96.

3  Sam Harris, "Believing the Unbelievable: The Clash Between Faith and Reason in the Modern World" (lecture, Aspen Ideas Festival, Aspen, Colorado, July 14, 2007, www.aifestival.org/library/transcript/believingtheunbelievable.pdf (October 8, 2007).

4  Friedrich Nietzsche, *Human, All Too Human*, trans. Walter Kaufman (New York: Viking, 1954), 54–55, quoted in Holloway, "The Church Organist," 98.

5  Emily Robison, Martie Maguire, Natalie Maines, and Dan Wilson, "Not Ready to Make Nice," *Taking the Long Way*, compact disc, Open Wide/Columbia, 82876 80739 2, ℗ © 2006 Sony BMG Music Entertainment.

6  John Shelby Spong, *A New Christianity for a New World: Why Traditional Faith Is Dying and How a New Faith Is Being Born* (New York: HarperCollins, 2001), 24–29.

7  John A.T. Robinson, *Honest to God* (London: SCM Press, 1963), 7–8.

8  Ibid.

9  A number of books have been published, including Tim Flannery's *The Weather Makers: The History and Future Impact of Climate Change* (Toronto: HarperCollins Canada, 2005), in which our actions are shown to have direct effect not only on the earth but on the forces of nature that affect it—rain, drought, hurricanes, and so on.

10  The Stewart brothers, wealthy oil magnates, financed the publication of a four-volume series edited by Reuben Archer Torrey, A.C. Dixon, et al., entitled *The Fundamentals: A Testimony to the Truth* in 1917. The books were to clarify, once and for all, the basic beliefs essential to a Protestant faith. They did not receive the response hoped for, but the books continue to serve as the bottom line set of beliefs of evangelical Christians.

11  The synoptic Gospels are Matthew, Mark, and Luke, named so because, side by side, they run through a similar account of Jesus' life. Some New Testament scholars use the differences between these Gospels to chart the development of early Christianity.

12  C. Kirk Hadaway and P. L. Marler, "Did You Really Go to Church This Week?" *The Christian Century*, May 6 (1998): 472–475. American polls consistently represent attendance at religious services at about 40 per cent of the population. That

figure is seriously challenged by researchers who sought to verify the claim. Their conclusions, found highly insulting by some, were that the reported attendance at services is roughly half what actually occurs. In the Canadian context, another survey provides similar results: "In 1946, about 67% of the adult population attended religious services on a weekly basis. According to the General Social Survey, by 2001 the weekly attendance rate had slipped to 20%; the monthly religious attendance rate also fell: from 43% in 1986 to 31% in 2001." Warren Clark, "Pockets of Belief: Religious Attendance Patterns in Canada," *Canadian Social Trends* Spring (2003), 2.

13   The 2005 Baylor Study on Religion (BSR) explores specific beliefs about Christianity. Available at www.thearda.com/Archive/Files/Search/BRS2005_AN.asp (accessed October 1, 2007). Baylor University, 2005. *The Baylor Religion Survey*. Waco, TX: Baylor Institute for Studies of Religion (producer).

14   "The Christmas Miracle," *Newsweek* Web Exclusive, December 10, 2004, www.msnbc.msn.com/id/6650997/site/newsweek/ (accessed October 1, 2007).

15   The official teaching of the Vatican is that the priest, through the Eucharistic Mass, transforms the bread and blood into the actual body of Christ as it is being sacrificed—the same sacrifice that originally took place. It isn't a rerun but a conflation of time. "Now," through the mystery of the Eucharist, becomes "then." That being the case, the individual's sins are then taken by Jesus onto himself so that they "will be/were" atoned for. Although that's the teaching, it would be interesting to find out exactly how many Roman Catholics know that.

16   A strong argument in favour of the ordination of women to the Roman Catholic priesthood is the dearth of male priests. Millions around the globe, according to Roman Catholic doctrine, exist from one month to the next in a state of sin brought about by their not having access to the Eucharist.

17   Robinson, *Honest to God*, 7.

18   D. L. Le Mahieu, "Honest to God and the Discourse on Patriarchy in Mid-Twentieth-Century Britain," *Christianity and Literature* 51.1 (2001).

19   Paul Tillich, "The Depth of Existence," *The Shaking of the Foundations* (New York: Scribner, 1948), 57.

20   See James Buchanan Given, *Inquisition and Medieval Society: Power, Discipline, and Resistance in Languedoc* (Ithaca, NY: Cornell UP, 1997); Mark Gregory Pegg, *The Corruption of Angels: The Great Inquisition of 1245–1246* (Princeton, NJ: Princeton UP, 2001); Simon Lemieux, "The Spanish Inquisition: Simon Lemieux Examines the Hard Facts about the Inquisition and Counters the Common Caricature," *History Review* December (2002).

21   "Notification on the Works of Father Jon Sobrino, SJ," *Congregation on the Doctrine of Faith*, March 14, 2007.

22   Mary Catherine Hilkert, "Feminist Theology: A Review of Literature," *Theological Studies* 56.2 (1995), www.questia.com/PM.qst?a=o&d=5000330759 (accessed October 8, 2007).

23   Henry Warner Bowden, *Church History in an Age of Uncertainty: Historiographical Patterns in the United States, 1906–1990* (Carbondale, IL: Southern Illinois UP, 1991), 2–5.

24   At Queen's Theological College, in 1987, the text for the course on Early Church History was Elaine Pagels' *The Gnostic Gospels* (London: Vintage, 1979), a challenging view of the development of the canon.

25   Jack Good, *The Dishonest Church* (Scotts Valley: Rising Starr, 2003), 12.

26   "Census Returns of the Jedi," BBC News, February 13, 2003, http://news.bbc.co.uk/2/hi/uk_news/2757067.stm (accessed October 8, 2007).

27   Catholic scholar Father Raymond Brown gives the scholarly consensus dates for the synoptic Gospels (the three that follow one another most closely) as follows:

Mark, 68–73 c.e.; Matthew 70–100 c.e.; Luke, 80–100 c.e. John is thought to be between 80 and 100 CE, dates that place all of them at least a generation following Jesus' death. Raymond Brown, *An Introduction to the New Testament* (New York: Doubleday, 1997), 127, 172, 226, 334.

28 Nigerian Anglican Archbishop Peter Akinola might be interested in this acronym. He has been encouraging the continued oppression of GLBTs by the church and has created the acronym TINA, There Is No Alternative (to the Bible), to galvanize support. TAWOGFAT might not be as catchy as TINA, but then, I'm not according it the positive status Akinola would like, either.

## Chapter 2

1 *An Inconvenient Truth*, DVD, directed by Davis Guggenheim (USA: Paramount Home Entertainment, 2006). Al Gore, former vice-president of the United States, in his documentary on global warming makes his point about the movement of the world's land masses by quoting a classmate who asked this same question decades ago.

2 Lamont-Doherty Earth Observatory, online audio recording, www.ldeo. columbia.edu/news/2005/images/tsun_eq.mp3 (accessed October 8, 2007).

3 Brooks Hanson, "Learning from Natural Disasters," *Science* 308, no. 5725 (2005): 1127–1133, www.sciencemag.org/cgi/content/summary/ sci;308/5725/1125 (accessed October 8, 2007).

4 Josephus, *The Wars of the Jews, of the History of the Destruction of Jerusalem*, 2.8.14. Trans. William Whiston, 1667–1752. www.gutenberg.org/etext/2850 (accessed December 13, 2007).

5 Josephus, *Wars*, 2.8.11.

6 Websites regularly present information as fact despite the ludicrous content found on them. One site carefully cited three hundred instances where the Hebrew scriptures "prophesied" Jesus' ministry. Its author is completely oblivious to the possibility that anyone at any time can write the fulfillment of a prophecy into someone's biography, especially if no one knows what actually happened. Those who wrote down the details of Jesus' life had the Hebrew scriptures in front of them and a blank slate in terms of Jesus' particulars. Adding an embellishment here and there as they filled in the blanks was a simple process of picking which prophecies the author wanted to include and writing in the details.

7 Baylor Study of Religion.

8 O. W. Holmes, *The Autocrat of the Breakfast Table* (Boston: M.A. Donahue & Co., 1895), 276.

9 Bart D. Ehrman, *Lost Christianities: The Battle for Scripture and the Faiths We Never Knew* (New York: Oxford UP, 2003), 118.

10 These are all indicators offered in Joel 2 of the coming of the Lord. If Jesus was that person, some of that should have happened. It didn't.

11 Ronald Wright, *A Short History of Progress* (Toronto: Anansi, 2004), 60.

12 Ibid., 63.

13 Robert Doran, *Birth of a Worldview: Early Christianity in Its Jewish and Pagan Context* (Boulder, CO: Westview Press, 1995), 11.

14 "If It Isn't Roman Catholic then It's Not a Proper Church, Pope Tells Christians," *The Times*, July 11, 2007, www.timesonline.co.uk/tol/comment/ faith/article2056515.ece (accessed October 8, 2007). Early in July 2007, Pope Benedict XVI clarified beliefs expressed in a document originally published in 2000, *Dominus Iesus*, in which he stated that the Roman Catholic Church was the

only true church of Christ established by God in the world. According to one Vatican spokesman, Father Augustine Di Noia (a senior doctrinal official at the Vatican), the Pope was merely clarifying his position so that ecumenical dialogue could take place honestly and without the suggestion that there would be any softening of the Vatican position. It does confuse the purpose of the ecumenical dialogue a bit, though, doesn't it?

15  Philip Jenkins, *The Next Christendom: The Coming of Global Christianity* (New York: Oxford, 2002), 40.

16  Hans A. Pohlsander, *The Emperor Constantine* (Routledge: New York, 2004), 49–50.

17  Ibid., 52.

18  Given, *Inquisition*, 73–74.

19  Ibid., 74.

20  Andrew Freeman, "Theology and the Church" (address, King's College, Cambridge, UK, July 14, 1994), Sea of Faith Network, www.sofn.org.uk/theology/freeman.html (accessed October 20, 2007).

21  Bill Phipps, transcript of statement, *Spirit Connection*, Vision TV, November 24, 1997, www.igs.net/~tonyc/mod14.html (accessed October 8, 2007).

22  Office of the General Assembly of the Presbyterian Church (U.S.A), *The Book of Confessions* (Louisville, KY: General Assembly of the Presbyterian Church, 2003), 252.

23  Josh Timonen, *The Four Horsemen: Discussions with Richard Dawkins*, http://richarddawkins.net/article,2025,the_four_horsemen,discussions-with-richard-dawkins-episode-1-rdfrs.

24  Lloyd Geering, "The Path of Faith to the Global Future," in *The Future of the Christian Tradition*, Robert J. Miller, ed. (Santa Rosa, CA: Polebridge, 2007) 170.

25  Wilfred Cantwell Smith, *The Meaning and End of Religion* (New York: Mentor, 1964), 141.

26  R. Scott Kearns, "The Light of Love," *The Wonder of Life: Songs for the Spirit* (Toronto, 2004), 63.

## Chapter 3

1  Extensive filing systems were the backbone of many a preacher's library, allowing him or her to draw on quotes, books, jokes, art, theatre, and many other sources for making connections in sermons. The Internet plays a huge role in this work now and may, for many, have completely eliminated the former need to collect materials for future use.

2  Anglican Houses of Laity of Clergy voted in favour of union and The United Church of Canada had agreed to accept Anglican episcopacy. The House of Bishops, however, fearing that the Anglican Church of Canada would be lost within the much larger United Church, vetoed the union. Since then, the two have moved further and further apart.

3  Corpora callosa is the plural of corpus callosum.

4  Information referring to these experiments is available at www.indiana.edu/~pietsch/split-brain.html (accessed October 8, 2007). For further information, see Michael S. Gazzaniga, "The Split Brain in Man," *Altered States of Awareness*, ed. T. J. Teyler (San Francisco: W. H. Freeman, 1972) and Gazzaniga, "Forty-five years of Split-brain Research and Still Going Strong," *Nature* 6 (2005), 653–659. With thanks to Paul Pietsch for access to these references.

5  Marcus Borg, *The Heart of Christianity: Rediscovering a Life of Faith* (New York: HarperCollins, 2003), 156–157.

6  Ibid., 159.

7  Ibid., 39–40.

8  Borg, *The Meaning of Jesus: Two Visions* (New York: HarperCollins, 1989), 156 (including a quote by John Hick). In his book, Hick concludes that he hopes "there will be a growing awareness of the mythological character of this [Christian] language as the hyperbole of the heart, most naturally at home in hymns and anthems and oratorios and other artistic expressions of the poetry of devotion." John Hick, *The Myth of God Incarnate* (Philadelphia: Westminster Press, 1977), 183.

9  One of Borg's earlier books, *Reading the Bible Again for the First Time*, explored this concept extensively.

10  The last crusade, in the technical sense of an expedition taken in the fulfillment of a vow, took place in 1669 when the Duke of Burgundy undertook to free Candia (Crete), which had been taken by the Turks. Louis Brehier, *The Catholic Encyclopedia*, Volume IV (New York: Robert Appleton, 1908). www.newadvent.org/cathen/04543c.htm (accessed October 8, 2007). The last legal execution of a witch took place in Poland in 1792; however, in 1999, Georgia Republican congressman Bob Barr launched a "witch-hunt" as the result of the presence of a Wiccan coven at Fort Hood military base. Barr threatened to instigate congressional hearings into the matter. His local supporters included Jack Harvey, pastor of Tabernacle Independent Baptist Church in Killeen, Texas, who quoted scripture as requiring witches be put to death. *Church & State*, July–August 1999, www.au.org/site/News2?abbr=cs_&id=9182&page=NewsArticle (accessed October 8, 2007).

11  For several decades, ending in the 1960s, Anglican and United Churches cooperated with the federal government in a program that removed Aboriginal children from their communities and placed them in residential schools in an effort to "Christianize" and civilize them. Aboriginal groups have recently been awarded compensation for the abuse, neglect, and cultural genocide they experienced under that program.

12  Fredrick William Faber, "There's a Wideness in God's Mercy," 1854. *Voices United* (Toronto: United Church, 1996), 271.

13  Sam Harris, *The End of Faith: Religion, Terror, and the Future of Reason* (New York: W.W. Norton & Co., 2004), 21–22.

14  Again, refer to the many instances in the Hebrew scriptures where God commands his people to care for strangers, widows, and orphans.

15  There are far too many situations in the world where this is not yet true. In China, the one-child-only law is believed to have led to a rise in the abortion of female fetuses, the reason behind the continued rise in the number of male births compared to female (figures have risen from a norm of 106 males and 100 females to 119 males and 100 females in the years since the one-child-only law was instituted). China has since outlawed the abortion of fetuses for reasons of sex in an attempt to correct the growing imbalance. See "China to outlaw aborting female fetuses," *CBC*, January 7, 2005, www.cbc.ca/story/world/national/2005/01/07/china-abortions050107.html (accessed October 8, 2007).

## Chapter 4

1  Northrope Frye, *Words with Power: Being a Second Study of the Bible and Literature* (San Diego: Harcourt Brace Jovanovich, 1992).

2  Richard Dawkins, *The God Delusion* (New York: Houghton Mifflin, 2006), 122–124.

The topic of evolutionary development is more highly explained in Dawkins' earlier book *The Blind Watchmaker*, (New York: Norton, 1996).

3 Since Thomas Aquinas' *Summa Theologiae*, thirteenth century, official teaching has been that heaven, hell, and purgatory are spiritual states, not places. I can't be sure if that teaching has trickled down to the pew.

4 International Theological Commission, "The Hope for Salvation of Infants Who Die Without Baptism," The Vatican, January 19, 2007, www.vatican. va/roman_curia/congregations/cfaith/cti_documents/ rc_con_cfaith_doc_ 20070419_un-baptised-infants_en.html# (accessed November 11, 2007).

5 On October 26, 2006, *The Guardian* quoted then U.S. vice-president, Dick Cheney as saying that the use of "waterboarding," a medieval practice of dunking a prisoner's head in water until the moment they are going to drown and then "rescuing" them, was a "no-brainer" when it came to getting information from terrorists and admitted the procedure had been used on detainees held at Guantanamo Bay after the 9/11 World Trade Center attacks. Mark Tran, "Cheney Endorses Simulated Drowning," *Guardian Unlimited*, October 27, 2006, www.guardian.co.uk/guantanamo/story/0,,1933317,00.html (accessed October 8, 2007).

6 Richard Dawkins, "Postmodernism Disrobed," *A Devil's Chaplain* (New York: First Mariner, 2004), 47–53.

7 "Language: A Key Mechanism of Control," FAIR, Fairness & Accuracy in Reporting, February 1995, www.fair.org/index.php?page=1276 (accessed October 8, 2007).

8 Scott Campbell, "The Challenge of Tectonic Change in the Church," Workshop, Barriers and Bridges Conference, Canadian Centre for Progressive Christianity, April 2005.

9 William Safire, *No Uncertain Terms: More Writing from the Popular "On Language" Column in* The New York Times Magazine (Toronto: Simon & Schuster, 2003), 151.

10 Ibid., 152.

11 Howard Gardner, *Changing Minds: The Art and Science of Changing Our Own and Other People's Minds* (Boston: Harvard Business School, 2004), 70–79.

12 Ken Wilber, *A Sociable God: Toward a New Understanding of Religion* (Boston: Shambhala, 2005), 4.

13 John Dominic Crossan, *The Birth of Christianity: Discovering What Happened in the Years Immediately After the Execution of Jesus* (New York: HarperCollins, 1998), 21.

14 I use the term *deconstruction* outside of its pure philosophical meaning, following Susan Adams and John Salmon, who, in their book *The Mouth of the Dragon*, use it to identify the process they apply to the Christian tradition. "We are not using the term 'deconstruction' in the precise way in which it is used in some threads of the postmodern approach. We are drawing on that, but broadening it to speak of a sustained critical appreciation of a received tradition, in order to identify what elements of that tradition are inappropriate to retain. We have pointed to the idea of deconstruction as used by postmodern writers such as Derrida. In that context the word is used in a technical sense to talk about problems in Western philosophical thought, including dualisms, as well as to expose aspects of the way we interpret texts. However, out of that background, the word has come to have a more general meaning, not unrelated, but not as narrowly defined. Thus it is used to speak of a process of critical re-appraisal, which 'unravels' a commonly accepted set of ideas or interpretations. It becomes the step beyond a hermeneutics of suspicion, for example, which identifies elements in a text or story that have the effect of protecting or enhancing the benefits to

those who promoted the text or story, to suggest a way in which the text of story might be understood if those elements were removed or radically reinterpreted." Susan Adams and John Salmon, *The Mouth of the Dragon: Theology for Postmodern Christians* (Ellerslie, New Zealand: Women's Resource Centre, 1996), 50.

15 Crossan, *The Birth*, 59–68.

16 Ibid., 580.

17 Jacques Derrida, *Deconstruction in a Nutshell: A Conversation with Jacques Derrida*, ed. John D. Caputo (New York: Fordham University Press, 1997), 21.

18 I am indebted to Susan Adams and John Salmon for their thoughtful development of parts of this process. While it is not a direct part of their work, their thoughtful considerations have so infiltrated my thinking that I have come to automatically apply their processes as I work my way through difficult theological and ecclesiological terrain.

19 Robinson, 11–14.

20 Crossan, *The Birth*, 419–444.

21 Alpina Begossi, "Food taboos at Búzios Island (SE Brazil): Their Significance and Relation to Folk Medicine," *Journal of Ethnobiology* 12, no. 1 (1992): 117.

22 Genesis 3:17–10; Romans 5:12; 1 Corinthians 15:21. Note that the concept of an everlasting stain of sin on humanity does not exist in the Genesis version but is assumed in the writings of the Epistles.

23 J. Maxwell Miller and John H. Hayes, *A History of Ancient Israel and Judah* (Philadelphia: Westminster Press, 1986), 33.

24 Carl F. Starkloff, *A Theology of the In-Between: The Value of Syncretic Process* (Milwaukee, WI: Marquette University Press, 2002), 145.

25 Tom Harpur, *The Pagan Christ: Recovering the Lost Light* (Toronto: Thomas Allen, 2004), 12, 56–65, 76–79.

26 W. Ward Gasque, "Defending the Faith: A Pagan's Christ," *Canadian Christianity*, June 23, 2004, www.canadianchristianity.com/cgi-bin/na.cgi? nationalupdates/040623 (accessed October 8, 2007).

27 Ronald Hutton, *Stations of the Sun: A History of the Ritual Year in Britain* (Oxford: Oxford University Press, 1996), 1.

28 This text is considered by Gaston H. Halsberghe, *The Cult of Sol Invictus* (Leiden, 1972), 174 and James George Frazer, *Adonis Attis Osiris: Studies in the History of Oriental Religion* (1906; repr., Whitefish, MT: Kessinger, 2003), 255, quoted in Hutton, *Stations of the Sun*, 1.

29 Owen Chadwick, *A History of the Popes, 1830–1914* (Oxford: Clarendon Press, 1998), 119.

30 Catherine Keller, "Inventing the Goddess: A Study in Ecclesial Backlash," *The Christian Century*, April 6, 1994, www.questia.com/PM.qst?a=o&d=5001659127 (accessed October 8, 2007).

31 Elaine J. Lawless, *Women Preaching Revolution: Calling for Connection in a Disconnected Time* (Philadelphia: University of Pennsylvania Press, 1996), 157, 159.

32 Terry Schlossberg, "Presbyterians Hold the Line," online report for Leadership University, Christian Leadership Ministries, www.leaderu.com/ftissues/ft9610/articles/schlossberg.html (accessed October 8, 2007).

## Chapter 5

1 It may be noted that the Israelites' history seems to be more one of loss than of victory. In the affairs of the world, as the story is told, very much of it tells of being defeated and captured by one kingdom after another. In the affairs of the spirit, however, in the eyes of God, the Israelites were the chosen people. They

were the victors in that story, and so the explanation of their losses is related to the winnowing of that relationship.

2  Abraham nearly gets himself killed on the way to Haran by passing his wife Sarai off as his sister and allowing her to be taken into the king's home, ostensibly as a new concubine or wife. God manages to save the three of them by keeping the king from actually having sex with her (if he hadn't done that, he'd have had to kill one of them in order to live up to the requisite biblical punishment for such a sin), and they are sent on their way. When Abraham is told, by God, to sacrifice his son Isaac, God subsequently provides a ram at the last minute, saving the terrified boy's life. Joseph, a few generations later, is thrown into a pit by his brothers but is saved by God. He ends up being taken into slavery in Egypt only to become its most important citizen and saves the butts of his pathetic brothers when they come seeking food to get them through a period of famine back home. And when the people, who have somehow all become slaves in Egypt, have had enough and aren't going to take it any more, Moses, who you will remember was supposed to be slaughtered as a baby boy but was saved by his very intelligent mother and raised as the brother of the prince of Egypt, and who has become a murderer, leads them off into the desert on their way to the promised land. God provides for their every need, despite the fact that they are a recalcitrant lot; they eventually make it to the promised land, where God girds up their loins and helps them slaughter anyone in their path so that they can get what they came for: milk and honey. Of course, he doesn't let Moses actually get to the promised land; only the people get there. Numbers 20:12.

3  Lloyd Geering, *Christianity Without God* (Santa Rosa, CA: Polebridge Press, 2002), 42. The word *elohim* is the plural form of God. In early Jewish texts, however, as the Israelites argued their way from polytheism to theism, the word continued to be used to describe the set of values by which an individual or a nation lived.

4  Ibid., 61–71.

5  Ibid., 52.

6  There are, of course, those whom history has judged to be inherently evil—Caligula, Nero, Adolf Hitler, Idi Amin, Jeffrey Dahmer. It is impossible, however, for us to assess these lives independent of those social, cultural, and emotional influences that moulded them.

7  As global warming moves from the realm of theory to that of fact, it may be that we will, actually, have something to blame for the majority of category 4 and 5 hurricanes: humanity. For further information on this topic, turn to Tim Flannery's *The Weather Makers*.

8  Jim Dollar, *The Evolution of the Idea of God* (Greensboro, NC: Outlands, 2006), 65.

9  You can find excellent parallel tools at the following website: John W. Marshall, "The Five Gospels Parallels," www.utoronto.ca/religion/synopsis/ (accessed November 11, 2007).

10  It is also very interesting to mark those Mark sections that you find in Matthew and Luke. If you are careful to underline (not the same as highlighting) only those words that appear in Mark, you can see how the passage evolved when it was included by the other evangelists in their versions of the gospel. While there are several analyses of this sort of work available, nothing beats discovering it for yourself!

11  I regret that I cannot offer an accurate citation for this quote other than to credit it to novelist P. D. James.

12  Jack Good (lecture, Barriers and Bridges: An Honest Wrestling with Faith conference, Canadian Centre for Progressive Christianity, Oshawa, Ontario, April 2005).

13 The prayer was first published anonymously in 1912 as "A beautiful prayer to say during the Mass," and may have been written by Father Esther Bouquerel, who was responsible for its printing. It is attributed to St. Francis because around 1920 it was published on the reverse of a little card with St. Francis' picture on it. Christian Renoux, "The Origin of the Peace Prayer of St. Francis," The Franciscan Archive, www.franciscan-archive.org/franciscana/peace.html (accessed October 8, 2007).

14 Scott Kearns and Gretta Vosper, "As I Live," © 2005 West Hill United Church.

15 While it may seem to make sense that the holy orders considered a sacrament are those made by male clergy because only men are allowed to be ordained in the Roman Catholic Church, we must remember that women take holy orders as well; they become nuns. Their vows are not, however, considered sacramental.

## Chapter 6

1 James W. Fowler, *Stages of Faith: The Psychology of Human Development and the Quest for Meaning* (San Francisco: Harper and Row, 1981).

2 Marcus Borg, lecture, *Living the Questions*, DVD series (Phoenix, AZ: Living the Questions).

3 Following the 2003 consecration of gay bishop Gene Robinson more than fifty Episcopal congregations have separated from the Episcopal Church and placed themselves under the authority of bishops who support anti-gay doctrine. Most of those bishops are African. Archbishop Peter Akinola of Nigeria, who heads the Anglican Communion's largest congregation, is a passionate leader in this factional movement.

4 John Shelby Spong, "A New Christianity for a New World: Bishop John Shelby Spong on the News and Christian Faith," September 7, 2007, www.johnshelbyspong.com (accessed December 20, 2007).

5 A modernized Anglican version goes as follows: "Glory to the Father and to the Son / and to the Holy Spirit; / as it was in the beginning is now / and shall be for ever. Amen."

6 Rick Warren, *The Purpose Driven Church: Growth Without Compromising Your Message and Mission* (Grand Rapids: Zondervan, 1995) 103–119.

7 T. R. Young, *The Drama of the Holy* (Red Feather Institute, MI) http://uwacadweb.uwyo.edu/RED_FEATHER/dramaholy/dramaholyindex. html (accessed October 8, 2007).

## Chapter 7

1 International Year of Freshwater, 2003, www.wateryear2003.org (accessed October 8, 2007).

2 "Warming of the climate system is unequivocal," reads an intergovernmental report issued in February 2007, the results of the most comprehensive scientific studies into global warming to date. Four points demand attention: (1) Greenhouse gases are at the highest atmospheric concentration in 650,000 years as determined by ice cores; (2) In the post-industrial period, the primary sources of atmospheric carbon dioxide are fossil fuel use and land-use change (for example, deforestation for the conversion of rainforest to pasture); (3) It is the increase in "anthropogenic greenhouse gas concentrations" that has adversely influenced such things as global average temperatures, ocean warming, continental-average temperatures, temperature extremes, and wind patterns;

and (4) Most disturbingly, global warming and sea level rise will continue for centuries even if we manage to stabilize greenhouse gas concentrations. IPCC, 2007: Summary for Policymakers, quoted in S. Solomon, D. Qin, M. Manning, Z. Chen, M. Marquis, K.B. Averyt, M.Tignor and H.L. Miller, eds., "Climate Change 2007: The Physical Science Basis," Contribution of Working Group I to the *Fourth Assessment Report of the Intergovernmental Panel on Climate Change* (New York: Cambridge University Press, 2004) http://ipcc-wg1.ucar.edu/wg1/wg1-report.html (accessed October 8, 2007). Identifying the current warming trend as the result of human activity on the planet, some also warn that possible future effects, such as the interruption of the ocean's thermohaline circulation (the "conveyor belt" that moves water around the globe), even by conservative estimates, are so catastrophic as to demand that our choice of action be to err on the side of caution. Eugene Linden, *The Winds of Change: Climate, Weather, and the Destruction of Civilizations* (New York: Simon & Schuster, 2006).

3   Identified as "a necessary and integral part of the liberal-capitalist political economy of production, consumption, and waste," the problem of toxic waste is systemic. As community activists challenge dumping in their own municipalities, the disposing of toxic by-products becomes more and more difficult due to increasingly stringent legal requirements. Our response, off-loading our toxic wastes to developing or depressed nations who need to take our garbage to pay their bills, only replicates the problems elsewhere. We remain culpable. Eddie J. Girdner and Jack Smith, *Killing Me Softly: Toxic Waste, Corporate Profit, and the Struggle for Environmental Justice* (New York: Monthly Review Press, 2002), 2.

4   The human demand for resources has resulted in an escalating destruction of the planet's ecosystems. For example, the global area of forest cover has been cut in half during the last three hundred years. We continue to lose thirteen million hectares of forest annually (equivalent to the area of Greece). Of all ecosystems, inland water systems have suffered the worst degradation of biodiversity: 50 per cent of inland water systems have been lost. Losses of both forests and inland water systems are a direct consequence of human demand for timber and food production. Millennium Ecosystems Assessment, *Ecosystems and Human Well-being Synthesis Reports* (Washington: Island Press, 2005) and Global Forest Resources Assessment, 2005, *Progress Towards Sustainable Forest Management* (Food and Agriculture Organization of the United Nations, Rome, 2005).

Particularly vulnerable is the Amazon basin, which is home to nearly 10 per cent of the world's mammals and 15 per cent of all known land-based plant species. *Eating Up the Amazon*, Greenpeace, 2006, www.greenpeace. org/international/press/reports/eating-up-the-amazon. At present rates of forest destruction, only 5 per cent of the rainforest will remain by 2020. Bruce E. Johansen, *Indigenous Peoples and Environmental Issues: An Encyclopedia* (Westport: Greenwood Press, 2003), 35.

Consequences include (1) Loss of an important carbon sink. Not only does this contribute to levels of greenhouse gasses but it also reduces the earth's capacity to treat future emissions; (2) Permanent loss of soil to runoff, and change of composition through intensive use of fertilizer; (3) Species extinction. The Living Planet Index, which tracks three thousand wild populations of species, shows a decline in species abundance of about 40 per cent for the period between 1970 and 2000. However, limitations in data availability mean that tropical forests are underrepresented. It is further estimated that species extinction rates have increased a thousand times above background rates revealed by fossil records. Secretariat of the Convention on Biological Diversity, *Global Biodiversity Outlook 2* (Montreal, 2006), 25–6; and 4. Destruction of indigenous cultures. There are 220,000 indigenous people living in the Amazon comprising

180 different nations. Greenpeace, *Eating Up the Amazon*. Many are forced off their land or, like the Awa, are poached to the brink of extinction by loggers and ranchers. Johansen, *Indigenous Peoples*, 33.

5  Our ecological footprint is an index that, since 1961, has tracked our consumption of resources against the earth's capacity to absorb the waste resulting from our consumption. "Humanity's Ecological Footprint," *Living Planet Report 2006* (Gland, Switzerland: World Wildlife Fund for Nature, 2006). www.panda. org/news_facts/publications/living_planet_report/index.cfm (accessed October 8, 2007).

In the late 1980s, we moved into "overshoot." (The term *overshoot* was first coined by William Catton in *Overshoot: The Ecological Basis of Revolutionary Change* [Urbana: University of Illinois Press, 1982].) And in 2003, we consumed 25 per cent more resources than the earth is capable of handling. In effect, we are consuming the earth's capital while simultaneously warehousing waste we have no way to dispose of. Perhaps the most obvious illustration of overshoot is our failure to manage our supply of fresh water. Although a renewable resource, we put pressure on ecosystems by withdrawing water faster than the rate of replenishment, drawing down water tables. *Living Planet Report 2006*, 12–13.

But the overshoot problem should be distinguished from our consumption of non-renewable resources such as oil, a cost which, by definition, cannot be absorbed by the earth. As of January 1, 2007, proven oil reserves were estimated at 1,317.447 billion barrels. Global oil consumption for 2005 was 84,538,000 barrels/day, or 30.8 billion barrels. Energy Information Administration, *Official Energy Statistics from the U.S. Government*, www.eia.doe.gov/neic/quickfacts/ quickoil.html (accessed October 8, 2007).

6  Many think of globalization as merely a description of reality in the twenty-first century. (See Jan Aart Scholte, *Globalization: A Critical Introduction*, 2nd edition, [New York: Palgrave Macmillan, 2005]. Scholte treats globalization as a phenomenon—the redefinition of the space in which social relations occur.) Others use the term to spread a neoliberal vision of how they think reality should look. For a critical summary of the rise of globalization as ideology, see Robert L. Borosage and William Greider, "Global Fairness: The Historical Debate," *The Next Agenda*, February 28, 2001, www.ourfuture.org/projects/next_agenda/ ch2.cfm (accessed October 8, 2007). What must concern us, in either case, is the way in which it is implemented and what it costs both humanity and the planet. Because of its broad sweep, globalization is an essential justice issue affecting everyone. (For a survey of current issues, see David McNally, *Another World is Possible: Globalization & Anti-Capitalism* [Winnipeg, MB: Arbeiter Ring Publishing, 2006]. McNally shows how these issues trace their roots to the West's long history of colonization and exploitation.)

In lockstep with neoliberal globalization is the concept of empire, drawn from a renewed sense of American exceptionalism, which aims to implement a global economic agenda by deploying the military to secure foreign markets and access to resources, primarily oil. This view is perhaps best expressed by the signatories to the "Statement of Principles" of the Project for the New American Century, which aspires to "American global leadership" in order to bring peace to Europe, Asia, and the Middle East by, among other things, modernizing the armed forces. Signatories to the "Statement of Principles" include such luminaries as Jeb Bush, Dick Cheney, Dan Quayle, and Donald Rumsfeld. "Statement of Principles," Project for the New American Century, www.newamericancentury. org/statementofprinciples.htm (accessed October 8, 2007).

Perhaps the most insidious aspect of imperialism is the notion of "colonization of consciousness": the hegemonic nature of imperialism through the global spread of Western culture makes it impossible even to think about the issues since we are unable to climb outside the box to gain a different perspective. The term "colonization of consciousness" was coined by Jean and John Comaroff in *Of Revelation and Revolution Vol I: Christianity, Colonialism, and Consciousness in South Africa* (Chicago: University of Chicago Press, 1991). Noam Chomsky provides a survey of American's hegemonic agenda in *Hegemony or Survival: America's Quest for Global Dominance* (New York: Metropolis Books, 2003).

7　While AIDS is not yet curable, it is both preventable and treatable. To the extent that we have failed to deliver prevention plans and treatment options, we have transformed this into an issue of justice. Our failures speak for themselves. According to the World Health Organization, in 2006 there were 39.5 million people living with HIV, there were 4.3 million new infections that year, 65 per cent of which were in sub-Saharan Africa, and there were 2.9 million AIDS-related deaths. *AIDS Epidemic Update: Special Report on HIV/AIDS*, UNAIDS, December 2006, www.unaids.org/en/HIV_data/epi2006/default.asp (accessed October 8, 2007). The institutions of global governance must shoulder the greatest share of the blame for these appalling statistics. Because the programs these institutions put in place require the dismantling of socialized health-care systems, few HIV/AIDS victims can afford the only alternative—privatized services. On the treatment side, the United States Trade Representative (USTR) to the World Trade Organization (WTO) has successfully pressured generic producers to abide by TRIPS (see note 8), prohibiting the production and distribution of affordable anti-retroviral medications in the name of free trade. "TRIPS, AIDS & Generic Drugs," Avert, 08 August 2007, www.avert.org/generic.htm (accessed October 8, 2007).

8　One of the multilateral treaties under the auspices of the WTO is the 1995 "Trade Related Aspects of Intellectual Property Rights Agreement" (TRIPS), which sets standards for the domestic Intellectual Property Regimes (IPRs) implemented by member countries. IPRs create time-limited monopolies in knowledge-based products so that creators (in the case of copyright) or inventors (in the case of patents) are rewarded for their efforts while allowing for the efficient dissemination of the work or knowledge that they have produced. Also subject to IPRs are trademarks. Because, traditionally, IPRs were enforceable only in the jurisdiction of the violation, countries without such laws became havens for piracy and the manufacture of knock-offs. TRIPS has expanded enforceability, and because it is supervised by the WTO, rights-based IPRs are swiftly becoming universal. Critics of rights-based copyright regimes argue that the commodification of creative works has a chilling effect upon culture and creativity. Furthermore, because the rights-based is becoming universal, it has a flattening effect, contributing to the "colonization of consciousness" by Americanizing all media. Lawrence Lessig offers a critical account of rights-based copyright in *Free Culture: How Big Media Uses Technology and the Law to Lock Down Culture and Control Creativity* (New York: Pilgrim Press, 2004). Critics of international patent enforcement contend that big pharma uses TRIPS to profit from misery. Nowhere is this more evident than in the subordination of the interests of those suffering from HIV/AIDS to the insistence upon compliance with TRIPS. For a concise discussion of this issue, see Christopher May, "Intellectual Property Rights," in *The Politics of International Trade in the Twenty-first Century: Actors, Issues and Regional Dynamics*, ed. Dominic Kelly and Wyn Grant (New York: Palgrave Macmillan, 2005), 164–182.

9　In addition to the military, the United States uses the International Monetary Fund (IMF) and World Bank to fulfill its world-domination agenda. These institutions were established as a result of an agreement reached in July 1944 with a view to European reconstruction and stabilizing the international monetary system. However, in the 1980s the role of global finance transformed into an agency of the neoliberal project—most notably through its euphemistically named Structural Adjustment Program (SAP). The SAP made the lending of funds conditional upon implementing "adjustments" to the borrowing country's economic policy and its institutional framework for managing that policy. The results have been particularly oppressive for sub-Saharan Africa, with mounting debt, civil wars, environmental degradation, famine, and epidemics. For a survey of crises that have been caused or aggravated by SAPs, see McNally, *Another World Is Possible*, 226 ff.

10  Neoliberal globalization contends that economies grow as barriers to trade are reduced or eliminated. However, it is well documented that such growth does not benefit everybody. The Human Development Report 2005 summarizes its findings thus: "The era of globalization has been marked by dramatic advances in technology, trade and investment—and an impressive increase in prosperity. Gains in human development have been less impressive. Large parts of the developing world are being left behind. Human development gaps between rich and poor countries, already large, are widening." The Human Development Report (UNDP, 2005).

11  McNally, *Another World Is Possible*, 54.

12  This is an enormous ethical dilemma. As our medical technology improves, the ability of individuals who would otherwise not have survived to adulthood to reproduce also improves. Genetic abnormalities, frailties, and faults all become protected by technology instead of evolving out of existence. Who makes the decisions around these types of technological progress has not been decided. If it ever is decided definitively, the probability of it being done in a fascist state is extremely high.

13  Margaret Wheatley, *Turning to One Another: Simple Conversations to Restore Hope to the Future* (San Franscisco: Berrett-Koehler, 2002), 29.

14  Frank Faulk, producer, "God and Other Dirty Words," *Tapestry*, CBC Radio, 2005.

15  The research reports of the Emerging Spirit project of The United Church of Canada can be found online at www.emergingspirit.ca.

16  "Terra Nova Discovery Workshop," Emerging Spirit, www.emergingspirit.ca (December 20, 2007).

17  Toronto United Church Council, *Church Development Resources Newsletter*, INV-002, www.tucc.ca/Articles/INV-002.pdf (accessed October 8, 2007).

18  Rita Healey, "The ATM in the Church Lobby," *Time*, July 30, 2007, www.time.com/time/business/article/0,8599,1648022,00.html (accessed October 8, 2007).

19  Leonard Sweet, *Soul Tsunami: Sink or Swim in the New Millennium Culture* (Grand Rapids, MI: Zondervan, 1999), 17.

20  Leonard Sweet, interview by Darren DeGraaf and Rick Hiebert, "The Missional Church: Interview with Leonard Sweet," *Canadian Baptist, Inspiration and News for the Baptist Convention of Ontario and Quebec Family*, PDF, Spring 2007: 2, www.baptist.ca/publications/cb-issues/cb-spring07.pdf (accessed October 8, 2007).

21  *More Voices*, Supplement to *Voices United, The Hymn and Worship Book of The United Church of Canada* (Toronto: United Church Publishing House, 2007), 6.

22  Sue Monk Kidd, *The Dance of the Dissident Daughter: A Woman's Journey from Christian Tradition to the Sacred Feminine* (New York: HarperCollins 1996), 28. Having "moved on" in my quest for spiritual truth, I had stopped buying and reading feminist Christian writers some time ago. *The Dance* came to me as a gift for my most recent birthday from my younger sister, Rebecca, partly because,

when she blurred her eyes, she thought the photo of Sue on the back cover looked like me. Although the book is ten years old, it reminds me of the challenge of the journey toward awakening and that the terrain I covered some time ago remains raw and scarred for many women yet. Thank you for the reminder, Becks.

23 "O Let the Power Fall on Me," author unknown.

24 For example, see the hymn "O Let the Power Fall on Me," author unknown.

25 Bill Hybels, *Courageous Leadership* (Zondervan: Grand Rapids, 2002) 187–188.

26 Lloyd Geering, *Fundamentalism: The Challenge to the Secular World* (Wellington, New Zealand: St. Andrew's Trust, 2003). www.religion-online.org/showchapter. asp?title=2732c=2437.

27 Sam Harris, "Believing the Unbelievable: The Clash Between Faith and Reason in the Modern World" (lecture, Aspen Ideas Festival, Aspen, Colorado, July 14, 2007, www.aifestival.org/library/transcript/believingtheunbelievable.pdf (accessed October 8, 2007).

28 More information about Salon Voltaire is available at www.salon-voltaire.com.

29 One of the very few lines of introduction you'll find on the front page of Green Drinks, www.greendrinks.org.

## Appendix

1 T. R. Young, *The Drama of the Holy* (Red Feather Institute) http://uwacadweb. uwyo.edu/RED_FEATHER/dramaholy/002theology.html (accessed November 11, 2007).

2 A quick trip (my unscientific method included searching the first congregational website page I could find in each of the states listing progressive congregations) through some fifty websites of progressive communities of faith, which are noted in Hal Taussig's *A New Spiritual Home: Progressive Christianity at the Grassroots* (Santa Rosa, CA: Polebridge Press, 2006), discloses that most congregations still use the word *worship*, while a few avoid it and refer only to *services*. Within that search only A New Life Metropolitan Community Church in Toledo, Ohio, advertises something else, calling its gatherings "Celebrations." Pathways Community Church in Markham, Ontario, avoids the term and holds a "Sacred Gathering" on Sunday mornings. Each of these alternatives offers possibilities but falls short of our goal. Only capturing one or another of the many important aspects of our coming together, "Celebrations" fails to reflect our need to communally attend to our griefs and laments and our need to be challenged. "Sacred Gatherings," while more comprehensive, has the potential to perpetuate the assumption that it is only on Sundays that we need turn our attention toward the sacred. It will likely be some time before a single term becomes common in our language.

3 William Murry, *Reason and Reverence: Religious Humanism for the 21st Century* (Boston: Skinner House, 2007), 2.

4 © 2005 Gretta Vosper.

5 © 2007 Gretta Vosper and Scott Kearns.

6 Murry, *Reason and Reverence*, 6.

7 Taussig, *New Spiritual*, 6.

8 This could be replaced with "We are not alone," a phrase familiar within The United Church of Canada. Since the phrase wraps a statement of faith affirming that we live in God's world and that God is with us, one or two things might result from its use. It may be very helpful for theists who recognize the

connection and use it to comfort themselves within a non-theistic prayer style. Or it may become a stumbling block if people begin adding "Thanks be to God" at its conclusion, the expected. If this is to be introduced, I would highly suggest including it in a cycle of responses, making it easier to discontinue if appropriate.

9  R. Scott Kearns, "The Light of Love," *The Wonder of Life: Songs for the Spirit* (Toronto, 2004), 63.

# INDEX

absolutism vs. relativism, 30–32
Acts, Book of, 86, 87
Adam and Eve, 198–99
Adams, Susan, 367n14, 368n18
advertising, 171–72
Africa, 90, 266
afterlife, 72
  assumptions of an, 122–29
  in Christianity, 74–75
  in Judaism, 73–74
  reward in, 72
  Roman Catholic Church on, 159–60
Agur, Colin, 308
AIDS, 286, 373n7
Akinola, Peter, 364n28, 370n3
anger, 265–67. See also respect
Anglican Church, 128. See also Church of
    England
  union talks with United Church of Canada,
    108, 110
Anglican Communion, 90, 266
animal sacrifice, 205–6
animism, 70
anti-Semitism. See Israelites
Apartheid, 90
Aphrodite, 200–202
apocalyptic prophets, 79–80
apostates, 265
Apostle's Creed, 93
Arius, 93
arrogance. See respect
assimilation, 210–11
assumptions
  basic, 16–18
  early, 261–63
atheists, 192n
  recent books by, 267
atonement, 58
authority. See also the authoritative word of God
    for all time (TAWOGFAT)
  questioning, 213–15
Axial age, 231

balance, 57, 182–88
baptism, 170, 274, 338–44. See also sacraments
  conceptions of, 345
Baptist Church, 35
Barth, Karl, 40
Baruch's Law, 277
Basis of Union, 99n
belief
  credo and, 115

creeds past, present, and future, 92–99
  disintegration of (see faith, experiencing the
    crash of losing)
  evolution of, 64–72 (see also change)
  guidelines for questioning, 214–15
  preserving, 80–85 (see also worldview)
belonging, 188–90. See also tribal distinction and
    prejudice
Bennett, Sanford F., 172n
Berry, Thomas, 42
Bible, 105–6. See also Christian Church, authority
    of; Gospels; Hebrew Scriptures; lectionary
    readings; New Testament; Old Testament
  and the Church, 84–85
  contemporaneous German theologians on, 40
  context in which it was written, 76–77, 139
  evangelicals and, 37–38
  as a human document, 217–25
  interpretations of and approaches to, 35–38,
    90–91, 138–39, 148–49, 200–202, 217 (see
    also biblical criticism)
    literal, 270–73
  liberal Christianity and, 35–37, 139
  as literature, 41, 149
  looked at like Shakespeare's sonnets, 223–25
  most valuable aspects of, 136
  purpose, 76, 84
  as recorded history of the victors, 218–20
  search for "The Meaning" of, 221–24, 240
  as TAWOGFAT, 53, 90, 103–4, 135, 146, 148,
    220–22, 224, 225
  values and ethics in, 136, 196–97
  well-loved passage from, 137–38
biblical criticism, 41–43, 138–39. See also Bible,
    interpretations of and approaches to; Jesus,
    as human being, a new view of
biblical scholarship, liberal, 35–38
biblical stories, 200–201, 219–22, 224
  as myth or metaphor, 268–73
  search for "The Meaning" of, 221–24, 240
biblical writings, accessibility of, 43–47
bishops. See also Anglican Communion; Spong,
    John Shelby
  African, 266
  Church of England, 95
  Western, 266
black women, 42
blame, 173–74, 209, 234. See also responsibility; sins
body and soul, separation of, 73–74
Bonhoeffer, Dietrich, 40
Borg, Marcus, 9–10, 114–16, 118, 138, 264, 268,
    269, 274

communion, 117, 253–54, 259, 345–49. *See also*
Eucharist
community(ies), 259, 309–13. *See also* belonging;
congregation(s)
of faith, 28
compassion, 275
confession(s), 94, 109
Confession of 1967 (Presbyterian Church), 97
prayer of, 329
congregational life, areas of, 277
congregation(s). *See also* evangelical congregations; Sunday morning services and sermons
change in, 252
Conjunctive stage of faith, 267–68
consciousness-raising, 288–91
Constantine, 90–91, 211
first council, 92–93
control. *See* security
conversation
essential principles of, 290
transformational nature of, 290
corpus callosum, theological training as severing,
104, 105, 111, 112, 119
cosmetics industry, 171–72
Council of Constantinople, 93
Council of Nicea, 92–93
courage, 175–78
creation, 198–99
creativity, 166–67
creeds, 115, 340. *See also under* belief
functions and purposes, 93–94
critical naïveté, 263, 268–69. *See also* naïveté
critical thinking, period of, 264, 268–69
cross, 326
Crossan, John Dominic, 194–95, 201–3, 205, 213
cross-disciplinary studies, 41, 207
crucifixion of Jesus, 86–87, 206
Jews blamed for, 86–87
*culpe*, 94
culture and religion, 209–10
Cupitt, Don, 43
curiosity, 162

da Vinci, Leonardo, 51
*Da Vinci Code, The* (Brown), 51
daemons, 336
Dawkins, Richard, 156, 168–69, 233, 267
Day of the Lord, 80
death, life after. *See* afterlife
deconstructionists, 202–3, 367n14
Derrida, Jacques, 203
dietary prohibitions, 207–8
Disciples' Prayer, 251
disfellowshipping, 161
divinity
embracing the being-ness of our, 237
experiencing and expressing our, 249, 279
Documentary Hypothesis, 41
dogma, 8, 24

avoiding creating new, 234–35
words related to theological, 292
Dollar, Jim, 234–35
Doran, Robert, 88–89
doubt, 159, 190–91
Doxology, 273, 274
*Drama of the Holy, The* (Young), 279
dress, 326

earth. *See also* ecological footprint; ecospirituality
theologians; environmental concerns, the
church and
birth and evolution of, 65–69
Easter Island. *See* Rapanui
*Eccelsia de Eucharistia*, 57–58
ecological footprint, 372n5
ecospirituality theologians, 42
ecosystems, destruction of, 284–86, 371n4
ecumenical council, 92–93
elephant(s) as symbols, 48–50, 54, 55, 57, 59–61
environmental concerns, the church and, 284–86,
371n4
Episcopal Church, 370n3. *See also* Anglican
Church; Anglican Communion; Church of
England; faith (development); Spong, John
Shelby; Statements of Faith
epistemology. *See* belief
equilibrium, 57
*Essay on the Development of the Christian Doctrine*
(Newman), 210
Essenes, 73
ethical dilemmas, 217
ethical living, things that prevent, 194, 196–97
Eucharist, 38, 57–58, 109, 117, 205, 363n15. *See
also* communion
Eusebius of Caesarea, 92
evangelical congregations, integrity in, 302–3
evangelicals, 37–38, 137, 257, 297, 299–300
community and, 311–12, 322
"soft," 296
Everything, beginning of, 64–65
evil, 73, 234. *See also* sinfulness of humanity
evolution, technology and, 287–89
excommunications, 159–61. *See also* heretics
experience, personal, 152–53. *See also* God,
experience of
Experimentalists (Radicals), 305
Ezer, Jonathan, 308

faith, 203. *See also* Statements of Faith
adult affirmations of, 342–44
changing language of, 25–26
communities of, 28
experiencing the crash of losing, 263–67
private and public, 318–19
faith (development), stages of, 261–68, 275–76,
306
family systems theory, 57
Fate, 73

unison prayers, 323
writing, 322–23
religious persecution, 34, 40, 41, 88–90, 94, 128, 160
religious training. *See* theological education
religiosity, extrinsic vs. intrinsic, 325
*Rescuing the Bible from Fundamentalism* (Spong), 138
respect, 179–81
responsibility. *See also* blame
taking personal, 161–62, 164, 174, 215, 249, 283
resurrection, 117, 200
rituals, 253–54. *See also* baptism; communion; Eucharist
handling the sacraments, 254–56 (*see also* sacraments)
testing the efficacy of, 208–9
Robinson, John A. T., 23–24, 39, 40, 43, 233, 235
*Honest to God*, 23–24, 39, 110, 204–5
Roman Catholic Church, 159–60
Roman Catholic Womanpriests movement, 324
Roman Empire, 88–89, 91
Ruether, Rosemary Radford, 41

sacramental traditions, 327. *See also* Anglican Communion; Roman Catholic Church
sacraments, 258–59. *See also* baptism; communion; symbols
handling, during rituals, 254–56
power, 254–55, 258–59
"Sacred Gatherings," 375n2
sacred objects and traditions, 195–96
sacred space, 320, 328
sacred values. *See* values
sacrifice, 205–6
eternal, 58
Saddleback Community Church, 293
Sadducees, 73
Safire, William, 185
Salmon, John, 367n14, 368n18
Salon Voltaire, 308
salvation, 38, 94, 109, 116, 127, 172, 243, 254–57
Satan, 59
Schlossberg, Terry, 212–13
scholarship, 43, 103–4, 113, 155, 190, 209, 249.
*See also* Jesus Seminar
contemporary, 35, 37, 43, 53, 55, 61, 76, 81, 89, 99, 110, 112, 119, 178, 181, 255, 265, 269, 301, 304, 306
on documentary hypothesis, 41
feminist, 41
liberal biblical, 37, 38
New Testament, 151, 153–54
postmodern, 304
progressive, 39, 103, 150, 307
Schweitzer, Albert, 151–53, 238
Sea of Faith, 43
Second Ecumenical Council, 40

secular society, 101
security, 187–88. *See also under* belief; belonging
need for sense of, 6–7 (*see also under* Christian Church)
*Seekers' Dialogue*, 308
self-preservation, 6, 275, 279
sensed presence. *See* Persinger, Michael
sermons, 44, 45
Shakespeare, William, 223
Shavuot, 86
silence theologians, 41
sinfulness of humanity, inherent, 208–9, 234. *See also* original sin
"Sing Praise to All," 334
sins
your personal share of the world's, 256–59
*Sins of Scripture, The* (Spong), 131, 138
Sobrino, Jon, 41
social concerns, the church and, 284–86
social status. *See* belonging
Song of Faith, A, 98, 99
songs, 294, 301. *See also* "Light of Love, The"; "Sing Praise to All"; "Then Sings My Soul"
soul, 73
spin, 183. *See also* manipulation
spiritual
dimension to life, 16
health and growth, 216
practices, reasons for, 63
quest, 195
questions, 278
spiritual toolbox
of the church, 216, 278–82
creating a, 276–82
spiritual ultimacy, quest for, 195
intuitive, 165–66
religion and, 291–92 (*see also under* values)
split-brain. *See* brain, two-sided
Spong, John Shelby, 21, 43, 85, 87, 96, 184–185, 266
*A New Christianity for a New World*, 21
*Rescuing the Bible from Fundamentalism*, 138
*The Sins of Scripture*, 131, 138
Spurrier, Les, 185
*Stages of Faith* (Fowler), 261–62
Statements of Faith, 96–99, 170
status, social. *See* belonging
Stoics, 232
Structural Adjustment Programs (SAPs), 286, 373n9
Sunday morning services and sermons, 119–20, 129–49, 375n2
assumptions of an afterlife, 122–29
in attendance, 120–22
chief purpose, 263
rates of attendance at religious services, 362n12
simple shifts in, 273–74
Sweet, Leonard, 9–10, 298–99